Kant's Ethics and the Same-Sex Marriage Debate - An Introduction

Christopher Arroyo

Kant's Ethics and the Same-Sex Marriage Debate - An Introduction

Springer

Christopher Arroyo
Philosophy Department
Providence College
Providence, RI, USA

ISBN 978-3-319-55731-1   ISBN 978-3-319-55733-5 (eBook)
DOI 10.1007/978-3-319-55733-5

Library of Congress Control Number: 2017937895

© Springer International Publishing AG 2017

This work is subject to copyright. All rights are reserved by the Publisher, whether the whole or part of the material is concerned, specifically the rights of translation, reprinting, reuse of illustrations, recitation, broadcasting, reproduction on microfilms or in any other physical way, and transmission or information storage and retrieval, electronic adaptation, computer software, or by similar or dissimilar methodology now known or hereafter developed.

The use of general descriptive names, registered names, trademarks, service marks, etc. in this publication does not imply, even in the absence of a specific statement, that such names are exempt from the relevant protective laws and regulations and therefore free for general use.

The publisher, the authors and the editors are safe to assume that the advice and information in this book are believed to be true and accurate at the date of publication. Neither the publisher nor the authors or the editors give a warranty, express or implied, with respect to the material contained herein or for any errors or omissions that may have been made. The publisher remains neutral with regard to jurisdictional claims in published maps and institutional affiliations.

Printed on acid-free paper

This Springer imprint is published by Springer Nature
The registered company is Springer International Publishing AG
The registered company address is: Gewerbestrasse 11, 6330 Cham, Switzerland

For Amy

Preface

I conceived of this book as a way to bring together two of my academic interests, Immanuel Kant's ethics and the debate over same-sex marriage. My conviction was, and still is, that Kant's ethical theory is viable and should be able to help us work through important practical ethical issues. Since the debate over same-sex marriage is one such practical issue, I wanted to write a book explaining the ways in which Kant's ethics can be a resource for those of us engaged in this debate. I realized from the start, however, that I would have to justify writing on Kant's ethics when it comes to same-sex marriage, since Kant's is far from the first name that comes to people's minds when they think of sexual ethics or the same-sex marriage debate. As I started writing, I realized that the prejudice (for that is what I think it is) against relying on Kant's ethics as a resource for a practical ethical issue such as same-sex marriage is born of an influential though mistaken reading of Kant's moral theory.

Unless you are a Kantian ethicist, or someone who otherwise has reason to be familiar with contemporary Kant scholarship, chances are that the account of Kant's ethics with which you are familiar is one that is informed by Elizabeth Anscombe and those critics of Kant who have taken their cue from her. The Anscombian reading, as I shall call it from here on, finds its source material in Elizabeth Anscombe's "Modern Moral Philosophy" (1958). In this essay, Anscombe, though a strong advocate of objective moral truth, recommends that the concepts of "moral" obligation and "moral" duty—indeed, the concepts of "morally" right and wrong—ought to be rejected by modern moral philosophers "because they are survivals, or derivatives from survivals, from an earlier conception of ethics which no longer generally survives, and [these concepts] are only harmful without it" (1). Anscombe believes that the concept of "moral" obligation, as it is used by modern moral philosophers, is a harmful concept leftover from an ethical theory that no longer holds sway; she concludes that this concept poses a serious impediment to doing moral philosophy well.[1]

---

[1] Anscombe's basic argument criticized what Bernard Williams (1985) would eventually call "morality," which he argues is a special system of ethical thought.

While Anscombe's essay has been widely influential, Alasdair MacIntyre has articulated the clearest and most extensively developed version of her reading of Kant's ethics. MacIntyre's *After Virtue* (1984) lays out this reading of Kant by attributing several features to Kant's moral theory.[2] According to MacIntyre, the main features of Kant's ethics, which takes "moral" obligation as its central concept, are as follows:

(1) It is committed to moral rigorism, which means that moral obligation applies universally and equally to all humans, regardless of circumstances; moral rules are like the rules of arithmetic (MacIntyre 1985, 45).[3]
(2) It is a version of ethical formalism, which means that universal moral rules are determined solely by a rational process of testing maxims, which entails an ethical intuitionism (MacIntyre 1986, 45; 236).[4]
(3) It abstracts from all material conditions, which means that Kant's ethics brackets any empirical considerations with respect to human beings and their circumstances and, therefore, severs all connection between human goodness and human desires, making the moral life a struggle against one's own wants and emotions (MacIntyre 1985, 44; 140).[5]

This "Anscombian reading" of Kant's ethics, unfortunately, is the reading of Kant's ethics that some of my readers will hold. It is unfortunate because each feature of it is demonstrably false or misleadingly exaggerated. Such a misreading is due largely to the fact that proponents of the Anscombian reading (as I shall call it) base their interpretation of Kant solely on his *Groundwork of the Metaphysics of Morals* and *Critique of Practical Reason*, which constitute but a fraction of Kant's writings on ethics, and not even the most important or substantive part of his moral theory. As a result, the Anscombian reading leaves one with a view of Kant's ethics that is remarkably unable to speak to many aspects of our moral lives, including concerns we may have regarding the ethics of sex and marriage.

In response to the Anscombian reading, and spurred in large part by the work of Mary J. Gregor (1963) and John Rawls (1971), contemporary Kant scholars and defenders of Kant have developed more holistic readings of Kant's practical philosophy, readings that draw on works that had been long ignored by English-speaking philosophers. As a result, these Kant scholars present us with accounts of

---

[2] Onora O'Neill (1983) criticizes MacIntyre's reading of Kant in the first edition of *After Virtue*. She identifies four features of MacIntyre's reading of Kant that she claims are mistaken. Although I agree that the four features she identifies involve misreadings of Kant, I think MacIntyre's mistakes are greater in number.

[3] Cf. MacIntyre (1985, 43–44): "If the rules of morality are rational, they must be the same for all rational beings, in just the way that the rules of arithmetic are; and if the rules of morality are *binding* on all rational beings, then the contingent ability of such beings to carry them out must be unimportant—what is important is their will to carry them out."

[4] According to MacIntyre, Kant believes that "the project of discovering a rational justification of morality therefore simply *is* the project of discovering a rational test which will discriminate those maxims which are a genuine expression of the moral law when they determine the will from those maxims which are not such an expression" (44).

[5] As MacIntyre puts it, "To act virtuously is not, as Kant was later to think, to act against inclination; it is to act from inclination formed by cultivation of the virtues" (149). On MacIntyre's Anscombian reading of Kant, the Kantian virtuous person is either completely unfeeling or constantly struggling against her feelings in order to act in ways that are morally worthy.

Kant's ethics that are quite different from the one we get from authors such as Anscombe and MacIntyre.

Commenting on what I am calling the Anscombian reading, Allen Wood makes the following observation:

> Critics have often questioned the deep distrust of human nature exhibited in Kant's insistence on the opposition of reason and inclination. But they display shortsightedness when they condescend to this feature of Kantian doctrine, making snide references to Kant's personality quirks or pietistic upbringing. They miss the connection between Kant's deep suspicion of our natural desires and his well worked-out theory of human nature and its history, which is generally optimistic rather than pessimistic in tendency and potentially quite radical in its social implications. (Wood 1991, 327).

I think Wood is onto something here. Indeed, I believe that one cannot have an adequate and charitable understanding of Kant's normative ethical theory, or of the practical implications of it, without seriously coming to grips with what he has to say about human nature. This conviction motivates my reading of Kant and the plan for the book, which I have divided into two parts. Part I develops a response to the Anscombian reading of Kant. I am aware that my interpretation of Kant's normative ethical theory and philosophical anthropology in Part I is rather apologetic, but this is because I am eager to disabuse readers of the Anscombian view (not because I think that there are no concerns with these parts of Kant's philosophy). Part II turns to a more critical discussion of Kant's treatments of gender, sex, and marriage and relies on these discussions in order to argue that Kant can be a valuable resource to those of us engaged in the debate over same-sex marriage.

Chapter 1 is an introductory chapter in which I lay out the most significant moral arguments against and for legalizing same-sex marriage. Although I present arguments that bear on the same-sex marriage debate in general, readers should realize that I am an American writing in an American context, which is what I know best. I do not think that what I have to say is inapplicable to those outside of the USA, but I think that I should acknowledge my cultural perspective at the outset.

In Chap. 2, I present the basics of the Anscombian reading of Kant's ethics and develop a reading of Kant on moral obligation to which Anscombe's criticisms do not apply.

In Chap. 3, I present Kant's philosophical anthropology, which takes "unsocial sociability" to be the central feature of human nature. I argue that Kant's understanding of humans as unsocially social motivates his practical philosophy as a whole and can help us understand the critical stance he takes toward human sexual relations.

In Chap. 4, which concludes Part I, I present Kant's theory of virtue, which serves to further disabuse readers of the Anscombian reading and anticipates the way in which Kant's ethics can help us develop a solution to the problem of sexual objectification.

Part II of the book turns more specifically to Kant's treatments of sex and marriage. In Chap. 5, I give an account of Kant's views on gender and sex, explaining the way in which Kant's philosophical anthropology and his sexist views on the relations between women and men inform his critique of sex acts as objatifying.

In Chap. 6 I distinguish between the legal problem of sexual objectification and the moral problem of sexual objectification and argue that Kant's account of marriage can only address the former. I then draw on Kant's account of friendship to develop a response to the latter, one that in principle can apply to both different-sex and same-sex couples.

In Chap. 7, which is the conclusion of the book, I develop a defense of same-sex marriage by drawing on Kant's writings, and I revisit the arguments I presented in Chap. 1 and evaluate them in light of the defense of same-sex marriage that I develop.

This book was a long time in the making. For various reasons, I was unable to finish the manuscript as quickly as I had planned. That I managed to finish it at all is due largely to the many people who helped me work through this project. First of all, I want to thank Neil Olivier, the executive editor of Social Sciences and Humanities at Springer. Neil is the first person to affirm my idea for this book, and he has patiently stood by me and encouraged me while I finished. For similar reasons, I also want to thank Diana Nijenhuijzen, Neil's assistant editor and the person with whom I've had the most contact at Springer. Diana, like Neil, has been a pleasure to work with, and I am forever grateful for her constant encouragement and seemingly infinite supply of understanding.

Parts of Chaps. 3 and 4 appear in my paper, "Kant on the emotion of love," which is published in the *European Journal of Philosophy*. I am grateful to the journal for permission to use those portions of my article.

Various people have read and commented on drafts of this manuscript and material that informed parts of the manuscript. I want to thank Eric Bennett, Sarah Braunstein, Licia Carlson, Peter Costello, Brian Davies, Joseph Gulezian, Bill Hogan, Michael Kelly, Darra Mulderry, Jeffery Nicholas, Anne Ozar, and Amy Peters for their feedback on the texts that I gave them. Nancy Kendrick invited me to Wheaton College in order to present some of my early work from Part II. I want to thank her, M. Theresa Celeda, John Partridge, and the philosophy students at Wheaton who attended my talk and gave me helpful feedback. Each of these people has, at various times and in various ways, been a source of strength and encouragement that helped me push through and get the manuscript finished.

Providence, RI, USA   Christopher Arroyo

References

Anscombe, G.E.M. 1958. Modern Moral Philosophy. *Philosophy* 33.124: 1–19.
MacIntyre, Alasdair. 1984. *After Virtue: A Study in Moral Theory*, 2nd ed. Notre Dame: University of Notre Dame Press.
O'Neill, Onora. 1983. Kant After Virtue. *Inquiry* 26.4: 387–405.
Williams, Bernard. 1985. *Ethics and the Limits of Philosophy*. Cambridge, MA: Harvard University Press.
Wood, Allen W. 1991. Unsocial Sociability: The Anthropological Basis of Kantian Ethics. *Philosophical Topics* 19.1: 325–351.

Contents

Part I The Same-Sex Marriage Debate & Some Basics of Kant's Ethics

1 For Better or for Worse: An Overview of the Same-Sex Marriage Debate 3
   1.1 The Case Against Same-Sex Marriage 4
      1.1.1 The Definitional Objection 4
      1.1.2 Marital Norms and the Harms of Same-Sex Marriage 6
      1.1.3 Same-Sex Marriage and the Harm Done to Children 7
      1.1.4 The Moral Objection to Homosexuality 8
      1.1.5 The Liberal Case Against Same-Sex Marriage 11
   1.2 The Case in Defense of Same-Sex Marriage 12
      1.2.1 The Equal Treatment Argument.. 12
      1.2.2 The Benefits of Same-Sex Marriage 14
      1.2.3 The Conservative Case for Same-Sex Marriage: Normalizing Homosexuality 16
      1.2.4 Marriage, the Changing Institution... 17
      1.2.5 Opening Up Marriage 18
   1.3 Looking Ahead.. 19
   References... 20

2 Finitude & Dependency: Kant's Conception of Moral Obligation 23
   2.1 Anscombe on Moral Obligation 25
      2.1.1 Anscombe's Brief History of Modern Ethics 25
      2.1.2 Moral Obligation: A Case of Language Gone on Holiday.. 27
   2.2 Kant on Moral Obligation... 29
      2.2.1 Finite Wills *vs.* Holy Wills 30
      2.2.2 Moral Necessitation and Human Imperfection...................... 33
      2.2.3 Kant *pace* Anscombe on Moral Obligation 36

	2.3	Kant's Account of Autonomy of the Will	37
		2.3.1 Setting the Stage: Autonomy and Heteronomy as Metaphors	38
		2.3.2 Kant's Moral Realism: Legislator *versus* Author of the Law	39
		2.3.3 Self-Legislation and Kant's Natural Dialectic	42
	2.4	Looking Ahead	44
	References		45
3	**Such Crooked Timber: Kant's Philosophical Anthropology**		**47**
	3.1	Unsocial Sociability and Radical Evil in Human Nature	49
		3.1.1 Human Development and Unsocial Sociability	50
		3.1.2 The Predispositions to Good and Propensities to Evil in Human Nature	53
	3.2	Desire and Emotion in Kant's Account of Sensible Nature	60
		3.2.1 Sensible Nature in the *Metaphysics of Morals*	60
		3.2.2 Moral Worth and Pathological Feelings in the *Groundwork*	62
		3.2.3 Affects and Passions as Detriments to Moral Disposition	65
	3.3	The Natural Desire for Happiness and Its Place in Kant's Ethics	68
		3.3.1 The Complete Satisfaction of All of One's Inclinations	68
		3.3.2 Worthiness to Be Happy	70
	3.4	Looking Ahead	71
	References		72
4	**All You Need Is Love, Respect, & Autocracy: Kant's Virtue Ethics**		**75**
	4.1	Kant's Doctrine of Virtue: Morally Obligatory Ends & Strength of Will	77
		4.1.1 Choice, Inner Constraint, & Morally Obligatory Ends	78
		4.1.2 Kant's Argument Against Virtue as Habit	81
	4.2	Misunderstanding Kantian Virtue: Self-Mastery and Sensible Nature	83
	4.3	Understanding Kantian Virtue: Controlling and Cultivating Sensible Nature	85
	4.4	Kant's Doctrine of Virtue: Self-Perfection and the Happiness of Others	87
		4.4.1 Self-Perfection and the Happiness of Others as Ends of Virtue	89
		4.4.2 Kant's Account of Respect for the Moral Law	91
		4.4.3 Kant's Account of the Emotion of Love	94
		4.4.4 Respect, Love, & Our Relations with Others	98
	4.5	Looking Ahead	99
	References		100

Part II Gender, Sex, and Marriage in Kant's Ethics

5 Dependency & Domination: Gender & Kant's Practical Sexual Ethic 105
- 5.1 Kant on the Character of the Sexes 107
  - 5.1.1 Kant on Feminine Nature 109
  - 5.1.2 Feminine Virtue, Masculine Virtue, and the Moral Agency of Women 111
  - 5.1.3 Kant on Gender Relations and the Precarious Status of Women 114
- 5.2 Kant's Account of Bodily Discipline and the Sexual Impulse 119
  - 5.2.1 Self-Perfection and Bodily Discipline 120
  - 5.2.2 Kant on Sexual Appetite 122
- 5.3 Kant on Lust and the *Crimina Carnis* 124
  - 5.3.1 *Crimina Carnis Secundum Naturam* 127
  - 5.3.2 *Crimina Carnis Contra Naturam* 130
- 5.4 Looking Ahead 132
- References 135

6 Love & Respect Redux: Kant on Sex, Marriage, and Friendship 137
- 6.1 Kant on Marriage 139
  - 6.1.1 Marriage and the Marriage Right 141
  - 6.1.2 The Marriage Right, Reciprocity, and Legally Permissible Sex 144
  - 6.1.3 Kant's Incomplete Solution: The Legal Problem & the Moral Problem of Sexual Objectification 147
- 6.2 Kant on Friendship 152
  - 6.2.1 Sex, The Enjoyment of Humanity, and Moral Friendship 157
  - 6.2.2 Sex, Reciprocity, and Moral Friendship 159
- 6.3 Looking Ahead 161
- References 162

7 Conclusion: Kant's Ethics & the Same-Sex Marriage Debate 165
- 7.1 Kant's Evaluation of Same-Sex Sexual Relations 166
  - 7.1.1 Sexual Activity and Procreation 166
  - 7.1.2 Same-Sex Sexual Activity and the Forfeiture of One's Person 169
  - 7.1.3 Same-Sex Sex Acts and the Behavior of Non-human Animals 170
- 7.2 The Arguments Against Same-Sex Marriage 171
  - 7.2.1 The Definitional Objection and Kant's Conception of Marriage 171
  - 7.2.2 Marital Norms and the Alleged Harms of Same-Sex Marriage 172
  - 7.2.3 Same-Sex Marriage and the Alleged Harm Done to Children 173
  - 7.2.4 The Liberal Case Against Marriage 173

7.3	The Case in Defense of Same-Sex Marriage		174
	7.3.1	The Equal Treatment Argument	175
	7.3.2	The Benefits of Same-Sex Marriage	
		and the Conservative Case	176
	7.3.3	Marriage the Changing Institution	178
7.4	Conclusion	179
References	180

Index 181

Abbreviations[6]

A   Kant, Immanuel. 2007 (1798). *Anthropology from a Pragmatic Point of View*, trans. Robert B. Louden. In *Anthropology, History, and Education*. Ed. Robert B. Louden and Günter Zöller, 227–429. Cambridge: Cambridge University Press.

CL   Kant, Immanuel. 1997 (1784–1785). "Collins Lecture Notes," trans. Peter Heath. In *Lectures on Ethics*. Ed. J.B. Schneewind and Peter Heath, 37–222. Cambridge: Cambridge University Press.

CPR   Kant, Immanuel. 1997 (1781/1787). *Critique of Pure Reason*, trans. And ed. Paul Guyer and Allen W. Wood. Cambridge: Cambridge University Press.

CPrR   Kant, Immanuel. 1996 (1788). *Critique of Practical Reason*. In *Practical Philosophy*. Trans. and ed. Mary J. Gregor, 133–271. Cambridge: Cambridge University Press.

G   Kant, Immanuel. 1996 (1785). *Groundwork of the Metaphysics of Morals*. In *Practical Philosophy*. Trans. and ed. Mary J. Gregor, 37–108. Cambridge: Cambridge University Press.

HL   Kant, Immanuel. 1997 (1762–1764). "Herder's Lecture Notes," trans. Peter Heath. In *Lectures on Ethics*. Ed. J.B. Schneewind and Peter Heath, 1–36. Cambridge: Cambridge University Press.

IUH   Kant, Immanuel. 2007 (1784). "Idea for a Universal History with a Cosmopolitan Aim," trans. Allen W. Wood. In *Anthropology, History, and Education*. Ed. Robert B. Louden and Günter Zöller, 107–120. Cambridge: Cambridge University Press.

---

[6] Given the frequency with which I refer to some of the works of Immanuel Kant, for the sake of ease and brevity, I decided to use abbreviations to refer to these works. The following is an alphabetical list of the abbreviations I use to refer to the works of Kant I cite, with the corresponding bibliographic information for each work. When I cite Kant's works in the text, I follow scholarly custom and refer to the volume and page number of the German text in the Academy Edition of the works of Immanuel Kant.

ML	Kant, Immanuel. 1997 (1785). "Mrongovius Lecture Notes," trans. Peter Heath. In *Lectures on Ethics*. Ed. J.B. Schneewind and Peter Heath, 223–248. Cambridge: Cambridge University Press.
MM	Kant, Immanuel. 1996 (1797). *Metaphysics of Morals*. In *Practical Philosophy*. Trans. and ed. Mary J. Gregor, 353–603. Cambridge: Cambridge University Press.
R	Kant, Immanuel. 1996 (1793). *Religion within the Boundaries of Mere Reason,* trans. George di Giovanni. In *Religion and Rational Theology*. Ed. Allen W. Wood and George di Giovanni, 39–215. Cambridge: Cambridge University Press.
TP	Kant, Immanuel. 1996 (1793). "On the Common Saying: That may be correct in theory, but it is of no use in practice." In *Practical Philosophy*. Trans. and ed. Mary J. Gregor, 273–309. Cambridge: Cambridge University Press.
VL	Kant, Immanuel. 1997 (1793). "Vigilantius Lecture Notes," trans. Peter Heath. In *Lectures on Ethics*. Ed. J.B. Schneewind and Peter Heath, 249–452. Cambridge: Cambridge University Press.
WIE	Kant, Immanuel. 1996 (1784). "An Answer to the Question: What is Enlightenment?" In *Practical Philosophy*. Trans. and ed. Mary J. Gregor, 11–22. Cambridge: Cambridge University Press.

Part I
The Same-Sex Marriage Debate & Some Basics of Kant's Ethics

Chapter 1
For Better or for Worse: An Overview of the Same-Sex Marriage Debate

Abstract This chapter presents what I take to be some of the most important ethical arguments against and in favor of same-sex marriage. This overview of the main arguments will provide the context for the treatment of Kant that follows, insofar as I will be able to trace certain recurring themes in these arguments, themes to which Kant's ethics will have to speak if his practical philosophy can serve as a resource for those engaged in the same-sex marriage debate.

According to the Pew Research Center (Masci and Sciupac 2015), there are twenty-three countries in which same-sex marriage is legal: Argentina (2010), Belgium (2003), Brazil (2013), Canada (2005), Colombia (2016), Denmark (2012), England/Wales (2013), Finland (2015), France (2013), Greenland (2015), Iceland (2010), Ireland (2015), Luxembourg (2014), The Netherlands (2000), New Zealand (2013), Norway (2009), Portugal (2010), Scotland (2014), South Africa (2006), Spain (2005), Sweden (2009), the United States (2015), and Uruguay (2013). For those who believe that same-sex couples should have the right to marry, in less than twenty years we have seen an extraordinary amount of progress on the issue of same-sex marriage and gay rights more generally, at least in these twenty-three countries.

It is still the case, however, that most countries in the world do not grant same-sex couples the right to marry. Some of those nations (e.g., Italy, Germany, and Chile, to name a few) allow for various legal designations for same-sex couples that offer some, but not all, of the rights and recognition that different-sex married couples enjoy. Moreover, according to the International Lesbian, Gay, Bisexual, Trans and Intersex Association (ILGA), seventy-five nations have laws criminalizing same-sex sexual activity (Carroll and Itaborahy 2015). And in some countries where same-sex marriage is legal, such as the United States, opponents of same-sex marriage insist that the issue is not settled. For example, Sherif Girgis, one of the most outspoken critics of same-sex marriage, has compared the debate to the debate over abortion, claiming that "continued argument and advocacy on the whole range of marriage and family issues—including [same-sex marriage]—remain crucial. Not only does social action make long term defeat less likely, it also serves the broader value for which legal victory is just a component and condition: the shaping of hearts and minds—and lives—in line with the truth" (Girgis 2014).[1]

In light of the preceding considerations it is fair to say that the issue of same-sex marriage is far from settled. In an effort to contribute helpfully to the contemporary debate, I have decided to write a book about the ethics of same-sex marriage, one that draws on Kant's writings on ethics as a resource in working through the contemporary debate. In order to contextualize my treatment of Kant and to help me focus on those issues in his practical philosophy that are relevant to the issue of same-sex marriage, the rest of this introduction sketches what I take to be some of the most important ethical (as opposed to, say, legal) arguments against and in favor of same-sex marriage. These will provide the context for the treatment of Kant that follows, insofar as I will be able to trace certain recurring themes in these arguments, themes to which Kant's ethics will have to speak if his practical philosophy can serve as a resource for those engaged in the same-sex marriage debate.

1.1 The Case Against Same-Sex Marriage

The debate over same-sex marriage has largely been driven by those who oppose allowing same-sex couples the right to marry.[2] Opponents of same-sex marriage often make their case by giving reasons against expanding the legal institution of marriage, which proponents of same-sex marriage subsequently work to refute. My presentation will follow suit, beginning with the main lines of argument against same-sex marriage and then moving on to the arguments made in its defense.

1.1.1 The Definitional Objection

Anyone who has followed the same-sex marriage debate is familiar with what is called the definitional objection to same-sex marriage. The definitional objection goes something like this: marriage *just is* the union of one woman and one man, and no law can change that any more than a law can make a shark a wombat. Of course, the "just is" motivating the definitional objection needs some explaining. The most philosophically sophisticated explanation appears in the writings of the new natural law theorists. Natural law is the name given to a host of related ethical, legal, and political theories that find their origin in the writings of Aristotle and Plato. Although it is difficult to identify a set of characteristics that all natural law theories share (Buckle 1993, 161), natural law theories of ethics are ones that purport to

---

[1] For some critics of same-sex marriage there is a causal relationship between legalizing same-sex marriage and the changing of people's beliefs about marriage. See, for example, Patrick Lee and Robert George (2014, 121–122).

[2] This is also true for the debate about the morality of homosexuality. See Corvino (2013, 15–16).

1.1 The Case Against Same-Sex Marriage

demonstrate that we can discover objective ethical standards by examining human nature and the nature of the world. Perhaps the most well-known classical natural law theorist is Thomas Aquinas (c. 1225–1274). New natural law theorists are so named because they claim to have developed their own interpretation of the natural law theory found in the writings of Aquinas.[3] By drawing on this interpretation they have developed a sophisticated sexual ethic that forms the basis of their definitional objection to same-sex marriage.

Recently, Sherif Girgis, Ryan T. Anderson, and Robert P. George (2012, 48) have developed their version of the definitional objection. They insist that marriage is a basic good with an "objective core," which is fixed by our nature as embodied, sexually reproductive (and, hence, sexually complementary) beings.[4] Marriage, they go on to argue, is not reducible to a changing and changeable societal conception of the institution. True marriage, according to Girgis, Anderson, and George, possesses three essential and related features: marriage should be understood as "a union of will (by consent) and body (by sexual union); inherently ordered to procreation and thus the broad sharing of family life; and calling for permanent and exclusive commitment, whatever the spouses preferences" (2012, 6). Same-sex couples cannot marry, according to this view, because same-sex couples are incapable of achieving the comprehensive union of persons that is characteristic of true, "conjugal marriage."

Girgis, Anderson, and George regard bodily union as a necessary component of a genuinely comprehensive union of persons, and their definitional objection turns on this conception (2012, 99). According to them, bodily union occurs when different-sex couples engage in coitus because only in this activity do the woman and man join to form an organic whole. They explain their position by way of an analogy with the human body: "your organs are one body because they are coordinated for a single *biological* purpose of the whole that they form together: sustaining your biological life. Just so, for two individuals to unite organically, *their bodies must coordinate toward a common biological end of the whole that they form together*" (2012, 25). On their view, only one biological (i.e., bodily) activity can unite two people in this way, namely, coitus, since "in coitus, and there alone, a man and a woman's bodies participate by virtue of their sexual complementarity in a coordination that has the biological purpose of reproduction—a function neither can perform alone" (26). Since, according to Girgis, Anderson, and George, two men or two women cannot achieve this kind of organic, bodily union, two men or two women cannot form a comprehensive union of persons, which is just to say that same-sex couples cannot marry.

---

[3] The founders of this school of thought are the philosopher and theologian, Germain Grisez, and the philosopher and specialist in jurisprudence, John Finnis. For a good overview of the basics of new natural law theory see Grisez (1983), Finnis (1980, second edition 2011), and George (2001).

[4] For a summary of the argument of Girgis, Anderson, and George, see Arroyo (2015).

1.1.2 Marital Norms and the Harms of Same-Sex Marriage

Closely related to the definitional objection is the argument that tries to establish that legalizing same-sex marriage will harm the marriages of different-sex couples. This argument is often misunderstood by defenders of same-sex marriage, since they take the harm at issue here to be material harm. According to this argument, however, the harm of same-sex marriage is much more subtle and pervasive than mere material harm. Proponents of this argument, such as David Blankenhorn (2007),[5] claim that it is not that same-sex marriage will cost different-sex married couples money, or result in damage to their property, or keep different-sex married couples from owning a home or starting a family; rather, the central harm of same-sex marriage is the erosion of marital norms. The thinking here is that just as reading trashy novels can erode one's capacity to identify, appreciate, enjoy, and produce great literature, so, too, bad marriage laws sap one's ability to identify, appreciate, enjoy, and achieve the goods of true marriage. John Finnis (2008), another proponent of the harm argument, for example, argues that marriages "are *factual* realities whose coming to be and lasting depends upon people's grasp of marriage's truth ("reality", "worth") as an *ideal*" (401). Finnis (2008, 398–399) insists that "concern for one's own people as a lasting community linking past, present, and future, justify and indeed mandate the defense even of modern marriage against such evacuations of [marriage's] meaning and intelligibility as an ideal and a summons to a thoroughgoing commitment for a non-illusory common good." Same-sex marriage, according to this argument, would amount to such an evacuation.

Girgis, Anderson, and George also predict that legalizing same-sex marriage will undermine what they take to be the central norms of true marriage. They hold that defenders of same-sex marriage want to replace true, conjugal marriage with "the revisionist view of marriage." In their telling of the revisionist view, marriage becomes nothing more than an intense emotional (loving) bond that distinguishes itself from other kinds of relationships by virtue of its intensity and that lasts only so long as both "married" partners feel this intense bond (2012, 1–2). Were such a conception of marriage to become the norm, Girgis, Anderson, and George believe that marriage would no longer be understood to be a sexually exclusive and permanent bond; on their view, the revisionists have no grounds for asserting such exclusivity and permanence (2012, 18–21), since, according to Girgis, Anderson, and George, procreation and the raising of children are the reasons why marriage is permanent and sexually exclusive.[6] Consequently, according to this argument, different-sex couples would have to persevere in the hard and permanent work of true marriage surrounded by the bad example of elective and merely transient bonds.

---

[5] Blankenhorn (2012) has since changed his position and no longer opposes the legalization of same-sex marriage.

[6] On the basis of this argument, some new natural law theorists, such as Patrick Lee and Robert George (2014, 90–96), develop a slippery slope argument, which charges that if we legalize same-sex marriage, we will have no principled objection to legalizing incest, bestiality, and polyamorous marriages. For a response to such arguments, see Corvino (2005).

There are, however, further harms to marriage, at least as far as this line of reasoning is concerned, ones that follow on the erosion of true marital norms. For example, some proponents of this way of thinking predict that legalizing same-sex marriage will result in a threat to moral and religious freedom, insofar as such legalization threatens to make defenders of conjugal marriage falsely appear to be bigots, which, they fear, will result in society outlawing "traditional" marriage (Girgis, et al. 2012, 62–64). They claim that legalizing same-sex marriage will also undermine genuine friendships, insofar as the revisionist view of marriage provides no clear way to distinguish a marital relationship from other kinds of committed relationships (65–66). Additionally, they argue, to redefine marriage law to allow for same-sex marriage is to threaten limited government, since redefining marriage will do away with the kinds of protections conjugal marriage provides for children, and this withering away of such safeguards will require the government to step in to play the role of protector (57–58).[7]

1.1.3 Same-Sex Marriage and the Harm Done to Children

This last point about the threat to limited government brings me to one final harm alleged by opponents of same-sex marriage, namely, the harm that same-sex marriage will do to children. The strongest proponent of this line of argument is Maggie Gallagher, co-founder of the National Organization for Marriage. Although Gallagher does not self-identify as a new natural law (NNL) theorist, she endorses many of their arguments (2012, 237 note 23). For example, she agrees with their conception of marriage as a comprehensive union of persons, and she endorses their version of the definitional objection (2012, 95–102). In particular, she shares Girgis, Anderson, and George's conviction that the United States needs a strong marriage culture in order to promote the values and norms of conjugal marriage. Central to Gallagher's account of a strong marriage culture is her claim that the norms of "traditional" marriage "stem from centuries of experience in the always-evolving, ever-adapting task of reconciling male and female in a way that is satisfying to both and most likely to protect the children they create" (2012, 142).

Gallagher grounds her argument about the importance of marriage for the well-being of children in what she takes to be three persistent truths about human beings everywhere: (1) "the overwhelming majority of us are powerfully attracted, and not by reason, to an act that makes new human life"; (2) "society needs babies"; and (3) "children ought to have a mother as well as a father" (108–109). Gallagher defends this third point by invoking the results of certain social scientific studies that conclude that children are better off when they are raised by their respective biological mothers and biological fathers. Quoting a Child Trends research brief from 2002, Gallagher claims that "research clearly demonstrates that family structure matters

---

[7] Girgis, Anderson, and George are thinking of the federal government of the United States, but their arguments apply equally well to any modern social-democratic nation.

for children, and the family structure that helps the most is a family headed by two biological parents in a low-conflict marriage" (110). According to Gallagher, a child *wants* to be raised by his biological mother and father, which stems from his "desire to experience both male and female love and to experience his own creation as an act of love by both his parents" (113). In other words, according to this way of thinking, differences between the way mothers and fathers love their children are real and not merely socialized, and a child needs both kinds of love in order to have the best chance of developing into a mature, flourishing adult. This is the case, according to Gallagher, because of basic, natural (i.e., not socially constructed/learned) differences between women and men. "We need a cultural mechanism," Gallagher summarizes,

> for attaching fathers to the mother-child bond and for communicating to young adults in the middle of erotic, romantic, psychological, and emotional dramas that they need to act with restraint and even self-sacrifice if they are to obtain this great good for their children. (113)

1.1.4 The Moral Objection to Homosexuality

What I am calling the moral objection to homosexuality (as opposed to an objection motivated merely by disgust or fear of what is different), consists in the view that homosexuality violates the natural law and is, therefore, immoral. When proponents of this objection write of "homosexuality," they have in mind what I would call same-sex sexual activity,[8] and they claim that engaging in same-sex sexual activity (of any kind, though the focus tends to be on penile-anal intercourse between two men) is by its nature bad for human beings, and, so, any choice to engage in such activity must be a bad choice, that is, it must be unethical or immoral. Two versions of this argument appear in the literature: a new natural law theory version (defended by thinkers such as John Finnis and Robert George) and a classical natural law theory version (defended by a thinker such as Thomas Aquinas).[9]

The New Natural Law Objection to Same-Sex Sex Acts NNL theorists such as Girgis, Anderson, George, and Gallagher insist that their objections to same-sex marriage are not motivated by an ethical condemnation of same-sex sex acts.[10] In making this claim, they rely on a metaethical distinction NNL theory makes between

---

[8] Natural law theorists tend to distinguish between homosexual acts (i.e., sexual acts between two men or between two women) and what they call the "homosexual condition/orientation" (i.e., the disposition that motivates one to want to engage in homosexual acts). See, for example, Joseph Ratzinger's "Letter to the Bishops of the Catholic Church on the Pastoral Care of Homosexual Persons" (1986). According to this distinction, we can truly designate someone a homosexual if she or he (a) engages in same-sex sexual acts, or (b) has the homosexual condition, even if she or he does not engage in same-sex sexual acts.

[9] Jean Porter (1999) explains some of the differences between the natural law theory defended by Aquinas and the moral theory articulated by the new natural law theorists.

[10] One may reasonably doubt whether this is the case. See for example Arroyo (2015).

1.1 The Case Against Same-Sex Marriage

(1) its account of fundamental practical principles that identify basic goods (recall that an account of marriage as a comprehensive union and as a basic good forms the basis of Girgis, Anderson, and George's Definitional Objection to same-sex marriage) and (2) NNL theory's account of the requirements for what it calls "practical reasonableness" (or, alternatively, "modes of responsibility"), which provide the criteria by which classical NNL theory distinguishes between moral and immoral acts.[11] Although different NNL theorists have formulated different versions of the modes of responsibility (Finnis 1980; Grisez 1983), there is one mode in particular on which NNL theorists rely: "one may never *intend* to destroy, damage, impede, or violate any basic human good, or prefer an illusory instantiation of a basic human good to a real instantiation of that or some other human good" (Finnis 1995, 31). Additionally, NNL theorists identify what they call "the first principle of morality": "In voluntarily acting for human goods and avoiding what is opposed to them, one ought to choose and otherwise will those and only those possibilities whose willing is compatible with a will toward integral human fulfillment" (Finnis 1980, 128). NNL theorists claim that they can demonstrate that all same-sex activity—indeed, all non-marital sexual activity—is unethical or immoral, simply by using the first principle of morality in conjunction with the mode of responsibility I identified.

According to NNL theory, all non-marital sex acts are immoral insofar as to choose to engage in any non-marital sex act is to choose in a way that intentionally violates the basic good of marriage. Accordingly, John Finnis (1995, 29–30) concludes that "there is no important distinction in essential moral worthlessness between solitary masturbation, being sodomized as a prostitute, and being sodomized for the pleasure of it." According to NNL theorists, same-sex sex acts in particular are wrong (a) because they violate the integrity of those who commit them, insofar as these acts lead to self-alienation via the treating of their respective bodies as mere instruments of pleasure (George 2004, 79–80), and (b) because same-sex sex acts violate the good of marital communion insofar as these acts mimic but fail to realize the two-in-one flesh communion of the marital act (Grisez 1983, 653–654).[12]

---

[11] Cf. Finnis (1980, 23): "There is (i) a set of basic practical principles which indicate the basic forms of human flourishing as goods to be pursued and realized, and which are in one way or another used by everyone who considers what to do, however unsound his conclusions; and (ii) a set of basic methodological requirements of practical reasonableness (itself one of the basic forms of human flourishing) which distinguish sound from unsound practical thinking and which, when all brought to bear, provide the criteria for distinguishing between acts that (always or in particular circumstances) are reasonable-all-things-considered (and not merely relative-to-a-particular-purpose) and acts that are unreasonable-all-things-considered, i.e., between ways of acting that are morally right or morally wrong—thus enabling one to formulate (iii) a set of general moral standards."

[12] Cf. Finnis (1995, 32): "It is not simply that [the deliberate genital coupling of persons of the same sex] is sterile and disposes the participants to an abdication of responsibility for the future of human kind. Nor is it simply that it cannot *really* actualize the mutual devotion which some homosexual persons hope to manifest and experience by it, and that it harms the personalities of its participants by its dis-integrative manipulation of different parts of their one personal reality. It is also that it treats human sexual capacities in a way which is deeply hostile to the self-understanding

Classical Natural Law's Objection to Same-Sex Sex Acts Classical natural law takes a different tack when arguing that same-sex sexual activity is unethical or immoral. This is primarily because classical natural law theorists do not subscribe to NNL theory's account of the division between fundamental practical principles and modes of responsibility. The *locus classicus* for classical natural law's objection to same-sex sex is the writings of Thomas Aquinas. In *On Evil,* for example, he writes:

> Sometimes along with disorder of concupiscence, there is also a disorder of the external act in itself, as happens in every use of the genital organs outside the marriage act. And that every such act is disordered in itself is apparent from the fact that every human act is said to be disordered which is not proportioned to its due end, just as eating is disordered if it is not proportioned to the health of the body, to which it is ordered as to an end. But the end of the use of the genital organs is the generation and education of offspring, and therefore every use of the aforementioned organs which is not proportioned to the generation of offspring and its due education is disordered in itself (2003, 15.1).

According to this argument, "disordered" means "defective" or "bad." An agent who engages in such disordered acts thereby acts in a way that is bad and harms her or his flourishing. The point of the argument is to establish that certain ways of acting are unethical precisely because they are inconsistent with (i.e., not properly related to) the natural purpose or end of one's sexual organs, regardless of the intentions or desires of the agents involved. According to this way of thinking, all same-sex sexual activity—even when such activity takes place between two people who love each other—is disordered and, therefore, is detrimental to the flourishing of those individuals who engage in such activity.

To summarize, there are two natural law versions of the ethical or moral objection to same-sex sexual activity: the NNL objection, which takes all non-marital sexual activity to be a violation of the basic good of marriage and, therefore, unethical or immoral; and the classical natural law objection, which takes all same-sex sexual activity to be contrary to the natural end of genitals and, so, always disordered and unethical or immoral. Some people object to same-sex marriage by relying on the classical natural law objection to same-sex sexual activity.[13] These people argue that all same-sex sexual activity is disordered and should not be sanctioned by legalizing same-sex marriage. Proponents of NNL can and do make a similar argument using their account of why same-sex sexual activity is unethical or

---

of those members of the community who are willing to commit themselves to real marriage in the understanding that its sexual joys are not mere instruments or accompaniments to, or mere compensations for, the accomplishment of marriage's responsibilities, but rather enable the spouses to *actualize and experience* their intelligent commitment to share in those responsibilities, in that genuine self-giving."

[13] I am not claiming that this objection to same-sex marriage is to be found in the work of Thomas Aquinas, just that he condemns same-sex sexual activity as always unethical or immoral. Actually, one can plausibly argue that despite his objections to homosexuality, Aquinas might have been open to legalizing same-sex marriage for the sake of the public good. I say this in light of Aquinas' admission in the *Summa Theologiae* that "the authorities rightly tolerate certain evils [such as prostitution] lest certain goods be impeded or greater evils incurred" (1975, 2a2ae, 10, 11).

immoral, but this is a different, additional argument from the definitional objection.

1.1.5 The Liberal Case Against Same-Sex Marriage

The final objection I am considering is not so much an objection to same-sex marriage as it is an objection to marriage, period. Although certain contemporary authors, such as Clare Chambers (2013), have criticized the state's involvement in marriage, Claudia Card's (1996) version of this argument has probably been the most influential.[14] In "Against Marriage and Motherhood" Card writes,

> I believe that women who identify as lesbian or gay should be reluctant to put our activist energy into attaining legal equity with heterosexuals in marriage and motherhood—not because the existing discrimination against us is in any way justifiable but because the institutions are so deeply flawed that they seem to me unworthy of emulation and reproduction (2).

Card does not object to erotic intimacy or to long-term romantic relationships, nor does she object to the education of and caring for children. Rather, she objects to the institutions of marriage and motherhood as they have existed in Western culture, given the central roles they have played in the systemic oppression of women. Since, according to Card, the institution of marriage has been and continues to be a systemic cause of the subjugation of women, Card believes that it is unjust.

In defending her position, Card identifies four problems with the institution of marriage. First, the government and employers tend to tie certain essential, basic benefits to one's marital status, which is unfair to the unmarried. Second, the consequences of divorce tend to be severe to one or both members of the formerly married couple, and they tend to be especially burdensome to women. Third, the government tends to understand marriage as a monogamous relationship between two people; this assumption on the part of government is a particular problem for gays and lesbians, according to Card, who are more open to polyamorous relationships than those who identify as heterosexual. Finally, "the legal right of access that married partners have to each other's person, property, and lives makes it all but impossible for a spouse to defend herself (or himself), or to be protected against torture, rape, battery, stalking, mayhem, or murder by the other spouse" (7–8). Historically, according to Card, the institution of marriage developed in large part as a way for men to control their property, including their wives (5). And this means, as far as Card is concerned, that marriage as it has developed as an institution in the West is inherently unjust—if not inherently oppressive and misogynistic—which is why Card does not hesitate to draw an analogy between the Western institution of marriage and the institution of chattel slavery (11). In light of these considerations, even though she thinks that laws precluding same-sex couples from marriage are unfair,

---

[14] Elizabeth Brake (2012) also criticizes the state institution of marriage as it currently exists, but she stops short of calling for its complete abolition.

Card concludes that lesbians (and gay men) should not put their energies into achieving the right to marry.

1.2 The Case in Defense of Same-Sex Marriage

In Sect. 1.1, I asserted that the debate over same-sex marriage has largely been determined by those who oppose legalizing same-sex marriage. The arguments in support of legalizing same-sex marriage are often developed as responses to the opposition and, as such, complement them in certain respects. With this in mind, I will present the arguments in defense of same-sex marriage in an order that reflects as best as I can the way in which the following arguments are responses to their numerical counterparts in the previous section.

1.2.1 The Equal Treatment Argument

What I am calling the equal treatment argument comes in a variety of forms, each of which draws the same basic conclusion: to allow different-sex couples to marry but not allow same-sex couples to do the same is unjust, since there are no morally relevant differences between different-sex and same-sex couples that can justify such different treatment. Hence, according to this line of reasoning, to allow different-sex couples the right to marry while denying this right to same-sex couples is discriminatory, plain and simple. Three versions of this kind of argument deserve attention: the analogy with anti-miscegenation, the sterility objection, and the sexual orientation caste system argument.

The Analogy with Antimiscegenation This argument concerns an analogy between race and sex; just as race is irrelevant when it comes to whether two people may marry, so, too, is sex. The key legal precedent in the United States, where this argument has particular sway, is *Loving v. Virginia* (1967), the United States Supreme Court case in which Richard Loving (a White man) and Mildred Jeter (a Black woman) challenged the Virginia court's ruling that their marriage entailed a violation of Virginia's Racial Integrity Act of 1959. The Court, in a majority opinion written by Chief Justice Earl Warren, judged that antimiscegenation laws are unconstitutional and that different-race couples enjoy the right to marry as much as same-race couples. Proponents of the analogy between antimiscegenation laws and laws against same-sex marriage invoke *Loving v. Virginia*, arguing that the position of those who would outlaw different-race marriages and the position of those who would outlaw same-sex marriages share a number of formal similarities. As William Eskridge (1996) explains:

> Those defending the prohibitions in both cases relied on arguments that deny marriage's social and contingent features. Specifically, the supporters of antimiscegenation statutes

made the same kind of definitional and natural law arguments that supporters of statutes barring same-sex marriage now make. *Loving* rejected all those arguments and exposed them as pretexts for a discriminatory race-based classification for which the state could advance no compelling interest. (153–154)

Since discrimination with respect to race is wrong when it comes to the issue of who may marry, it is equally wrong, according to this line of reasoning, to discriminate with respect to sex.

The Sterility Objection The second equal treatment argument I want to present emerges directly as a response to the definitional objection. Just like the analogy with antimiscegenation, this argument relies on the formal notion of consistency. Although he did not invent the phrase,[15] the strongest proponent of the sterility objection is Stephen Macedo. Macedo (1996) develops the sterility objection within the context of his more general critique of the sexual ethics of the new natural law theorists. According to Macedo, opponents of same-sex marriage such as the new natural law theorists are committed to an "unexplained inconsistency" in their position. They insist that an essential condition for morally good sex is the organic (biological) unity that is achieved in coitus, which is open to procreation, yet these same people also insist that different-sex couples who are sterile can and do achieve the kind of unity requisite for genuine marriage, despite the impossibility of procreation. In Macedo's own words,

> What is the point of sex in an infertile marriage? Not procreation: the partners know they are infertile. If they have sex, it is for pleasure and to express their love or friendship or some other shared good. It will be for precisely the same reasons that committed, loving gay couples have sex. Why are these good reasons for sterile or elderly married couples but not for gay and lesbian couples? And if, on the other hand, sex detracts from the real goods shared by homosexual couples, and indeed undermines their friendship, why is that not the case for infertile heterosexual couples as well? (36)

The crux of the definitional objection to same-sex marriage is that same-sex couples cannot achieve the kind of bodily union available to different-sex couples in the form of coitus, the so-called reproductive-type of act. According to Macedo and those who agree with him, if we allow sterile different-sex couples to marry despite being unable to procreate or to engage in sexual acts that are open to procreation, then we should, on pain of contradiction, allow same-sex couples to marry, too.[16]

The Sexual Orientation Caste System Argument This version of the equal treatment argument differs from the previous two insofar as it tries to make a substantive moral case (and not merely a formal case on the basis of equal treatment) for same-sex marriage. The chief proponent of this line of reasoning is Cheshire Calhoun (2000). Although she is not directly responding to "Against Marriage and Motherhood," Calhoun takes seriously the arguments of Claudia Card regarding the

---

[15] It is widely agreed that the first person to use the phrase "the sterility objection" was Paul J. Weithman (1997).

[16] John Corvino (Corvino and Gallagher 2012, 36–39) also makes a case for the sterility objection.

institution of marriage and, so, sets herself the task of establishing the importance of the right to marry and why refusing same-sex couples this right entails a serious injustice (109). She rejects those arguments which take a certain heterosexual conception of marriage as the normative ideal, and she also criticizes arguments for same-sex marriage that claim barring gays and lesbians from marriage entails sex discrimination. Instead, she examines the reasoning behind the Defense of Marriage Act (1996)[17] in order to uncover the ways in which a marriage bar (i.e., ban) for same-sex couples entails a moral privileging of different-sex couples in a way that seriously displaces gays and lesbians from participating fully in civil society:

> Specifically, marriage bars enact the view that heterosexual love, marriage, and family have a uniquely prepolitical, foundational status in civil society. As a result, heterosexuals can claim for their own relationships not just moral superiority, but a uniquely privileged status beyond the reach of liberal political values. Marriage bars also enact the view that because only heterosexuals are fit to participate in this foundational marital institution, only heterosexuals are entitled to lay claim to a unique citizenship status. Heterosexuals are not *just* free, rational, self-defining persons. They are also naturally fit to participate in the one institution that all societies, liberal or otherwise, must presuppose. (127)

By revealing this alleged privileging of heterosexual status that marriage bars entail, Calhoun believes that she has thereby demonstrated these bars to be immoral, at least insofar as they play a significant role in oppressing and marginalizing gays and lesbians, making it significantly more difficult for them to participate fully in civil society. So, she concludes, formal marriage rights for same-sex couples are worth pursuing in places where they do not exist since establishing these rights can effectively undermine the unjust privileging of heterosexual status.

1.2.2 The Benefits of Same-Sex Marriage

Just as a number of opponents of same-sex marriage argue that granting same-sex couples the right to marry would cause a number of significant harms, a number of defenders of same-sex marriage argue that legalizing it would in no way cause the harms alleged and would, in fact, lead to a number of goods. For example, William Eskridge and Darren Spedale (2006) examined almost twenty years of data concerning same-sex domestic partnerships in Scandinavia and found no evidence to support the harm claims and predictions of opponents of legalizing same-sex marriage. Indeed, they argue that legalizing same-sex domestic partnerships has had a significant positive impact on many different aspects of Scandinavian society, and not merely for gays and lesbians (131–167). For example, they argue that legalizing same-sex domestic partnerships tends to foster closer relationships between

---

[17] The Defense of Marriage Act (DOMA) was passed in the United States and had two main provisions: (1) no state would be required to recognize the same-sex marriage of another state, and (2) the word "marriage" would be defined as the union of one man and one woman for the purposes of the federal government. DOMA passed both the House of Representatives and the Senate with overwhelming majorities. On September 21, 1996, President Bill Clinton signed it into law.

members of same-sex couples and their respective friends and family members (149–154). Additionally, defenders of same-sex marriage are quick to point out, these kinds of benefits extend to the children of gays and lesbians. For example, contrary to the view of someone such as Maggie Gallagher, defenders of same-sex marriage can cite social scientific evidence that purports to show that children who are part of gay or lesbian families are not thereby harmed, and, in fact, seem to do as well as children raised by parents who are in a different-sex relationship, even though the sample sizes tend to be small in these studies (Meezan and Rauch 2005).[18]

Jonathan Rausch (2004) has made his case for expanding the institution of marriage to gays and lesbians on the grounds of the alleged benefits of same-sex marriage. Rauch argues that despite the various functions marriage has had throughout history and across cultures, one of the main points of the institution today is caregiving (18). In other words, marriage is good for married people because "they have someone to look after them, and they know it" (23). On his view, there is, therefore, no good reason to deny this good to same-sex couples. Actually, he argues that such a denial positively harms gays and lesbians, particularly in our marriage-positive culture: "With all due respect to opponents of same-sex marriage, discriminating in order to pin a badge of inferiority on some group or another is not a legitimate use of law….The law's job is not to punish the disadvantaged by excluding them but to help them make the most of their lives, or at least to give them the same benefit of doubt which is accorded everyone else" (100–101). The benefit of allowing same-sex couples to marry, according to Rauch, goes well beyond granting these couples the same rights and legal benefits of different-sex married couples. As he puts it:

> Sex, love and marriage go together. Each works better in conjunction with the other two; each gives shape and direction to the others. Sex without love and love (at least romantic love) without sex both tend to be hollow, unstable, and difficult to integrate into healthy emotional life. And marriage is just as important as the other two. From early adolescence, the prospect of marriage and the expectation of marriage (and the knowledge that society expects marriage) condition the meaning of love. Every kiss, every passion, from the first crush and the first date, has a different, deeper meaning in the context of possible marriage. (59)

According to Rauch, legalizing same-sex marriage would signal an important cultural change for gays and lesbians, one that would allow them to embrace and enjoy the rights, responsibilities, and norms of marriage. In other words, the norms of married life, as they currently exist, would have a knock-on effect, creating more stability for lesbians and gays communities and their families, particularly as they get older.[19]

Standing behind these arguments is the conviction that same-sex relationships and same-sex sexual activity can be every bit as good as different-sex relationships and different-sex sexual acts. That is, the foregoing proponents of the good of same-sex marriage insist that homosexuality (i.e., engaging in same-sex sex acts) is not immoral. John Corvino, for example, has consistently argued this point. Corvino

---

[18] See, for example, Doug Allen's (2015) review of the literature.

[19] I have more to say about this line of reasoning in the next section.

(2013) considers all the arguments about the allegedly harmful "gay lifestyle" (49–76) and the various ways in which some critics claim that homosexuality is "unnatural" (77–97).[20] With respect to the argument I considered above regarding the purpose of sexual organs, Corvino responds by pointing out that sexual organs, and the activities in which we use them, have a variety of purposes beyond mere procreation, and some of these purposes are good (85–86). Also, he argues, "the failure to pursue a good—in this case, procreation—is not equivalent to undermining or attacking that good" (86). In other words, just as my decision to pursue a career as a college professor rather than a career as a physician does not undermine or attack the good of pursuing a career as a physician, so, too, my decision to pursue a childless sexual relationship does not undermine the good of procreation. So, according to Corvino, there are no good reasons for thinking that same-sex relationships are any less capable of ensuring or enhancing the happiness of couples than different-sex relationships.[21] Accordingly, his reasons for supporting the legalization of same-sex marriage are nearly identical to Rauch's.[22]

1.2.3 The Conservative Case for Same-Sex Marriage: Normalizing Homosexuality

Much of Rauch's argument hangs on the current norms for different-sex marriage and the way in which these norms will allegedly have a positive effect on gays and lesbians. This line of thinking originates with Andrew Sullivan (1997) and what is known as the conservative case for same-sex marriage (147). The conservative case critiques the claim that legalizing same-sex marriage harms "traditional" marriage by offering same-sex relationships as a legitimate alternative to different-sex ones, thereby undermining the norms of "traditional" marriage. The main worry for conservatives, as Sullivan acknowledges, concerns the alleged viciousness of a "homosexual lifestyle," which Sullivan eloquently captures:

---

[20] Corvino (2005) also develops a detailed rebuttal of the slippery-slope argument regarding homosexuality (i.e., the view that sanctioning same-sex sexual acts leaves one with no grounds to object to polygamy, incestuous relations, or bestiality).

[21] Gareth Moore (1992) deals directly and more extensively with Aquinas' arguments against homosexuality (71–78). Moore identifies and criticizes three arguments that Aquinas makes against same-sex sex acts: that nature has taught all animals (including humans) that same-sex sex acts are bad; that every emission of semen where there can be no procreation is contrary to the good of humans; and same-sex acts, insofar as they are vices of lechery, are sins against one's neighbor.

[22] As Corvino (2012) puts it, his positive case for same-sex marriage is fairly simple and straightforward: "Generally speaking, it is good for human beings to commit to someone else to have and to hold, for better or for worse, and so on, for life. It is good regardless of whether they happen to be straight or gay. It is good, not only for them, but also for their neighbors, because happy stable couples make happy, stable citizens. And marriage helps sustain this commitment like nothing else" (180).

They mean by a "homosexual life" one in which emotional commitments are fleeting, promiscuous sex is common. Disease is rampant, social ostracism is common, and standards of public decency, propriety, and self-restraint are flaunted. They mean a way of life that deliberately subverts gender norms in order to unsettle the virtues that make family life possible, ridicules heterosexual life, and commits itself to an ethic of hedonism, loneliness, and deceit. (149)

But, according to the conservative case, the extent to which such a "homosexual lifestyle" prevails is due in no small part to the absence of the kinds of social and familial support different-sex couples can get from the institution of marriage. The idea is that legalizing same-sex marriage would open the sexual and familial norms of different-sex marriage to gays and lesbians, and this opening would have a domesticating effect, for lack of a better word, on those gays and lesbians who engage in a "homosexual lifestyle."[23]

1.2.4 Marriage, the Changing Institution

Part of the argumentative strategy of the conservative case is to use the idea of "traditional" marriage to its advantage. This strategy emerges because some opponents of the right of same-sex couples to marry claim that they are merely defending "traditional" marriage—that is, the idea that marriage is between one woman and one man and has procreation and the raising of a family as its essential ends. But some defenders of same-sex marriage are quick to respond that there is no such thing as "traditional" marriage. The institution of marriage, so the argument goes, is an invention of humans, one with no natural purpose or structure. Historian Stephanie Coontz (2005) has done significant work to document the history of marriage. According to her, the history of marriage is the history of an ever-changing and evolving institution, one whose purpose and structure was shaped by, and helped to shape, the societies in which it existed.[24] According to Coontz, "for most of history marriage was not primarily about the individual needs and desires of a man and a woman and the children they produced. Marriage had as much to do with getting good in-laws and increasing one's family labor force as it did with finding a lifetime companion and raising a beloved child" (6). The reality is that for much of human history the institution of marriage was primarily a way for families (i.e., the male heads of families) to build political alliances and gain economic security (Coontz 2005, Part Two). Only in the seventeenth century did we begin to see the changes take place that result in the idea of marrying for love (Coontz 2005, 145–154).

---

[23] It is important to note that talk of a "homosexual life" or "gay lifestyle" almost always concerns gay men, not lesbians. Actually, as Sullivan acknowledges (152–153), lesbian relationships tend to be extremely stable and suffer from none of the alleged defects of a "homosexual life."

[24] Actually, Coontz's research reveals that marriage is not even a universal practice among humans; the Na people of China seem to have had no concept of marriage (Coontz 2005, 24).

Actually, some thinkers would contest the idea that legalizing same-sex marriage signals a new development in human history. William Eskridge (1996) gives a detailed history of the ways in which a variety of cultures—including Western European, Christian cultures— at various points in history have allowed for same-sex unions and marriages. For example, he describes the ways in which certain civilizations (such as those in classical Greece, the Roman Empire, medieval China, and certain Native American tribes, to name a few) recognized same-sex marriages or at least recognized some same-sex relationships as equivalent to marriages (Eskridge 1993, 1437–1469; 1996, Chapter 2). Accounts such as Eskridge's are not trying to say that same-sex marriage was the norm in those cultures and societies (Eskridge 2011). Rather, Eskridge's point is to provide what he calls a "social constructionist history of marriage," which is one that "emphasizes the ways in which marriage is 'constructed' by society over time, with 'exclusions' from the institution being viewed as reflecting larger social power relations" (1993, 1421–1422). If marriage is a social construction in Eskridge's sense, and if throughout history there have been various ways in which the institution has functioned and been understood, then, so proponents of this line of argument contend, there is no such thing as "traditional marriage," and there is no *prima facie* reason why the institution of marriage in the United States cannot change yet again to include same-sex couples.

1.2.5 Opening Up Marriage

These considerations about the historically contingent and changing nature of the institution of marriage leads to the final argument in defense of same-sex marriage that I am going to consider, namely the argument that marriage as it currently exists is incompatible with the ideals of political liberalism and is, therefore, unjust. Elizabeth Brake (2012) defends this view by arguing for something that she calls "minimal marriage." According to Brake, "political liberalism requires the disestablishment of monogamous amatonormative[25] marriage" since "under the constraints of public reason, a liberal state must refrain from basing law, in matters of great import, solely on a comprehensive moral, religious, or philosophical doctrine" (6). According to minimal marriage, "a liberal state can set no principled restrictions on the sex or number of spouses and the nature and purpose of their relationships, except that they be caring relationships" (158).

Brake identifies caring relationships as worthy of legal protection and promotion because she takes caring relationships to be what John Rawls (1971/1999) called a "primary good."[26] As she develops her case for caring relationships as a primary good (173–185), Brake argues for a conception of marriage that would allow differ-

---

[25] "Amatonormativity" is a term of art original to Brake. She defines it as "the focus on marital and amorous love relationships as special sites of value" (5).

[26] According to John Rawls (1971/1999), a primary good is one that "every rational man is presumed to want. These goods normally have a use whatever a person's rational plan of life" (54). Rawls identifies rights, liberties, opportunities, and self-respect as primary goods.

ent-sex and same-sex couples to minimally-marry, along with many other kinds of caring relationships: polyamorous relationships, friendships, caring relationships between relatives, and others. According to Brake's conception of minimal marriage, an individual would be allowed "to exchange all her marital rights reciprocally with one other person or distribute them through her adult care network" (161). Brake's position is a radical one, insofar as it calls for a significant change to our current marriage laws. Such radicalism is justified, on her view, because current legal systems that enshrine amatonormative marriage into law are inconsistent with the ideals of political liberalism, since any "more-than minimal" conception of marriage presupposes particular substantive conceptions of the good, which political liberalism rules out. As such, they are all unjust and should be rejected in favor of a system that supports and legally protects caring relationships of all kinds, including same-sex sexual relationships.

1.3 Looking Ahead

This chapter was dedicated to outlining some of the most important arguments against and for same-sex marriage. Such an account, particularly in a book such as this one, cannot help but be incomplete, but I have aimed to sketch some major lines of argument in the contemporary debate. Looking back on this chapter, I think one might see a handful of themes common to both opponents and proponents of the move to legalize same-sex marriage. Perhaps the most prominent theme is that of the nature and purpose of marriage. In particular, both sides of the debate are keen to argue that their respective understanding of marriage is central to both the good life for individuals and the concerns of justice (Sects. 1.1.1, 1.1.2, 1.1.5, 1.2.1, 1.2.2, 1.2.3, 1.2.4, and 1.2.5). Closely related to this theme is the issue of the relationship between marriage and procreation—or, more broadly, between marriage and children (Sects. 1.1.3 and 1.2.2). A final recurring theme is the place of sexual activity in a good life for some human beings and the way in which sexual activity—both same-sex and different sex—relates to marriage (Sects. 1.1.4 and 1.2.2).

I will return to these arguments in the conclusion of the book, in order to evaluate them in light of resources, I will argue, to be found in Kant's practical philosophy. In the meantime, keeping these three major themes (the purpose of marriage, the relationship of marriage to procreation, the role of sex in marriage) in mind will help inform my presentation in Part I of some of the basics of Kant's ethics and philosophical anthropology.

In my Preface I considered the question as to whether the ethics of Immanuel Kant, an eighteenth-century Prussian philosopher, could have anything to offer those engaged in the contemporary debate over same-sex marriage. This question, I argued, finds its motivation in an influential though misguided reading of Kant's practical philosophy, what I called "the Anscombian reading of Kant." The

Anscombian reading, I argued, mistakenly takes Kant's ethics to be committed to a rigorism and formalism that abstracts from the material conditions and particularities of human life and agency. The remainder of Part I presents an overview of Kant's ethics that is meant to function as an alternative and corrective to the Anscombian reading. In order to clear the way for my overview, I need first to address Anscombe's critique of moral obligation and demonstrate why it does not apply to Kant. This, then, is the concern of the next chapter.

References

Allen, Doug. 2015. More Heat Than Light: A Critical Assessment of the Same-Sex Parenting Literature, 1995–2013. *Marriage & Family Review* 51 (2): 154–182.

Aquinas, Thomas. 2003. *On Evil*. Trans. Richard Regan, ed. with an Introduction and Notes by Brian Davies. Oxford: Oxford University Press.

———. 1975. *Summa Theologiae, Volume 32: Consequences of Faith (2a2ae. 8–16)*. Trans. Thomas Gilby. London: Blackfriars & Eyre and Spottiswoode Limited.

Arroyo, Christopher. 2015. Is the Same-Sex Marriage Debate Really Just about Marriage? *Journal of Applied Philosophy* 33: 2.

Blankenhorn, David. 2007. *The Future of Marriage*. New York/London: Encounter Books.

———. 2012. How My View on Gay Marriage Changed. *The New York Times*. June 22. http://www.nytimes.com/2012/06/23/opinion/how-my-view-on-gay-marriage-changed.html?_r=0.

Brake, Elizabeth. 2012. *Minimizing Marriage: Marriage, Morality, and the Law*. Oxford/New York: Oxford University Press.

Buckle, Stephen. 1993. Natural Law. In *A Companion to Ethics*, ed. Peter Singer, 161–174. Malden: Blackwell Publishing, Ltd.

Calhoun, Cheshire. 2000. *Feminism, the Family, and the Politics of the Closet: Lesbian and Gay Displacement*. Oxford/New York: Oxford University Press.

Card, Claudia. 1996. Against Marriage and Motherhood. *Hypatia* 11 (3): 1–23.

Carroll, Aengus & Lucas Paoli Itaborahy. 2015. *State-Sponsored Homophobia: A World Survey of Laws: Criminalisation, Protection and Recognition of Same-Sex Love*. http://old.ilga.org/Statehomophobia/ILGA_State_Sponsored_Homophobia_2015.pdf.

Chambers, Clare. 2013. The Marriage-Free State. *Proceedings of the Aristotelian Society* 113 (2): 123–143.

Coontz, Stephanie. 2005. *Marriage, A History: How Love Conquered Marriage*. New York: Penguin Books.

Corvino, John. 2005. Homosexuality and the PIB Argument. *Ethics* 115: 501–534.

———. 2013. *What's Wrong with Homosexuality?* New York: Oxford University Press.

Corvino, John, and Maggie Gallagher. 2012. *Debating Same-Sex Marriage (Point/Counterpoint)*. New York: Oxford University Press.

Eskridge, William N. Jr. 1993. A History of Same-Sex Marriage. *Faculty Scholarship Series*. Paper 1504. http://digitalcommons.law.yale.edu/fss_papers/1504

———. 1996. *The Case for Same-Sex Marriage: From Sexual Liberty to Civilized Commitment*. New York: The Free Press.

———. 2011. Six Myths that Confuse the Marriage Equality Debate. *Valpariso University Law Review vol.* 46 (1): 103–116.

Eskridge, William N. Jr., and Darren R. Spedale. 2006. *Gay Marriage: For Better or for Worse? What We've Learned from the Evidence*. Oxford/New York: Oxford University Press.

Finnis, John. 1980 (2011). *Natural Law and Natural Rights*. Oxford: Clarendon Press.

References

Finnis, John M. 1995. Law, Morality, and Sexual Orientation. *Notre Dame Journal of Law, Ethics, and Public Policy* 9 (1): 11–39.

Finnis, John. 2008. Marriage: A Basic and Exigent Good. *The Monist* 91.3–91.4: 388–406.

George, Robert P. 2001. *In Defense of Natural Law*. New York: Oxford University Press.

———. 2004. What's Sex Got to Do with It? Marriage, Morality, and Rationality. *American Journal of Jurisprudence* 49 (1): 63–85.

Girgis, Sherif. 2014. Why Fight for Marriage? *The Public Discourse*, February 6, 2014. http://www.thepublicdiscourse.com/2014/02/11982/.

Girgis, Sherif, Ryan T. Anderson, and Robert P. George. 2012. *What is Marriage? Man and Woman: A Defense*. New York: Encounter Books.

Grisez, Germain. 1983. *The Way of the Lord Jesus, Volumes 1 & 2*. Chicago: Franciscan Herald Press.

Lee, Patrick, and Robert P. George. 2014. *Conjugal Union: What is Marriage and Why It Matters*. New York: Cambridge University Press.

Macedo, Stephen. 1996. Against the Old Sexual Morality of the New Natural Law. In *Natural Law, Liberalism, and Morality*, ed. Robert George, 27–48. Oxford: Oxford University Press.

Masci, David & Elizabeth Sciupac. 2015. Gay Marriage Around the World. *Pew Research Center* http://www.pewforum.org/2015/06/26/gay-marriage-around-the-world-2013/.

Meezan, William, and Jonathan Rauch. 2005. Gay Marriage, Same-Sex Parenting, and America's Children. *The Future of Children* 15 (2): 97–115.

Moore, Gareth. 1992. *The Body in Context: Sex and Catholicism*. London/New York: Continuum.

Porter, Jean. 1999. *Natural and Divine Law: Reclaiming the Tradition for Christian Ethics*. Grand Rapids: Eerdmans.

Ratzinger, Joseph. 1986. Letter to the Bishops of the Catholic Church on the Pastoral Care of Homosexual Persons. http://www.vatican.va/roman_curia/congregations/cfaith/documents/rc_con_cfaith_doc_19861001_homosexual-persons_en.html.

Rauch, Jonathan. 2004. *Gay Marriage: Why It Is Good for Gays, Good for Straights, and Good for America*. New York: Holt Paperback.

Rawls, John. 1971 (1999). *A Theory of Justice*, Rev ed. Cambridge, MA: The Belknap Press of Harvard University Press.

Sullivan, Andrew. 1997 (2004). The Conservative Case. In *Same-Sex Marriage: Pro & Con, A Reader*, ed. Andrew Sullivan, 147–155. New York: Vintage Books.

Weithman, Paul J. 1997. Natural Law, Ethics, and Sexual Complementarity. In *Sex, Preference, and Family*, ed. Martha Nussbaum and David Estlund, 227–246. Oxford: Oxford University Press.

Chapter 2
Finitude & Dependency: Kant's Conception of Moral Obligation

Abstract The concept of moral obligation is central to Kant's ethics. According to the Anscombian reading of Kant's ethics, this concept is conceptually confused and, therefore, corrupts much, if not all, of what Kant has to say about ethics. This critique of moral obligation forms the cornerstone of the Anscombian reading of Kant's ethics, which is why I need to address it directly. Accordingly, I devote this chapter to dealing with the classical source for this critique of moral obligation, Elizabeth Anscombe's "Modern Moral Philosophy" (1958). My main contention regarding Anscombe's critique of "moral obligation" is that she and Kant are working with two very different understandings of moral obligation, and, therefore, Anscombe's criticism of the modern sense of "moral" obligation does not apply to Kant. More specifically, I argue that for Kant moral obligation is not some irreducible, inexplicable metaethical concept, leftover from a divine command theory of ethics and robbed of its metaphysical underpinnings; instead, I argue, we should understand Kant's concept of moral obligation as his way of acknowledging how human beings—finite, imperfect beings that we are—experience the normative constraints that an objective account of human goodness makes on us, namely, as something with which, in some sense, we do not want to comply.

In the Preface to his *Groundwork of the Metaphysics of Morals* Kant famously claims that the book is "nothing more than the search for and establishment of the *supreme principle of morality,* which constitutes by itself a business that in its purpose is complete and to be kept apart from every other moral investigation" (G 4:392). The supreme principle turns out to be the moral law, which Kant understands to be an objective practical principle that holds for every rational being (CPrR 5:19). As he sees it, the moral law can be formulated in a variety of ways, each of which Kant calls "the categorical imperative," and he defines "obligation"—a central concept of his ethical theory—as "the necessity of free action under a categorical imperative" (MM 6:222). Kant even conceives of virtue in terms of our duties to pursue certain ends (MM 6:379–388).

The concept of moral obligation (and the closely related concept of duty), therefore, is central to Kant's ethics. Accordingly, whatever Kant has to say about the ethics of marriage and sex is going to be expressed in terms of one's moral obligation to do X, or one's duty to behave in Y manner, or what one owes to others.

Despite such expressions seeming unproblematic to some, according to the Anscombian reading of Kant's ethics, they actually rest on a conceptual confusion, one that allegedly lies at the heart of Kant's moral theory and, therefore, corrupts much, if not all, of what he has to say about ethics. This critique of moral obligation forms the cornerstone of the Anscombian reading of Kant's ethics, and if I am to make a cogent case for the relevance of Kant's ethics to the contemporary same-sex marriage debate, I need to address it directly. In order to do so, I devote this chapter to dealing with the classical source for this critique of moral obligation, Elizabeth Anscombe's "Modern Moral Philosophy" (1958).[1] Anscombe argues that the concept of a particularly "moral" obligation is one that pervades modern moral philosophy, but this concept, she maintains, makes no sense in our modern context, since it originates in a divine command ethics, which we no longer accept. According to her, the concept of "moral" obligation should be jettisoned along with those moral theories that rely on it. For those persuaded by Anscombe's argument, Kant's ethics—with its focus on obligation and duty—is the paradigmatic case of a modern moral theory committed to the confused notion of "moral" obligation and should, therefore, be condemned to the historical dustbin.

My main contention regarding Anscombe's critique of "moral obligation" is that she and Kant are working with two very different understandings of moral obligation, and, therefore, Anscombe's criticism of the modern sense of "moral" obligation does not apply to Kant.[2] More specifically, I argue that for Kant moral obligation is not some irreducible, inexplicable metaethical concept that is leftover from a divine command theory of ethics and robbed of its metaphysical underpinnings; instead, I maintain, we should understand Kant's concept of moral obligation as his way of acknowledging how human beings—finite, imperfect beings that we are—experience the normative constraints that an objective account of human goodness makes on us, namely, as something with which, in some sense, we do not want to comply.

This chapter proceeds as follows. First, I expound the relevant sections of Anscombe's "Modern Moral Philosophy," drawing attention to the parts of her text that explicitly address Kant's ethics. I distinguish between Anscombe's critique of Kant's ethics and her critique of the modern sense of "moral" obligation, and I argue that there are good reasons for thinking that she did not primarily have Kant in mind when she formulated her critique of "moral" obligation as confused. Nonetheless, we can distinguish between (1) what Anscombe took her primary target to be in criticizing "moral" obligation, and (2) which ethical theories are susceptible to

---

[1] Perhaps the other most influential critic of Kant's ethics is Bernard Williams (1985). Williams is influenced by Anscombe's work but develops his criticisms of Kant by examining what he takes to be Kant's understanding of "morality." For responses to Williams' version of the Anscombian reading, see Stephen Darwall (1987) and Korsgaard (1996a)

[2] Given the influence of Anscombe's criticisms of the modern concept of moral obligation, it is somewhat surprising that few defenders of Kant's ethics address them. For example, although J.B. Schneewind (1997) and Allen Wood (1999, 2008) acknowledge Anscombe's criticism of the concept of moral obligation, neither of them engage in an extended defense of Kant's use of the concept.

Anscombe's critique. With this distinction in mind, I go on to present Anscombe's critique of moral obligation in order to discern the extent to which it may apply to Kant's ethics, regardless of her intentions. I argue that it actually does not apply at all, since Kant understands moral obligation to be the way in which humans subjectively experience the rational requirement to be good. Finally, I turn to Kant's concept of autonomy and develop an interpretation of this concept that is consistent with my reading of his understanding of moral obligation, thereby demonstrating that Anscombe's critique of Kantian autonomy (the centerpiece of her criticisms aimed directly at Kant) also misses its mark.

2.1 Anscombe on Moral Obligation[3]

Anscombe begins "Modern Moral Philosophy" with three theses for which she argues. The first is that it is no longer profitable to do moral philosophy. The second is that the concepts of "moral" obligation and "moral" duty "ought to be jettisoned if this is psychologically possible; [*sic.*] because they are survivals, or derivatives of survivals, from an earlier conception of ethics which no longer generally survives, and are only harmful without it" (1958, 1). Her final thesis is that there are no significant differences between British moral philosophers from Sidgwick until 1958, when the essay was published. Given my aim in this chapter, I focus exclusively on her second thesis.

2.1.1 *Anscombe's Brief History of Modern Ethics*

Anscombe claims that "all the best-known writers on ethics in modern times, from Butler to Mill, appear to me to have faults as thinkers on the subject which make it impossible to hope for any direct light on it from them. I will state these objections with the brevity which their character makes possible" (2). If we exclude her extended discussion of Hume, for whom she has a particular esteem (despite thinking he gets things wrong), her dismissal of 150 years of Western European moral philosophy spans about one page of the text. One might take issue with her dismissiveness, but that is not my concern. Rather, I want to look at what she says about Kant, who figures prominently in this part of the essay. Here is what she says, in full:

---

[3] I first developed my reading of Anscombe and defense of Kant in "The Experience of Duty and the Kingdom of Ends: A Reply to Anscombe's critique of Kant's Ethics," which I presented at the 2011 meeting of the Northern New England Philosophical Association. In what follows, I develop the argument I presented in that paper, and I rely on the work of Robert Stern, which I subsequently discovered and which makes a similar argument to the one I made.

Kant introduces the idea of 'legislating for oneself,' which is as absurd as if in these days, when majority votes command great respect, one were to call each reflective decision a man made a *vote* resulting in a majority, which as a matter of proportion is overwhelming, for it is always 1-0. The concept of legislation requires superior power in the legislator. His own rigoristic convictions on the subject of lying were so intense that it never occurred to him that a lie could be relevantly described as anything but just a lie (e.g., as 'a lie in such-and-such circumstances'). His rule about universalizable maxims is useless without stipulations as to what shall count as a relevant description of an action with a view to constructing a maxim about it. (2)

In the preceding passage Anscombe identifies three particularly egregious mistakes of Kant: (1) Kant's notion of self-legislation (i.e., autonomy), (2) Kant's rigoristic views on lying,[4] and (3) Kant's failure to explain how to formulate maxims (i.e., what he defines as a "subjective principle of volition" [G 4:401, note; cf. 4:420, note]); this failure, according to Anscombe, results in our inability to use his universalizability test for discerning whether a course of action is permissible or not.[5] Of the three criticisms, only the first, which Robert Stern (2012, 13–14) calls "the Kantian paradox," is relevant to my purpose in this chapter, and I shall address it in the last section. What I want to note at this point is that the preceding passage is Anscombe's only explicit discussion of Kant in her essay, which is one reason why I think that Anscombe does not have Kant in mind when she goes on to formulate her critique of "moral" obligation as confused. Actually, I think there are three additional reasons for drawing this conclusion.

First of all, in her brief catalogue of Kant's philosophical sins, Anscombe does not identify Kant's use of the term "moral" as one of them. This is unsurprising, since the point of her discussion of the failures of the most noteworthy modern philosophers from Butler to Mill is to show that their respective moral theories are inadequate quite apart from their troubling use of the term "moral." To put the issue bluntly, Anscombe thinks that the three other problems she identifies in Kant's ethics are so profound that it is not worth the trouble to take issue with his conception of moral obligation. Second, no evidence exists that Anscombe made a detailed study of Kant's ethics, though she likely read the *Groundwork*.[6] Third, throughout

---

[4] Kant believed that one should never lie, that lying always constitutes a violation of the moral law. For Kant on lying, see "On a Supposed Right to Lie from Philanthropic Concerns" (1797) and the *Metaphysics of Morals* (6:429–431). There have been many attempts to defend Kant's position on lying, often by interpreting his moral theory as at odds with his explicit universal prohibitions on lying. See, for example, Allen W. Wood (2011) and Sally Sedgwick (1991). It is worth noting that Anscombe herself believed that it is always wrong to lie.

[5] Anne Margaret Baxley (2010) explains maxims thusly: "A maxim is a subjective principle of action according to which an agent tends to act in relevantly similar situations, expressing a generalized intent or policy of action that can be characterized by the formula: 'When in S-type situation, perform Y-type actions for purpose P'" (22). On the so-called universalizability test, the literature is too vast to summarize in a note. For an example of someone who tries to defend Kant's universalizability test of maxims, see Korsgaard (1996a). For an example of someone who downplays the importance of the universalizability test in favor of other formulations of Kant's categorical imperative see Wood (1999, 2008).

[6] The same is true of Peter Geach (1969), who defends Anscombe's criticism of "moral" obligation.

2.1 Anscombe on Moral Obligation

her essay, when Anscombe writes about "modern moral philosophy" she almost always has in mind British moral philosophers. Indeed, the only non-British philosopher she mentions is Kant, which she does only to dismiss him as hopelessly confused.

So, I do not think that Anscombe had Kant especially in mind when she developed her criticism of "moral" obligation, but this should not stop us from asking whether the criticism applies to him nonetheless. Actually, given that Kant develops his account of moral obligation in response to a metaethical debate that started in the late medieval ages between natural law theorists and divine command theorists (Stern 2012, 43–52),[7] not surprisingly, some contemporary philosophers have read Anscombe's criticism of "moral" obligation as applying to Kant. For example, Maria Alvarez and Aaron Ridley (2007), and Reshef Agam-Segal[8] (2012, 2013) all argue that Anscombe's criticisms successfully apply to Kant, while Stephen Darwall (2006), Christine Korsgaard (1996a), and Eric Wilson (2008, 2009) have each attempted in their own respective ways to defend Kant from Anscombe's criticism of the "moral" ought.[9] I think, however, that each of these critiques and defenses of Kant is misguided insofar as I think Anscombe's criticism of "moral" obligation does not actually apply to Kant's use of the concept. In order to prepare the way for my argument defending my reading of Kant on obligation (which I present in Sect. 2.2), I want first to exposit Anscombe's criticism of "moral" obligation.

2.1.2 Moral Obligation: A Case of Language Gone on Holiday

Anscombe distinguishes between a perfectly acceptable use of "ought" or "should" and an allegedly special "moral" ought or "moral" should. The acceptable uses of these terms are ones that we encounter with some frequency in ordinary affairs. For example, according to Anscombe, we sometimes say that "a machine should be oiled," or that "it ought to be oiled." Such uses of "should" and "ought" are fairly straightforward. As she explains, these phrases only mean, e.g., "that running without oil is bad for it, or it runs badly without oil" (5). She distinguishes these acceptable uses of "ought" or "should" from the "special so-called 'moral' sense—i.e. a sense in which they imply some absolute verdict (like one of guilty/not guilty on a man) on what is described in the 'ought' sentences used in certain types of contexts"

---

[7] J. B. Schneewind (1997) gives the definitive historical account of this debate.

[8] Agam-Segal (2013) agrees with me that Anscombe most likely did not have Kant in mind when she formulated her criticisms, but he thinks they apply nonetheless.

[9] Korsgaard and Wilson attempt to defend Kant from Anscombe's criticisms while Alvarez & Ridley argue that Korsgaard misinterprets Anscombe and, therefore, does not defend Kant successfully from Anscombe's critique of the modern sense of "moral." Darwall argues that Anscombe's critique can be "turned on its head" (115) by relying on his account of the second-person standpoint (i.e., the idea that the normative force of obligation proceeds from the demand that others make on oneself). For a critique of Korsgaard's response to Anscombe, see Agam-Segal (2013). For a critique of Darwall, see Stern (2015, 243–263).

(5). An example of such a special use of "ought" might be, "You ought to keep your promises." In cases of such imperatives, were someone to ask, "But why should I keep my promises?", the reply would be, "Because you should, *period.*" Hence, Anscombe's remark about the "moral" ought implying some absolute verdict.

Given that a classical thinker such as Aristotle did not have the concept of "moral" obligation, what accounts for the difference between his conceptual framework and our modern one? According to Anscombe, the answer is Christianity, which subscribes to a law conception of ethics (one that Christians took over and adopted from the Torah). To be clear, Anscombe is *not* claiming that a divine law ethic could only arise within a Christian or Jewish culture, since she readily acknowledges that the Stoics had a law conception of ethics without the Jewish or Christian conceptions of a creator God who legislates the law.[10] Rather, she claims that the particular, special "moral" ought as it appears in modern ethical theories has its roots in the use of "moral" that was at home in Christian divine law ethics:

> To have a *law* conception of ethics is to hold that what is needed for conformity with the virtues [*sic.*] failure in which is the mark of being bad *qua* man (and not merely, say, *qua* craftsman or logician)—that what is needed for *this,* is required by divine law. Naturally it is not possible to have such a conception unless you believe in God as a lawgiver; like Jews, Stoics, and Christians. But if such a conception is dominant for many centuries, and then is given up, it is a natural result that the concepts of 'obligation,' of being bound or required as by a law, should remain though they had lost their root; and if the word 'ought' has become invested in certain contexts with the sense of 'obligation,' it too will remain to be spoken with a special emphasis and a special feeling in these contexts. (6)

According to Anscombe, a Christian divine law conception of ethics explains what is required for a human being to be a good human being by reference to what God has commanded us to do, by reference to what God, as Creator, requires of us: "Why should I do X?" "Because God demands it.". Within such a divine command theory of ethics, any account of why, e.g., being just or temperate is normative for humans must, at bottom, appeal to the authority of God as requiring humans to be just and temperate, period. To get at this central point in yet another way, according to a divine command theory framework, *that* God commands X, or Y, or Z is what makes it right and good. Accordingly, as Anscombe explains things, a whole vocabulary was developed within a Christian divine law ethic, one that used legalistic language (e.g., "bound," "required," "obligated," "illicit") to describe human goodness and badness. This way of thinking and talking about ethics reigned for many hundreds of years, though, as far as Anscombe is concerned, it no longer does.

Given the longevity of a Christian divine law ethics, we should not be surprised, thinks Anscombe, that some of the language that was at home in *that* worldview would still be with us and would still carry with it some of the psychological force that it had when most people actually subscribed to such an ethic. In other words, the psychological force a word such as "moral" has on us is a mere remnant of a long-since rejected moral framework—a kind of conceptual analog of a vestigial

---

[10] In this respect, it seems that some of Charles Pigden's (1988) criticisms of Anscombe miss their mark.

organ (think, for example, of the way in which people of a certain age still talk about "taping" some song or television program despite almost all of our media being digital). Insofar as the divine command framework has been rejected, so, too, has the normative justification for the distinctive vocabulary developed with that framework. So, as far as Anscombe is concerned, we should no longer use the special, "moral" sense of ought because it is out of place in our secular worldview. As she writes, "the situation, if I am right, was the interesting one of the survival of a concept outside the framework of thought that made it a really intelligible one" (6). The problem with the modern, special sense of "*moral* ought," according to Anscombe, is that it suggests "a *verdict* on my action, according as it agrees or disagrees in the 'ought' sentence. And where one believes no judge or law exists, the notion of a verdict may retain its psychological effect, but not its meaning" (8). Therefore, reasons Anscombe, we should jettison this peculiar concept, since "it has no reasonable sense outside a law conception of ethics" and "you can do ethics without it, as is shown by the example of Aristotle" (8). In short, without a divine legislator, the concept of moral obligation, according to Anscombe, is senseless.

2.2 Kant on Moral Obligation

Keeping in mind the long, British philosophical tradition that criticizes Kant's moral theory, Barbara Herman (1993) claims that "Kant's ethics has been the captive of its critics" (vii). She means that the basic way in which Kant's ethics is understood, the language that is typically used to characterize it, has been foisted upon Kant by those who take issue with his moral theory. Herman identifies J.H. Muirhead (1932) as the first to sort moral theories into two basic types: deontological theories, which prioritize obligation and the moral law, and teleological theories, which focus on ends and our pursuit of them. According to Muirhead's typography, Kant's ethics is a paradigmatic case of a "deontological moral theory." To say that Kant's ethics is "deontological" is to say that it is primarily "rule-based, centered on duty rather than on good, without concern for the place of morality in a good human life, and so on" (Herman 1993, vii). In other words, to characterize Kant as a deontologist is to buy into the Anscombian reading of Kant's ethics. Like Herman, I think such a sweeping generalization does more to obscure than to clarify.[11] To push her observation a bit further, though, I also think that Kant's ethics has occasionally been the captive of his defenders, thinkers such as those I named at the end of Sect. 2.1.1: Darwall, Korsgaard, and Wilson. I think philosophers such as they do not fully appreciate what Kant means by the phrase "moral obligation" and related concepts

---

[11] There is not enough space to give a representative list of the thinkers who have sought to defend Kant's ethics from misreadings, even if I were to limit myself to the last twenty-five years. Nonetheless, some of the most influential interpreters of Kant have been Allison (1990), Baron (1995), Baxley (2010), Guyer (2000), Herman (1993), Korsgaard (1996a, b), O'Neill (1989), Rawls (2000), and Wood (1999, 2008).

such as "law" and "duty." I contend that the failure to appreciate the way these concepts function in Kant's practical philosophy leads them to assume that Anscombe's criticism of "moral" obligation is supposed to apply to Kant. More specifically, I think philosophers such as these have overlooked the way in which Kant's understanding of moral obligation is informed by his philosophical anthropology, particularly Kant's understanding of humans as finite, imperfect rational beings.[12] Adequately acknowledging the role this conception of human beings plays in his practical philosophy holds the key to seeing why Anscombe's criticism of "moral" obligation does not apply to Kant's ethics.

2.2.1 *Finite Wills vs. Holy Wills*

Kant's distinction between finite rational wills and holy wills has not received the attention it deserves (Stern 2012, 75), which I think is the main reason why misunderstandings remain when it comes to the sense of moral obligation in Kant's ethics.[13] The distinction is between beings, such as human beings, who have what Kant calls "finite wills" and beings, such as God, who have what he calls "holy wills." Kant draws this distinction in various places in his writings. Here is a typical statement from his *Critique of Practical Reason:*

> For human beings and all created rational beings moral necessity is necessitation, that is, obligation, and every action based on it is to be represented as duty, not as a kind of conduct which we already favor of our own accord or could come to favor—as if we could ever bring it about that without respect for the law, which is connected with fear or at least apprehension of transgressing it, we of ourselves, like the Deity raised beyond all dependence, could come into possession of *holiness* of will by an accord of will with the pure moral law becoming, as it were, our nature, an accord never to be disturbed (in which case the law would finally cease to be a command for us, since we would never be tempted to be unfaithful to it). (CPrR 5:81–82).

In this passage Kant contrasts human beings (i.e., created rational beings) with God. God, on his view, is a being whose will is, in principle, in perfect accord with what is genuinely good—that is, with what reason correctly deems good. Kant, therefore, says that God possesses "holiness of will," which is just to say that God is not the kind of being who can act badly, since God cannot be tempted to act badly.[14]

---

[12] For some examples of commentators who have argued that Kant's philosophical anthropology is integral to his moral theory overall see Baxley (2010), Louden (2000), and Wood (1999, 2003).

[13] I do not mean to imply that no one has recognized this distinction. Baxley (2010) and Wood (2008), for example, draw attention to it in ways that point to its importance for understanding Kant's moral theory. Rather, I mean to say that very few people have emphasized the distinction sufficiently. One exception to this is Stern (2012), on whom I rely heavily in the current section.

[14] I realize that this passage, and others that I shall cite, raise many questions about the cogency of Kant's concept of God, particularly in light of more traditional, orthodox understandings of God found in Christianity and Judaism (e.g., is God a moral agent? Does it make sense to say that God acts freely? Etc.). These are important questions, but they do not need to be answered in order for me to make my argument about Kant's understanding of moral obligation. Hence, I set them aside.

2.2 Kant on Moral Obligation

According to Kant, therefore, it does not make sense to say that God is under obligation (i.e., is subject to what Kant calls "moral necessity"), since God cannot but do what reason shows to be genuinely good.[15] The case is very different, thinks Kant, when it comes to human beings. Human beings do not have a holy will, and, as the above passage maintains, humans *cannot* have a holy will. They cannot, according to Kant, because human beings are imperfect rational beings.

When I say that Kant thinks that human beings are imperfect, I do not mean to draw attention to the fact that people sometimes calculate incorrectly, or that they occasionally fail to follow directions, or that sometimes musicians play the wrong note (though each of these observations is correct). When I write of the imperfection of human beings in this context I mean it as a direct contrast to the perfection of what Kant calls a holy will. So, as I read Kant, to say that human beings are finite, imperfect beings means that, unlike a morally perfect being (i.e., a being with a holy will), it is possible for human beings to act in ways that are inconsistent with what is objectively good for human beings in general. This is the case, according to Kant, because human beings are not purely rational beings. We are rational, to be sure, but we are embodied rational beings, finite beings who are also animals. This means, on his view, that in addition to the ends proper to human beings merely in virtue of our being rational we also have ends proper to us in virtue of our being embodied animals. Kant's most common way of expressing the distinction that applies to human beings (but not, for example, to God) is to talk about finite rational beings "possessing two natures," but this phrase needs some elbaoration.

On the one hand, humans have what Kant calls "rational nature," by which we can understand Kant to mean that human beings are able to reason practically in order to discern what is genuinely good to do, and humans can then act on the results of such reasoning. But humans are not purely rational beings (as Kant believes God to be). We are, according to Kant, also sensible, dependent beings: embodied beings with sensuous desires and appetites and who are subject to emotions and who need others. Kant understands these "sensible" (i.e., sensuous) desires and emotions to be geared toward the individual's own well-being, what Kant calls "happiness."[16] So, unlike God, according to Kant, human beings have competing concerns: on the one hand, an interest in doing what reason rightly discerns is good; on the other, the incentive of one's own happiness (i.e., one's own satisfaction and well-being). In a famous passage from the *Groundwork*, Kant describes the relationship between these two concerns:

---

[15] Cf. LE 29: 604: "In the Gospel we also find an ideal, namely that of holiness. It is that state of mind from which an evil desire never arises. God alone is holy, and man can never become so, but the ideal is good." One philosopher who picks up on this line of thinking in Kant is William P. Alston (1990).

[16] Kant, of course, recognizes that there are other-regarding emotions such as sympathy, but he thinks that these are only genuinely other-regarding after we have done the work of cultivating them under the guidance of our reason and willing, putting these emotions under what Kant calls "the discipline of reason" (CPrR 5:82). Prior to such work, these emotions may seem other-regarding but Kant thinks that they really are primarily expressions of one's self-love.

> Now reason issues its precepts unremittingly, without thereby promising anything to the inclinations [i.e., habitual, sensuous desires], and so, as it were, with disregard and contempt for those claims, which are so impetuous and besides so apparently equitable (and refuse to be neutralized by any command). But from this there arises a *natural dialectic*, that is, a propensity to rationalize against those strict laws of duty and to cast doubt upon their validity, or at least upon their purity and strictness, and, where possible, to make them better suited to our wishes and inclinations. (4:405)[17]

In the preceding passage Kant has in mind a phenomenon he believes pervades the moral lives of imperfect beings such as humans. Let us imagine the case of Melinda. Melinda is a sculptor and has been commissioned by a local college to produce a work of art to inhabit the foyer of a new building on campus. She has a strict deadline that she has promised to meet, and she knows that she cannot lollygag and waste time if she is going to follow through on her promise. But, for various reasons, Melinda is disinclined to get started on the piece. Let's suppose that she feels insecure about her own talents as an artist, or that she is simply overwhelmed with the idea of the task at hand, or that (for whatever reason) on this particular day, she would much prefer to be doing just about anything else besides working on the sculpture. Here, then, we have the case of someone who knows what she should do but does not want to do it. Following Kant, one might metaphorically say that there is a tug-o-war going on with Melinda between her concern to do what is right (i.e., what is objectively good) and her desire to do what satisfies her.[18] This tug-o-war is what Kant means by a natural dialectic between reason and inclination (i.e., our sensuous, habitual desires).

Before moving on I must make two further points, each of which I will explore further in the next chapter. First, when it comes to making choices, Kant thinks that human beings in general have a tendency (he calls it a "propensity") to side with their own respective conceptions of happiness rather than with what their practical reasoning tells them is truly good.[19] Second, he thinks that the natural dialectic he identifies and the propensity to side with inclination and one's own happiness is a constitutional defect of human beings (CPrR 5:25). In other words, moral imperfection is part of human nature and, therefore, cannot be completely overcome or eliminated, even in the best of us. Hence, Kant's claim (in the passage from the second *Critique* that I quoted at the start of this section) that it is absurd to think that humans could ever achieve holiness, since this achievement would involve human beings bringing it about that they cannot be tempted to act immorally, which is impossible (i.e., it would consist in human beings becoming something no longer human).

---

[17] Cf. G 4:424: "If we now attend to ourselves in any transgression of a duty, we find that we do not really will that our maxim should become a universal law, since that is impossible for us, but that the opposite of our maxim should instead remain a universal law, only we take the liberty of making an *exception* to it for ourselves (or just this once) to the advantage of our inclination."

[18] Some might say that were Melinda more virtuous, she would be satisfied by doing her work and keeping her promise. Kant would not disagree with such a claim, but what I am concerned to emphasize at present is that on Kant's view human beings can never completely exterminate the desire to pursue one's own well-being over-and-against what is truly and objectively good.

[19] This propensity will be the subject of Chap. 3.

At this point one might want to voice an objection: are not there cases of people who *simply want to do what is good*? If so, are not these same cases ones where there is no reluctance, and, therefore, no opposition from the inclinations? To borrow an example that the philosopher D.Z. Phillips once used in a lecture, are there not cases where a father *just wants* to play with his children and enjoys doing so? I will have more to say in response to this kind of objection when I get to Chap. 4. At this point, however, I can briefly anticipate my full response. First, of course, Kant acknowledges such cases (i.e., he acknowledges that someone might "just want" to do what is good because she or he enjoys doing it); this is why in the *Groundwork* he considers the example of the sympathetic benefactor (G 4:398–399), someone who *just enjoys* helping people in need. Second, Kant would want to distinguish cases where someone wants to do what is good because they just "naturally" enjoy it and cases where someone wants to do what is good as a result of a considered and deliberate resolution to cultivate such a disposition. Kant praises the latter as virtuous but views the former as the expression of some natural and unreflective disposition that is no more deserving of moral praise than having green eyes or being six feet tall. Lastly, even when one cultivates a virtuous disposition, Kant's philosophical anthropology and understanding of human imperfection motivates him to insist that there always remains some competing desire, however, slight, which stands in contrast to doing what is good, since there is always the "demand" our animal natures make on us with respect to our happiness. This notion of competing desires in human beings is what Kant has in mind when he explains their experience of what he calls "moral necessitation."

2.2.2 *Moral Necessitation and Human Imperfection*

Although Kant insists that the moral law applies equally to all rational beings,[20] he thinks that moral obligation only applies to human beings—to finite, imperfect, dependent rational beings such as ourselves. Kant uses the term "law" or "moral law" as applicable to both finite rational wills and holy wills, but he does so because he takes "law" to pick out what reason correctly judges is good for rational beings

---

[20] There seems to be an obvious problem with Kant's insistence that the moral law applies to all rational beings alike, namely, that it stands to reason that what is good for human beings would not be good for a being such as God. I think that this problem can be addressed by keeping in mind that, according to Kant, we do not determine what is good for humans merely by reference to some formal law of practical reason. We also, on his view, need to take into account the particular constitution and circumstances of human beings in order to discover what is good for them, what is required of them in order for them to act well. As he writes in his introduction to the *Metaphysics of Morals*, "a metaphysics of morals cannot dispense with principles of application, and we shall often have to take as our object the particular *nature* of human beings, which is cognized only by experience, in order to *show* in it what can be inferred from universal moral principles" (6:217). Accordingly, although the moral law in principle applies to all rational beings insofar as they are rational, this law does not yield content until it is applied to the nature of the rational being in question, which, in our case, is human beings.

qua rational beings. Kant, as I have observed, believes that the moral law takes the form of an imperative for finite rational beings such as human beings—"You ought to do X," or "You ought to refrain from Y"—because human beings "are beings affected by needs and sensible motives" (CPrR 5:32) and, so, experience the moral law as a constraint, as what Kant calls "necessitation."[21].

Kant defines duty as "that action to which someone is bound" (MM 6:222),[22] but he distinguishes between two ways in which someone can be bound or constrained: "the constraint may be an *external constraint* or a *self-constraint*" (MM 6:379). This distinction between two ways in which someone can be constrained corresponds to the distinction Kant makes in his practical philosophy between a doctrine of right and a doctrine of virtue. This distinction will play an important role in understanding Kant's conception of marriage as a solution to the problem of sexual objectification, which I treat in Chap. 6.[23] In anticipation of that discussion, and by way of explaining what Kant means by necessitation, I can give a preliminary account of the difference between right and virtue. The Doctrine of Right, according to Kant, deals with external constraint, which is accomplished via positive law or contract (e.g., my duty as a United States citizens to obey U.S. laws, or my duty to fulfill my contractual obligations with my employer). External constraint has to do with the ways in which human beings can be coerced by others into performing certain acts or refraining from certain acts.[24] The Doctrine of Virtue, by contrast, deals with self-constraint insofar as virtue, according to Kant, concerns not merely the acts human beings perform but also the motives with which we act. He characterizes virtue in terms of self-constraint because agents must freely adopt motives, and, in so doing, human beings have to subordinate some desires in order to pursue other ones. Self-constraint is, according to Kant, the kind of constraint we exercise with respect to our inclinations and what the moral law commands, but Kant's view can be easily misunderstood. It is easy, though incorrect, to read him as saying that every time any human being acts, there is a felt temptation to act contrary to what is truly good (i.e., to what the moral law commands). And so it is easy, though incorrect, to read Kant as saying that the best kind of character of which humans are capable is what

---

[21] Cf. MM 6:222: "An imperative is a practical rule by which an action in itself contingent is *made* necessary. An imperative differs from a practical law in that a law indeed represents an action as necessary but takes no account of whether this action already inheres by an *inner* necessity in the acting subject (as in a holy being) or whether it is contingent (as in the human being); for where the former is the case there is no imperative." For an account of Kant's indebtedness to Baumgarten with respect to the concept of necessitation, see Clemens Schwaiger (2009).

[22] Cf. G 4:397.

[23] To foreshadow that discussion, insofar as Kant's practical philosophy distinguishes between juridical lawgiving and ethical lawgiving, it allows for a distinction between the legal problem of sexual objectification (i.e., how can the rights of sexual partners be protected) and the moral problem of sexual objectification (i.e., how can the dignity of sexual partners be acknowledged and respected). Kant's account of marriage is meant to be a solution to the former, not the latter.

[24] It is under the heading of right that Kant recognizes what Anscombe characterizes as the everyday, unproblematic uses of "duty" and "obligation."

2.2 Kant on Moral Obligation

Aristotle called "continence."[25] In order to explain why the preceding readings of self-contraint are incorrect, I need to return to a point I made above about the wills of finite rational beings.

When Kant claims that finite rational beings have a propensity to rationalize their behavior in favor of the interests of their sensible natures (i.e., in favor of the interest of their respective conceptions of happiness over and against what is genuinely good and required of them), he is making a conceptual point about human agency. In the *Critique of Practical Reason,* Kant explains that for finite, imperfect beings such as human beings.

> the moral law is for them an *imperative* that commands categorically because the law is unconditional; the relation of such a will to this law is *dependence* under the name of obligation, which signifies a *necessitation,* though only by reason and its objective law, to an action which is called *duty* because a choice that is pathologically affected (though not thereby determined, hence still free) brings with it a wish arising from *subjective* causes, because of which it can often be opposed to the pure objective determining ground and thus needs a resistance of practical reason which, as moral necessitation, may be called an internal but intellectual constraint. (CPrR 5:32).

As Anne Margaret Baxley (2010, p. 111) puts it, "morality is obligatory for us human beings because it is always possible for our sensible feelings, desires, and interests to run contrary to the demands of morality." In other words, even if on a particular occasion one's inclinations are in line with what is genuinely good, it is nonetheless the case that they might not be (i.e., things could have been otherwise on that occasion and may be otherwise on other occasions). Hence, according to Kant, human beings' experience of genuine goodness as obligation, as restraint or necessity. Here are Kant's own words from the *Groundwork*:

> A perfectly good will would, therefore, equally stand under objective laws (of the good), but it could not on this account be represented as *necessitated* to actions in conformity with law since of itself, by its subjective constitution, it can be determined only through the representation of the good. Hence, no imperatives hold for the *divine* will and in general for a *holy* will: the 'ought' is out of place here, because volition is of itself necessarily in accord with the law. Therefore imperatives are only formulae expressing the relation of objective laws of volition in general to the subjective imperfection of the will of this or that rational being, for example, of the human will. (4:414)[26]

---

[25] Baxley (2010, Chapter 2) responds to this criticism of Kant. I take up Kant's account of virtue in Chap. 4.

[26] It is telling that Kant consistently maintains that human beings have no obligation to pursue their own happiness, since "*his own happiness* is an end that every human being has (by virtue of the impulses of nature), but this end can never without self-contradiction be regarded as a duty. What everyone already wants unavoidably, of his own accord, does not come under the concept of *duty,* which is *constraint* to an end adopted reluctantly" (MM 6:386). Cf. CPrR 5:37.

2.2.3 Kant pace Anscombe on Moral Obligation

I am now in a position to explain why Kant's understanding of moral obligation is immune to Anscombe's critique. Recall her account of the normative justification of moral obligation in a divine command theory of ethics: "to have a *law* conception of ethics is to hold that what is needed for conformity with the virtues…is required by divine law" (6). In other words, on a law conception of ethics, the answer to the question, "Why should I do X?" boils down to, "Because God commands it of you." On such an ethic, moral claims are justified by appeal to God's command. And, argues Anscombe, without belief in such a God, the notion of "moral" obligation has no legitimate normative force and sense. Put differently, according to Anscombe, modern moral philosophers have retained the concept of a "moral" obligation as their basic ethical concept: what makes some action morally good is that you are *"morally"* obligated to perform it (just as what makes some action morally bad is that you are "morally" required to refrain from performing it); these modern moral philosophers go wrong insofar as we secular, twentieth-century philosophers cannot, according to Anscombe, explain the normative force of this "moral" obligation, since there is no superior lawgiver to obligate us morally. As a result, observes Anscombe, modern moral philosophers who subscribe to a concept of "moral" obligation can only answer the question, "Why should I do X?", with "Because it is your *moral* duty." And that, she maintains, does not cut it.

Kant's concept of moral obligation, however, does not function in this way. To borrow Robert Stern's (2012, 47) expression, Kant's talk of moral obligation is best understood in "phenomenological" terms, that is, as an attempt to capture the way in which morally imperfect beings such as ourselves experience what is genuinely and objectively good for us. Kant does not invoke moral obligation or the feeling of obligatoriness as an answer to the normative question, "Why should I do X?" He uses the concept of moral obligation as a way of capturing the extent to which we are finite, imperfect beings (i.e., as a way of expressing the possibility on any given occasion that a human being may be motivated to act in favor of her own subjective happiness rather than because of considerations about what is genuinely, objectively good for her to do *qua* human being). An important part of the reason he can use the concept of moral obligation in this way is because he is committed to moral realism (i.e., because he believes that a cogent answer to the normative question, "Why should I do X," has to make reference to facts about human beings and the kind of life that is good for human beings).[27] "Moral obligation" is not a basic moral concept for Kant in the way that it is for the divine law theorists and the modern moral philosophers whom Anscombe criticizes. As I read Kant, what is basic for him, morally-speaking, is what practical reason discerns as genuinely good, and these genuine goods do not depend on the desires or emotions of human beings for their

---

[27] I have more to say about Kant's moral realism in Sect. 2.3.2.

goodness, nor do they depend for their goodness on the will of God.[28] But because humans are constitutionally imperfect and can be tempted to act in ways inconsistent with what reason prescribes (i.e., since it is always possible for even the best humans to act immorally), Kant asserts that our *experience* of what is genuinely good, of what reason judges to be good, results in a feeling of obligation, of being required to do something that one, in some sense, does not want to do. Hence, Kant's claim that the moral law, when it comes to humans, takes the form of a command or an imperative.

In light of these considerations, I think that Kant's concept of moral obligation does not commit him to the kind of conceptual confusion that Anscombe claims infects modern uses of the concept "moral" obligation. So, I think this aspect of the Anscombian reading of Kant is mistaken. I have not, however, addressed the other, related criticism Anscombe makes of Kant, namely, that his notion of self-legislation is absurd. Drawing on the preceding account of moral obligation in Kant, I am going to argue that Anscombe's critique of Kantian self-legislation rests on a misunderstanding of Kant's concept of autonomy, one analogous to the way in which some have misunderstood Kant's concept of moral obligation to be a concept of "moral" obligation.

2.3 Kant's Account of Autonomy of the Will

Recall that Anscombe takes the notion of self-legislation to be absurd, since "the concept of legislation requires superior power in the legislator" (1958, 2). Her critique gets at what has come to be known as the Kantian paradox (Stern 2012, 13–14), which for my purposes entails two related criticisms. First, the notion of self-legislation is absurd because she who "binds" herself at will can also "unbind" herself, which is just to say that the notion of "binding oneself" makes no sense (as anyone who has made and failed to keep a New Year's Eve resolution knows). Second, since self-legislation requires superior power in the legislator (i.e., power to make and to enforce the law), and since one cannot be superior to oneself in the way required, the notion of self-legislation is absurd.

As Anscombe represents Kant's concept of autonomy, she makes it out as though Kant believes that each person makes laws for herself and hands them down, as the members of a parliament might make and promulgate the laws of a State. The question, however, is whether Kant's concept of autonomy is as blatantly nonsensical as Anscombe insists. I argue that it is not and that it actually coheres with the understanding of moral obligation that I have already presented.

---

[28] Kant readily admits that we can think of our moral duties as divine commands (R 6:153), but he does not think that this admission commits him to a divine command theory of ethics. For a good discussion of Kant on duties as divine commands, see Wood (1999, 160–161, 317–320).

2.3.1 Setting the Stage: Autonomy and Heteronomy as Metaphors

Near the end of *Section II* of the *Groundwork*, Kant makes the following claim: "the will is not merely subject to the law but subject to it in such a way that it must be viewed [*angesehen*] as also giving the law to itself and just because of this as first subject to the law (of which it can regard itself as the author)" (4:431). Such a passage seems to support Anscombe's reading of Kant, but only when one ignores Kant's important qualification: he does not say that the will gives itself the law; he says that the will "must be viewed as giving the law to itself." One can more easily see his non-literal use of the image of "giving the law to oneself" in Kant's characterization of heteronomy:

> If the will seeks the law that is to determine it *anywhere else* than in the fitness of its maxims for its own giving of universal law—consequently if, in going beyond itself, it seeks this law in a property of any of its objects—*heteronomy* always results. The will in that case does not give itself the law; instead the object, by means of its relation to the will, gives the law to it. (4:441).[29]

When he says that the will "gives the law to itself" or that the will "legislates the moral law to itself," Kant is making a point about how human beings determine (i.e., choose) the objects of their wills, namely, that in acting autonomously an individual is motivated to pursue an end that she has reasoned to be good (as opposed to an end that she merely adopts because of inclination), and her interest in pursuing said end is one that arises from reason (as opposed to an interest of inclination). Put more colloquially, to act heteronomously is to allow one's actions to be determined unreflectively by one's needs and wants; it is to give in to one's contingent, natural desires without asking whether or not these desires are truly good, without exerting any self-discipline or control with respect to those desires. To act autonomously, on the other hand, is to act so that one's end and the motive for pursuing one's end are products of successful practical reasoning.[30] Think, for example, of the difference between, one the one hand, having a glass of red wine because you might as well finish the bottle now that you've started it, and, on the other, having a glass of red wine because you recognize the cardiovascular benefits of drinking red. This kind of distinction between acting merely on unreflective and uncritical natural desires and

---

[29] Cf. 5:33: "If, therefore, the matter of volition, which can be nothing other than the object of a desire that is connected with the law, enters into the practical law **as a condition of its possibility,** there results heteronomy of choice, namely dependence upon the natural law of following some impulse or inclination, and the will does not give itself the law but only the precept for rationally following pathological law."

[30] According to Stern (2012, 24–25), "at the centre of Kant's conception of the autonomy/heteronomy distinction is a contrast between reason controlling the will on the one hand, and reason acting as a 'handmaid' to achieve some end given to it by desire on the other." Baxley (2010, 58) claims that "according to Kant's particular conception of autonomy, the laws we give ourselves are prescriptions of our own reason, through which we constrain ourselves in virtue of the recognition of their validity for all rational agents."

acting on considered reasons does not merely apply to our appetites for food, drink, and sex. It applies to any choice we might make, including (for example) the choice to donate our time to charity and the choice to visit aunt Beatrice in the hospital.

Kant's talk of autonomy, therefore, should not be taken literally but, rather, is best understood metaphorically,[31] that is, as a helpful way for human beings to conceive of the way in which we are able to pursue what is genuinely good for considered reasons rather than being a slave to our inclinations and merely pursuing what makes us happy. Commenting on Kant's discussion of autonomy in the *Groundwork*, Allen Wood (2008, 111) observes, "we should be struck by the frequency with which Kant uses expressions conveying the thought that autonomy of the will is only a way of *considering* or *regarding* the objectively valid moral law.".[32]

Kantian autonomy, then, is not a literal binding of oneself—he is not committed to the view that people become "morally" obligated through their own respective sheer fiats. Hence, in a serious way, the alleged Kantian paradox of autonomy rests on a misreading of Kant, since Kant's concept of autonomy should be understood metaphorically. Actually, over 150 years prior to "Modern Moral Philosophy," Kant anticipated the kind of criticism Anscombe makes of his position:

> If the I *that imposes obligation* is taken in the same sense as the I *that is put under obligation*, a duty to oneself is a self-contradictory concept....[since] the one imposing obligation (*auctor obligationis*) could always release the one put under obligation (*subiectum obligationis*) from the obligation (*terminus obligationis*), so that (if both are one and the same subject) he would not be bound at all to a duty he lays upon himself. This involves a contradiction. (MM 6:417)

For the sake of argument, however, I want to pursue the notion of the paradox of autonomy in order (hopefully) to disabuse readers of this misreading once and for all. Drawing on my reading of Kant thus far, I think that there are two resources in Kant's ethics that can be used to flesh out a response to the Kantian paradox (the second of which I have already mentioned): (a) Kant's distinction between the legislator of the law and the author of the law, and (b) Kant's account of the natural dialectic between our rational and sensible natures.

2.3.2 Kant's Moral Realism: *Legislator* versus *Author* of the Law

The first part of the Kantian paradox claims that self-legislation is absurd because someone who makes a law to bind or obligate herself can just as easily unbind or "unobligate" herself. Implicit in this argument is the idea that Kantian self-legislation

---

[31] Cf. Wood (2008, 112–113): "Strictly speaking, *our own will is neither the legislator nor the author of the moral law*. (To speak of it in either of these ways is at most merely an appropriate way of *considering* or *regarding* the matter.)"

[32] Consider, e.g., the passage from the *Groundwork* at the start of this subsection. There, Kant says that the will "must be viewed as" giving the law to itself and that it "can regard itself" as its author.

entails human beings creating the moral law that is supposed to obligate them, but this view is not Kant's, since he clearly distinguishes between what he calls the legislator of the law and the author of the law. As he puts it in the *Metaphysics of Morals,* "A (morally practical) *law* is a proposition that contains a categorical imperative (a command). One who commands (*imperans*) through a law is the *lawgiver* (*legislator*). He is the author (*autor*) of the obligation in accordance with the law, but not always the author of the law" (MM 6:227). He explains the distinction more fully in his lectures on ethics:

> The legislator is not always simultaneously an author of the law; he is only that if the laws are contingent. But if the laws are practically necessary, and he merely declares that they conform to his will, then he is a legislator. So nobody, not even the deity, is an author of moral laws, since they have not arisen from choice but are practically necessary. (LE 27: 283, translation modified)[33]

And

> All laws are either natural or arbitrary. If the obligation has arisen from the *lex naturalis,* and has this as the ground of action, it is *obligation naturalis;* but if it has arisen from *lex arbitraria,* and has its ground in the will of another, it is *obligatio positive*....All morality, however, rests on the fact that the action is performed because of the inner nature of the act itself. (LE 27:262)

Patrick Kain (2004, 276) explains these passages succinctly: "an author *makes* a law through his will; whereas a legislator declares that a law is in accord with his will, whether or not it is something that he makes."

My reading of Kant's distinction between the legislator of the law and the author of the law is consistent with the reading of moral obligation and autonomy that I have developed in this chapter. Human beings legislate the moral law insofar as we recognize what is truly good through a process of rational deliberation and reflection. Hence, the appropriateness, according to Kant, of thinking of human beings as autonomous or self-legislating: because of our ability to reason practically we are capable of acknowledging genuine goods and then acting on the fruits of our reasoning. But because we are not purely rational beings and have habitual desires (inclinations) that are directed to our own respective conceptions of happiness, we experience the normative force of these genuine goods as obligatory. In other words, human beings are the author of obligation, insofar as our imperfect natures results in our experiencing genuine goods as obligatory, but we are not the author of the

---

[33] Cf. G 4:433–434: "A rational being belongs as a *member* to the kingdom of ends when he gives universal laws in it but is also himself subject to these laws. He belongs to it *as sovereign* when, as lawgiving, he is not subject to the will of any other. A rational being must always regard himself as lawgiving in a kingdom of ends possible through freedom of the will, whether as a member or as sovereign. He cannot, however, hold the position of sovereign merely by the maxims of his will but only in case he is a completely independent being, without needs and with unlimited resources adequate to his will"; CPrR 5:82–83; and LE 27: 263–264: "In the divine will the subjective laws of that will are identical with the objective laws of the universally good will, but God's subjective law is no ground for morality; it is good and holy because His will is in conformity with this objective law. So the question of morality has no relation at all to subjective grounds; it can only be framed on objective grounds alone."

content of the moral law, since the content is determined by the nature of things. As Wood (2008, 113) puts it, "Who, then, is the author of the moral law? The plain answer given here is: *no one*. The only laws that have an author at all are positive (contingent), arbitrary (or 'statutory') laws. Moral laws, however, are *natural* laws."

Kant's distinction between the legislator of the law and the author of the law points to an underlying feature of the reading of Kant I have developed throughout this chapter, namely, his moral realism. In asserting that Kant is a moral realist, I am following the lead of a number of prominent interpreters of Kant,[34] but I also am going against the grain of an influential school of Kant scholarship, namely the constructivism of John Rawls and his students.[35] As Alison Hills notes (2008, 182–183), "according to Kantian constructivism, values are not part of the fabric of the world. Instead, rational agents construct values by carrying out certain procedures." Hence, we find John Rawls (2000, 230) asserting that "practical reason constructs for the will its own object out of itself and does not rely on a prior and antecedent order of values." And as Christine Korsgaard, a student of Rawls, reads Kant (1996a, 241), "it is rational beings who determine what is good; rational nature confers value on the objects of its choices and is itself the source of all value."[36]

I do not have the space to address the debate between those who read Kant as a constructivist and those who read him as a realist,[37] but engaging this debate is not necessary for my purposes. Instead, I want briefly to point to two pieces of textual evidence that speak in favor of reading Kant as a moral realist.[38] First, there is Kant's conception of the good will. According to him, "it is impossible to think of anything at all in the world, or indeed even beyond it, that could be considered good without limitation except a **good will**" (G 4:393). Kant goes on to claim that the good will "is good in itself and, regarded for itself, is to be valued incomparably higher than all that could merely be brought about by it…" (G 4:394). These passages make clear that Kant understands a good will to be good itself (i.e., not merely because human beings value a good will but because it possesses value).[39] Second, Kant insists that human beings, considered as ends in themselves, possess dignity, which means that human beings have an "inner worth" (G 4:435) that is "raised

---

[34] Some examples of commentators who read Kant as a value realist are Paul Guyer (2000), Alison Hills (2008), Patrick Kain (2004), and Allen Wood (1999, 2008)

[35] Rawls' constructivism is most evident in his *Lectures on the History of Moral Philosophy* (2000). Students of Rawls, such as Christine Korsgaard (1996a, b, 2009), Onora O'Neill (1989), and Andrews Reath (2006) have each developed their own versions of constructivism.

[36] I raise some criticisms of Korsgaard's constructivism (Arroyo 2011) to which she responds (Korsgaard 2011).

[37] And, so, neither can I explain the varieties of Kantian constructivism and realism. See Galvin (2011).

[38] Stern (2012, 29–31) cites a third piece of evidence concerning Kant's discussion of our ability to take a moral interest (G 4:449–450).

[39] Cf. G 4:396: "the true vocation of reason must be to produce a will that is good, not perhaps *as a means* to other purposes, but *good in itself,* for which reason was absolutely necessary. This will need not, because of this, be the sole and complete good, but it must still be the highest good and the condition of every other, even of all demands for happiness."

above all price and therefore admits of no equivalent" (G 4:434).[40] In other words, according to Kant, human beings really possess an absolute worth or value in virtue of the kind of beings that we are (namely, beings endowed with practical reason). So, we have some good reasons for taking Kant to be a moral realist, not the least of which is the fact that such a reading coheres well with the account of moral obligation and autonomy that I have developed in this chapter, an account that shows Kant not to run afoul of Anscombe's criticisms of moral obligation. It also means that Kant avoids the first component of the Kantian paradox, namely, that Kantian autonomy commits him to the view that human beings can (and do) "morally" obligate themselves by acts of our respective wills.[41]

At the very end of the previous subsection I claimed that there are two resources in Kant that can be used to develop a response to the supposed paradox of self-legislation, the first of which is his distinction between the legislator and the author of the law. The second resource speaks directly to the second component of the Kantian paradox (i.e., that legislation requires superior power in the legislator), and it is one I have already discussed in a different context, namely, what I have called Kant's description of the tug-o-war between our rational and sensible natures.

2.3.3 Self-Legislation and Kant's Natural Dialectic

The second component of the Kantian paradox claims that the notion of self-legislation is absurd because the concept of legislation requires a superior power in the legislator. Since an individual human being cannot have superior power over herself, so the reasoning goes, an individual human being cannot legislate to herself. As I have already noted, Kant was sensitive to this criticism. He claims to avoid it by drawing on his distinction between human beings considered as sensible/natural beings and human beings considered as intelligible/noumenal beings. According to Kant, as natural, sensible beings with reason, human beings are capable of exercising practical reason and acting in the (sensible) world. "But," argues Kant,

---

[40] Cf. G 4:428: "But suppose there were something the *existence of which in itself* has an absolute worth, something which as *an end in itself* could be a ground of determinate laws; then in it, and in it alone, would lie the ground of a possible categorical imperative, that is, of a practical law. Now I say that the human being and in general every rational being *exists* as an end in itself, *not merely as a means* to be used by this or that will at its discretion." Hills (2008, 190), commenting on this passage, concludes that "Kant could hardly make his views any clearer: the existence of rational beings has in itself an absolute value."

[41] One might think that constructivists can equally claim that we are not, on their reading of Kant, the author of the law. But I am not sure that this is true. According to constructivists, we come to recognize our moral duties as a result of the (allegedly best) rational procedure that answers the question, "What should I do?" But this procedure is one that we come to develop (or perhaps discover) and use to construct the law. Hence, it seems to me fair to describe this process of construction as "authoring the law."

2.3 Kant's Account of Autonomy of the Will

the same human being thought in terms of his *personality,* that is, as a being endowed with *inner freedom* (*homo noumenon*), is regarded as a being that can be put under obligation and, indeed, under obligation to himself (to the humanity in his own person). So, the human being (taken in these two different senses) can acknowledge a duty to himself without falling into contradiction (because the concept of a human being is not thought in one and the same sense). (MM 6:418)[42]

Unfortunately, in explaining how human beings can self-legislate and, therefore, be morally obligated, Kant relies on his questionable metaphysical distinction between a "noumenal" (intelligible) realm and a "phenomenal" (sensible) realm. This reliance is unfortunate because this distinction in Kant has been criticized as untenable.[43] But I think that his point regarding autonomy and obligating oneself can be explained without relying on his dubious metaphysical distinction, so long as we keep in mind his understanding of obligation as a phenomenon exclusive to finite, imperfect wills. I take Kant's point in passages such as the one I just quoted to be that human beings are embodied rational animals, subject to needs, wants, desires, and emotions, but we are not merely animals, since we possess the power to reason, both theoretically and practically. When each person considers herself as an embodied rational animal, she considers herself as this particular human being—a dependent being (to use Kant's term) that has as a central concern her own happiness (her own well-being). This individual, however, is also a person,[44] that is, a being capable of free—and, therefore, moral—action, and the power to reason practically and choose (i.e., set ends). This power to set ends as a result of reasoning practically is what endows us with what Kant calls "humanity," which is the source of our dignity (G 4:436). To say that a human being possesses dignity, according to Kant, is to say, in part, that she possesses a worth that is incalculably greater than any value to be placed on her comfort or well-being, and this worth is what you might call "the better part" of herself. It is this "part" of her that obligates her, since it is this part of her that is the root of her capacity to reason correctly about what is truly good. When this "part" of her does this, that is, when she comes to recognize what is truly good, the "lower part" of herself, the part that considers herself as a merely sensible individual concerned with her own happiness, results in her experiencing this good as obligatory.[45]

---

[42] Cf. CPrR 5:43.

[43] For someone who thinks that one can defend Kant's ethics while rejecting his dubious metaphysics, see Wood (2008).

[44] "A *person* is a subject whose actions can be *imputed* to him. *Moral* personality is therefore nothing other than the freedom of a rational being under moral laws (whereas psychological personality is merely the ability to be conscious of one's identity in different conditions of one's existence)" (MM 6: 223).

[45] Cf. LE 27:510: "if the obligator is personified as an ideal being or moral person, it can be none other than the legislation of reason; this, then, is man considered solely as an intelligible being, who here obligates man as sensory being, and we thus have a relationship of man *qua* phenomenon towards himself *qua* noumenon. The situation is similar in obligations towards others."

2.4 Looking Ahead

I have spent this chapter addressing what I take to be the most serious criticism of Kant's ethics, one that forms the cornerstone of the Anscombian reading, namely, that his conception of moral obligation is confused and his related notion of autonomy is nonsensical. By way of a response, I have argued that Kant's understanding of moral obligation has to do with the way imperfect rational beings such as human beings experience the normative demands of what is genuinely good for us. Put differently, I have argued that Kant is a moral realist who makes the concept of moral obligation central to his ethical theory because he takes human beings to be imperfect beings who cannot but experience the normative claims of morality *as demands*. On this reading of Kant, Anscombe's criticisms (i.e., both her criticism of "moral" obligation and the two components of the Kantian paradox) don't apply.

I contend that my reading of Kant on moral obligation speaks to the way in which his moral theory is particularly suited to dealing with practical ethical issues concerning sex and marriage. As I will argue in Part II, when it comes to his treatment of sexual relations Kant's central preoccupation is the way in which human beings can be and often are tempted to treat their sexual partners merely as instruments of gratification and to allow their sexual partners to do the same in return. That is, Kant's ethics of sex and marriage is concerned to address the ways in which our sexual behavior tends to objectify human beings, including oneself, instead of being consistent with and expressive of the dignity Kant believes human beings possess. This is due in no small part, he thinks, to the way in which we can and often do prioritize our own respective satisfaction, often at the expense of what is genuinely good. But this claim—that human beings often can and do prioritize their own happiness over what is genuinely good—might motivate yet another potentially significant criticism of Kant's ethics, one that readers might think poses just as serious a challenge to Kant as the Anscombian reading's criticism of "moral" obligation. The new criticism might be expressed thusly: doesn't Kant hold an overly pessimistic and untenable view of human beings, one that corrupts his understanding of human goodness? And if his view of human beings is overly pessimistic and untenable, then insofar as his philosophical anthropology functions as the central influence on his ethics, his ethics must also be overly pessimistic and untenable. In light of this potential criticism, I need to explain why, according to Kant, we can and often do prioritize our own respective happiness over what is genuinely good, which is why the next chapter focuses on Kant's philosophical anthropology, particularly what he takes to be a central feature of human nature, namely, our unsocial sociability.

References

Agam-Segal, Reshef. 2012. Kant's Non-Aristotelian Conception of Morality. *Southwest Philosophy Review* 28 (1): 121–133.
———. 2013. A Splitting "Mind-Ache": An Anscombian Challenge to Kantian Self-Legislation. *Journal of Philosophical Research* 38: 43–68.
Allison, Henry E. 1990. *Kant's Theory of Freedom*. Cambridge: Cambridge University Press.
Alston, William P. 1990. Some Suggestions for Divine Command Theorists. In *Christian Theism and the Problems of Philosophy*, ed. Michel D. Beaty, 303–325. Southbend: University of Notre Dame Press.
Alvarez, Maria, and Aaron Ridley. 2007. The Concept of Moral Obligation: Anscombe *contra* Korsgaard. *Philosophy* 82: 543–552.
Anscombe, G.E.M. 1958. Modern Moral Philosophy. *Philosophy* 33.124: 1–19.
Arroyo, Christopher. 2011. Freedom and the source of value: Korsgaard and Wood on Kant's formula of humanity. *Metaphilosophy* 42 (4): 353–359.
Baron, Marcia W. 1995. *Kantian Ethics Almost Without Apology*. Ithaca/London: Cornell University Press.
Baxley, Anne Margaret. 2010. *Kant's Theory of Virtue: The Value of Autocracy*. Cambridge: Cambridge University Press.
Darwall, Stephen L. 1987. Abolishing Morality. *Synthese* 72: 71–89.
Darwall, Stephen. 2006. *The Second-Person Standpoint: Morality, Respect, and Accountability*. Cambridge, MA: Harvard University Press.
Galvin, Richard. 2011. Rounding up the Usual Suspects: Varieties of Kantian Constructivism in Ethics. *The Philosophical Quarterly* 61 (242): 16–36.
Geach, Peter. 1969. The Moral Law and the Law of God. In *God and the Soul*, 2nd ed. South Bend: St. Augustine's Press.
Guyer, Paul. 2000. *Kant on Freedom, Law, and Happiness*. Cambridge: Cambridge University Press.
Herman, Barbara. 1993. *The Practice of Moral Judgment*. Cambridge, MA/London: Harvard University Press.
Hills, Alison. 2008. Kantian Value Realism. *Ratio* 21 (2): 182–200.
Kain, Patrick. 2004. Self-Legislation in Kant's Moral Philosophy. *Archiv für Geschichte der Philosophie* 86 (3): 257–306.
Korsgaard, Christine M. 1996a. *Creating the Kingdom of Ends*. Cambridge: Cambridge University Press.
———. 1996b. *The Sources of Normativity*. Cambridge: Cambridge University Press.
———. 2009. *Self-Constitution: Agency, Identity, and Integrity*. Oxford: Oxford University Press.
———. 2011. Natural goodness, rightness, and the intersubjectivity of reason: Reply to Arroyo, Cummisky, Moland, and Bird-Pollan. *Metaphilosophy* 42 (4): 381–394.
Louden, Robert B. 2000. *Kant's Impure Ethics: From Rational Beings to Human Beings*. New York/Oxford: Oxford University Press.
Muirhead, J.H. 1932. *Rule and End in Morals*. Oxford: Oxford University Press.
O'Neill, Onora. 1989. *Constructions of Reason: Explorations of Kant's Practical Philosophy*. Cambridge University Press.
Pigden, Charles. 1988. Anscombe on 'Ought'. *Philosophical Quarterly* 38 (150): 20–41.
Rawls, John. 2000. In *Lectures on the History of Moral Philosophy*, ed. Barbara Herman. Cambridge, MA: Harvard University Press.
Reath, Andrews. 2006. *Agency and autonomy in Kant's moral theory*. Oxford: Oxford University Press.
Schneewind, J.B. 1997. *The Invention of Autonomy: A History of Modern Moral Philosophy*. Cambridge: Cambridge University Press.

Schwaiger, Clemens. 2009. The theory of obligation in Wolff, Baumgarten, and the early Kant. In *Kant's moral and legal philosophy*, ed. Karl Ameriks, Otfried Höffe, and Nicholas Walker, 58–76. Cambridge: Cambridge University Press.

Stern, Robert. 2012. *Understanding Moral Obligation: Kant, Hegel, Kierkegaard*. Cambridge: Cambridge University Press.

———. 2015. *Kantian Ethics: Value, Agency, and Obligation*. Oxford: Oxford University Press.

Williams, Bernard. 1985. *Ethics and the Limits of Philosophy*. Cambridge, MA: Harvard University Press.

Wilson, Eric Entrican. 2008. Kantian Autonomy and the Moral Self. *The Review of Metaphysics* 62: 355–381.

———. 2009. Is Kant's Concept of Autonomy Absurd? *History of Philosophy Quarterly* 26 (2): 159–174.

Wood, Allen W. 1999. *Kant's Ethical Thought*. Cambridge: Cambridge University Press.

———. 2003. Kant and the Problem of Human Nature. In *Essays on Kant's Anthropology*, ed. Brian Jacobs and Patrick Kain, 38–59. Cambridge: Cambridge University Press.

———. 2008. *Kantian Ethics*. Cambridge: Cambridge University Press.

Chapter 3
Such Crooked Timber: Kant's Philosophical Anthropology

Abstract This chapter takes Kant's understanding of our finitude and imperfection as a central theme by examining the main feature of Kant's philosophical anthropology, namely, Kant's account of what he calls "unsocial sociability" or "the propensity to radical evil in human nature," which are but two ways to describe our dependency and moral imperfection. First, I examine what Kant has to say about the "unsocial sociability" of human beings. I then turn to Kant's treatment of radical evil in human nature in *Religion within the Boundaries of Mere Reason*, since that is a work in which Kant more precisely explains the ways in which human nature possesses the animal tendency to easy living and happiness. Next I look closely at Kant's treatment of the inclinations in the *Groundwork* and their relation to what he calls "moral worth," since critics of Kant often wrongly take this text to commit Kant to a wholesale rejection of sensible/sensuous nature as the cause of moral evil and the obstacle standing in the way of our acting genuinely morally. After providing a correct understanding of the relevant parts of the *Groundwork*, I then turn to Kant's account of affects and passions, two particular species of emotion and desire. I conclude the chapter by considering Kant's view of happiness, which he identifies as the natural end of human beings.

In the previous chapter I defended Kant from Anscombe's critique of "moral" obligation, arguing that she and Kant work with two very different understandings of "moral obligation." Kant, I argued, expresses his normative ethical theory in terms of moral obligation and duty because he conceives of human nature as finite and, therefore, morally imperfect. Our finitude, according to Kant, takes the form of our having two "natures" with two competing ends: sensible nature, which is his phrase for connoting our being (embodied) animals with appetites, desires, and emotions, and which results in our having happiness as an end; and rational nature, which is the phrase he uses to pick out our capacity for making choices as a result of reasoning practically, and which, he thinks, endows us with dignity and entails our having the development of moral character as an end. Because we have these two ends, Kant thinks that an individual can opt for her own happiness over-and-against opting for what is genuinely morally good. More to the point, he thinks that our having two ends results in what he calls a "natural dialectic," that is, on the one hand, a tendency to prioritize one's own well-being and satisfaction, and, on the other, the ability to recognize and act on what one reasons to be genuinely morally good. In light of this view of human beings, Kant often characterizes human life in terms of the struggle between these two ends. In the final pages of his *Anthropology from a Pragmatic Point of View*, Kant claims that a

> human being is destined by his reason to live in a society with human beings and in it to *cultivate* himself, to *civilize* himself, and to *moralize* himself by means of the arts and sciences. No matter how great his animal tendency may be to give himself over *passively* to the impulses of ease and good living, which he calls happiness, he is still destined to make himself worthy of humanity by *actively* struggling with the obstacles that cling to him because of the crudity of his nature. (7:324–325)

Although I exposit Kant's account of the finitude and moral imperfection of human beings as a way of responding to Anscombe's criticism of "moral" obligation, my reading of Kant seems to reinforce another aspect of the Anscombian reading. Specifically, my reading of Kant might appear to commit him to an untenable philosophical anthropology, insofar as my reading depicts Kant's account of human nature (and, specifically, human happiness) as fundamentally antagonistic to moral goodness. On this line of reasoning, the problem seems to be that his philosophical anthropology precludes our genuinely acting morally, since each of us always wants to do something other than what is good, namely, pursue our own respective conceptions of happiness.

In order to answer this new potential criticism, I once again take Kant's understanding of our finitude and imperfection as a central theme by examining the main feature of Kant's philosophical anthropology, namely, Kant's account of what he calls "unsocial sociability" or "the propensity to radical evil in human nature," which are but two ways to describe our moral imperfection and dependency (i.e., our need for others and the vulnerability due to that need). Just as importantly, unsocial sociability plays a significant role in Kant's account of gender relations and sexual relations, particularly when it comes to the central problem of his sexual ethics, sexual objectification. By making unsocial sociability my focus in the present chapter, I hope to explain Kant's understanding of the moral imperfection of human beings in a way that presents a defensible account of his philosophical anthropology and sets the stage for his account of the problem of sexual objectification in Part II. I proceed as follows. First, I examine what Kant has to say about what he takes to be the defining feature of human nature, what he calls the "unsocial sociability" of human beings. I then turn to Kant's treatment of radical evil in human nature in *Religion within the Boundaries of Mere Reason*, since there Kant more precisely explains the ways in which human nature possesses the animal tendency to easy living and happiness. Next I look closely at Kant's treatment of the inclinations in the *Groundwork* and their relation to what he calls "moral worth," since critics of Kant often wrongly take this text to commit Kant to a wholesale rejection of sensible/sensuous nature as the cause of moral evil and the obstacle standing in the way of our acting genuinely morally. After providing a correct understanding of the relevant parts of the *Groundwork*, I then turn to what Kant has to say about affects and passions, two particular species of emotion and desire, respectively, focusing on one passion in particular that Kant identifies: the passion for dominion over other human beings, since this passion plays an important role in his practical sexual ethics. I conclude the chapter by considering Kant's view of happiness, which he identifies as the natural end of human beings.

3.1 Unsocial Sociability and Radical Evil in Human Nature

Kant defines practical (or moral) anthropology as the empirical study of human nature (G 4:388), which he envisions as the component of practical philosophy that "would deal only with the subjective conditions in human nature that hinder people or help them in *fulfilling* the laws of a metaphysics of morals" (MM 6:217). In other words, he takes practical anthropology to be the discipline that studies human beings in order to discover those aspects of human beings that are conducive to us being good and those aspects of human beings that stand in the way of our efforts to be good. His approach to the subject is pragmatic,[1] which he contrasts with the then-dominant physiological approach to anthropology: "physiological knowledge of the human being concerns the investigation of what *nature* makes of the human being; pragmatic the investigation of what *he* as a free-acting being makes of himself, or can and should make of himself" (A 7:119).[2] Kant proceeds on the assumption that human nature is at least in part formed by human action, that it is not something merely determined by the physical constitution of the human animal.[3] More than that, as Allen Wood (2003, 41) observes, "Kant also holds that the development of our human predispositions is a social process, a result of the collective actions of society (most of which are unknown to and unintended by individual agents)." So, Kant's practical anthropology focuses on human beings as individual agents and as agents who are members of certain social communities and who depend on the members of those communities to help them develop as human beings. According to Kant, the main characteristic of the human species is "that nature has planted in

---

[1] Robert Louden (2000, 68–70) and Allen Wood (2003, 40–42) identify four senses of "pragmatic" in Kant's use of it to describe his anthropology. According to Louden, "pragmatic" in Kant's writings can mean (1) skillfulness in interacting with others, (2) prudence in achieving one's ends, (3) the capacity to act freely in developing one's character, or (4) being of concern to moral living (as opposed to being of merely theoretical concern).

[2] Cf. R 6:21: "let it be noted that by 'the nature of a human being' we only understand here the subjective ground—wherever it may lie—of the exercise of the human being's freedom in general (under objective moral laws) antecedent to every deed that falls within the scope of the senses." Alix Cohen (2008) develops this theme in Kant's anthropology by expounding what she calls "man's praxis."

[3] Nell, the main protagonist in Lily King's *Euphoria* (2014), is an anthropologist studying different cultures in Southeast Asia. At one point her husband, Fen, suggests that the people they are studying are seriously less human than he and Nell, to which she responds, "If I didn't believe they shared my humanity entirely, I wouldn't be here….I'm not interested in zoology." Nell's contrast between anthropology and zoology seems to me to get at Kant's point about the way in which his philosophical anthropology is pragmatic rather than physiological insofar as human beings, unlike animals, do not merely act on instinct but are also capable of acting rationally and freely.

it the seed of *discord*, and has willed that its own reason bring *concord* out of this, or at least the constant approximation to it" (A 7:322). Using a phrase he derives from Montaigne,[4] Kant takes humans to be unsocially sociable.

3.1.1 Human Development and Unsocial Sociability

Kant's first published discussion of the unsocial sociability of human beings appears in his "Idea for a Universal History with a Cosmopolitan Aim." In the introduction to the essay, Kant gives a nod to his pragmatic understanding of human beings, insofar as he asserts that "human beings, in their endeavors, do not behave merely instinctively, like animals," but he also acknowledges that humans also do not "on the whole [act] like rational citizens of the world in accordance with an agreed upon plan" (UH 8:17). These two observations point to why history as a discipline, according to Kant, seems to be impossible: human freedom and irrationality make it extraordinarily difficult to come up with a coherent narrative of human events. Insisting on our moral imperfection, and foreshadowing what he will write just a few pages later, Kant makes the following wry observation:

> One cannot resist feeling a certain indignation when one sees their doings and refrainings on the great stage of the world and finds that despite the wisdom appearing now and then in individual cases, everything in the large is woven together out of folly, childish vanity, often also out of childish malice and the rage to destruction; so that in the end one does not know what concept to make of our species, with its smug imaginings about its excellences. (UH 8:17–18)

In the world Kant describes, things look bleak, indeed.[5] Kant's essay attempts to address this bleakness by developing an account of the way in which nature—specifically, human nature—allows human beings to develop despite their own folly (Wood 1991, 329).

Kant begins his case by asserting that all living beings possess distinguishing, species-specific capacities, and that reason is our distinguishing capacity. Reason, he adds, can develop fully only in the species and not in an individual (UH 8:18–19). Kant then identifies what he takes to be the means by which nature encourages such development, namely, "antagonism" among humans in society, which he

---

[4] Cf. Michel de Montaigne (1965, 175): "There is nothing so unsociable and so sociable as man: the one by his vice, the other by his nature." Accordingly, conceiving of human beings as both sociable and unsocial is not an invention of Kant. J.B. Schneewind (2009, 94–105) gives a history of the two concepts in early modern philosophy and how Kant relates to that history.

[5] Onora O'Neill (2008) argues that Kant holds that the notion of human progress at work in "Idea for a Universal History" is a regulative ideal for him. A regulative ideal, according to Kant does not give us theoretical knowledge (CPR A180/B223). Rather, it is an idea that allows us to organize experience for practical purposes (CPrR 5:48). As O'Neill puts it, regulative ideals "are practical principles adopted to regulate any search for scientific or other order in the natural world, and any practical attempt to introduce order into human affairs, for example by constitutional or political change" (531).

insists ends up motivating the efforts of humans to establish lawful order and peaceful living among themselves. Kant calls this antagonism "unsocial sociability," by which he understands human beings' "propensity to enter into society, which, however, is combined with a thoroughgoing resistance that constantly threatens to break up this society" (UH 8:20). He continues,

> The human being has an inclination to become *socialized*, since in such a condition he feels himself as more a human being, i.e., feels the development of his natural predispositions. But he also has a great propensity to *individualize* (isolate) himself, because he simultaneously encounters in himself the unsociable property of willing to direct everything so as to get his own way, and hence expects resistance everywhere because he knows of himself that he is inclined on his side toward resistance against others. (UH 8:20–21).

The concept of unsocial sociability captures the way in which human beings are dependent beings. In the previous chapter, I emphasized the way in which Kant conceives of our dependency in terms of our sensible needs and wants, since this aspect of dependency was most relevant for the reading of moral obligation I was developing. But in this context, and with an eye on Kant's ethics of sex and marriage, it is worth emphasizing the other implication of our dependency, namely, that we are not self-sufficient beings. We are vulnerable and need others. Indeed, Kant claims that we feel ourselves become more human around others. But the social aspect of human nature, the need we have for others, entails a certain degree of vulnerability, which expresses itself, on Kant's account, in the unsocial aspect of our nature.

The unsocial drive in human beings, according to Kant, consists of two parts. First, we all want everything to go our way; we long to satisfy our subjective, empirical, self-centered desires. Second, to some degree Kant thinks that we recognize the same want in every other human being, and we resist their attempts to fulfill it.[6] Another way to put this point is to say that each person wants to be happy, which just means that each person wants to satisfy all of her needs and wants, often without regard for what other people desire. Each person also recognizes that this strong desire for happiness is one that all people possess. So, each person expects that others will act in ways that prioritize their own respective needs and wants, and each of us is reluctant to indulge others in this respect—we don't want to help others become happy because we are preoccupied with trying to become happy ourselves. You might say that our need for others (sociability) gives rise to our antagonism toward them (unsociability).

Paradoxically, Kant identifies this self-centeredness and resistance to others as the natural impetus for the development of our talents, including our rational capacities. Here's how it works, according to Kant. The unsocial part of our human nature

---

[6] So, I think Michaele Ferguson (2012) misconstrues unsocial sociability as "plurality," that is, as due to the fact that there are multiple humans with multiple desires. Ferguson seems to think that antagonism arises merely as a result of there being a multitude of people with a multitude of desires that need to be satisfied, which makes Kant sound much more like Thomas Hobbes (1994). For Kant, however, antagonism is not due to the fact that desire satisfaction is a zero-sum game. Rather, it is due to each person *anticipating* the same drive to ease and happiness in her fellows, which, as it were, puts each person on the defensive (and the best defense is a good offense).

gives rise to a competitive spirit, and during the early stages of our development as a species, we are driven by "ambition, tyranny, and greed to obtain a rank" amongst our fellow human beings, each of whom we cannot stand but we "also cannot leave alone" (UH 8:21). Nature has implanted this competitive drive in us in order to use it as a means to our development. The competitive spirit provides part of a "foundation of a mode of thought which can with time transform the rude natural predisposition to make moral distinctions into determinate practical principles and hence transform a *pathologically* compelled agreement to form a society finally into a *moral* whole" (UH 8:21). The idea is that the unsocial aspect of our natures instrumentally contributes to our moral development in two ways: first, by motivating us to perfect ourselves as a way of attaining our own happiness (i.e., having things 'go my own way'); and, second, by motivating us to perfect ourselves as a way of satisfying our natural, competitive drive to feel superior to our fellows. Kant thinks that one way our unsociability expresses itself is in terms of a desire to be superior to our fellows, to be better than them. This competitiveness, combined with each person's realization that others may not help her as she pursues her happiness, motivates each of us to develop our talents and abilities. Were it not for our unsociability, Kant thinks, we would never cultivate our rational capacities and develop into moral agents who live in a moral community.[7] Kant actually expresses gratitude for this: "thanks be to nature, therefore, for the incompatibility, for the spiteful competitive vanity, for the insatiable desire to possess and or even to dominate" (UH 8:21)!

I want to draw attention to the way in which human dependency (and, more specifically, Kant's claim that human beings have two competing ends, namely happiness and their vocation to become morally good) lies at the heart of his account of our unsocial sociability.[8] Humans, according to Kant, want to live in society with others and cooperate with them. Indeed, he thinks we *need* this, that in a serious way we become human through our socialization in community. As I have suggested, this need for others points to a vulnerability in humans, to a lack of self-sufficiency. Our lack of self-sufficiency gets expressed in our needs and wants, which gives us one of our ends, namely happiness. And Kant thinks that the natural drive that each

---

[7] When Kant writes of cultivating and developing our talents and rational capacities, he should not be understood to mean that through practice human beings come to have reason. In fact, Kant explicitly claims the contrary in his discussion of the predispositions to good in human nature (R 6:26–28). In thinking about the sense in which humans cultivate and develop their talents, it is helpful to keep a distinction of Aristotle in mind, namely the distinction between first and second potentiality. First potentiality is the capacity to acquire a capacity that one does not currently have (e.g., the capacity for someone who does not know how to play the piano to learn how to play the piano). Second potentiality is the capacity to exercise some ability one in fact has but is not currently exercising (e.g., the capacity a piano player has to sit down at a piano and play). When I write of developing our rational capacities, I mean this in the sense of second potentiality.

[8] Wood (1991, 329) points to the importance of Kant's "Idea for a Universal History" by noting that it precedes Kant's publishing of the *Groundwork* by just one year. Wood argues that the *Groundwork* should be read as part of an overall project that starts with "Idea for a Universal History" and "What is Enlightenment" (which is published the same year as UH). But Wood (2009, 112) is also careful to acknowledge that "to regard Kant's main project in *Idea for a Universal History* as motivated by morality is totally to misunderstand the essay from the ground up."

human has to secure her own satisfaction and comfort, in a word, to secure her happiness, motivates our antagonism toward others. So, once again, we see the way in which Kant's understanding of human beings as dependent beings (i.e., as embodied, vulnerable, rational beings with needs and wants) gives rise to a natural dialectic between our respective conceptions of happiness and our developing moral dispositions. This dialectic, I shall argue, lies at the heart of the problem of sexual objectification, according to Kant. On the one hand, he thinks that sexual desire strongly inclines us to use our sexual partners as mere objects for our gratification. On the other hand, our status as rational beings who possess dignity requires us to treat our sexual partners (and ourselves) with respect. As I have been arguing, the tension between our two ends, happiness and developing moral character, informs Kant's thinking on ethics through and through, and we see this tension perspicuously on display in our sexual relations.

Before I can turn to Kant's discussions of sex and gender, I need to continue to elaborate the philosophical anthropology that underpins his normative ethical theory and informs his understanding of gender and sex. Specifically, the foregoing account of unsocial sociability invites two questions, both of which speak to the potential criticism of Kant that I articulated at the start of this chapter. First, does Kant dismiss human needs, wants, and emotions—indeed, human happiness overall—as antithetical to morality. Second, is Kant's view that human beings cannot help but act unsocially and, so, cannot help but prioritize their own happiness? In order to answer these questions, I turn to Kant's account of radical evil in human nature, which really is just another name for our unsocial sociability (Wood 2008, 227).[9]

3.1.2 The Predispositions to Good and Propensities to Evil in Human Nature

In Part I of *Religion within the Boundaries of Mere Reason* Kant asks the question, "Are human beings good or evil by nature?" Unsurprisingly, Kant rejects both the idea that we are completely good and the idea that we are completely evil. He insists that, when it comes to the moral evaluation of human beings, we are what we make of ourselves: "whenever we therefore say, 'The human being is by nature good,' or, 'He is by nature evil,' this only means that he holds within himself a first ground (to us inscrutable) for the adoption of good or evil (unlawful) maxims…" (R 6:21).[10]

---

[9] Cf. Wood (2010, 162): "Another Kantian name, therefore, for the radical evil in human nature is 'unsocial sociability'—the sociable need that human beings have as *rational* beings for society with others, which, however, is also the unsociable need to gain superiority over them in honor, power, and wealth." Also cf. Wood (2009, 125). Jeanine Grenberg (2005, 2010) takes issue with Wood's emphasis on the social nature of evil and what she takes to be the way in which his account cannot accommodate Kant's conception of transcendentally free acts.

[10] Cf. UH 8:19: "Nature has willed that the human being should produce everything that goes beyond the mechanical arrangement of his animal existence entirely out of himself, and participate in no other happiness or perfection than that which he has procured for himself free from instinct through his own reason."

Accordingly, the moral evaluation of human beings is really the evaluation of our dispositions, which Kant thinks are largely the result of our choices. But these choices, he thinks, are conditioned by certain predispositions towards good and propensities toward evil that, when taken together, help explain in more detail the unsocial sociability in human beings. These predispositions and propensities are both original and essential to human beings: you're born with them; they can't be extirpated; and they form part of what it is to be human. Insofar as it makes sense to speak of there being a "radical evil"[11] in human nature, Kant believes that this source is in the propensities he identifies, and these propensities to evil ought to be sharply distinguished from our predisposition to good.

The Predisposition to Good Kant maintains that we have a single predisposition to goodness, but he distinguishes three elements to this predisposition. He thinks that it makes sense to distinguish three elements to this predisposition because he thinks we can describe this aspect of human beings in three basic ways, depending on our focus. The first element, Kant calls "animality," which is the predisposition to good when we consider human beings merely as living, animal beings. Animality "may be brought under the general title of physical or merely *mechanical* self-love, i.e., love for which reason is not required" (6:26). Kant, further, divides animality into three: (1) the predisposition to self-preservation, (2) the predisposition to propagate the species through the sexual drive and the preservation of any offspring that result from this drive, and (3) the predisposition to community with other human beings (i.e., the social drive). One can see here some important features of Kant's view of human beings, features that incline us toward prioritizing happiness: the desire to preserve oneself in life (which ideally involves not merely freedom from harm but also comfort) and the sexual drive, which, on Kant's view, is the drive associated with the most powerful pleasure. Since the power of the sex drive in humans is part of what makes it so dangerous, according to Kant, it is worth emphasizing at this point that the sex drive, along with each of the elements of animality, are good, as far as he is concerned.[12]

In anticipation of my discussion in Part II of Kant's account of the problem of sexual objectification, I want to note that Kant identifies vices he associates with our animality. He calls them "vices of the *savagery* of nature, and, at their greatest deviation from the natural ends, are called the *bestial vices of gluttony, lust, and wild lawlessness* (in relation to other human beings)" (R 6:26–27). These are vices of what Kant calls our mechanical self-love (i.e., our natural/instinctive self-love).

---

[11] When Kant writes of "radical evil" in this context, the sense of radical has to do with the way in which this evil "corrupts the ground of all maxims" (R 6:37).

[12] Insofar as Kant locates the social drive at the level of animality, he distinguishes his view of human nature from thinkers such as Hobbes (1994) and Jean-Jacques Rousseau (1992), each of whom take human beings to be originally solitary beings.

There is nothing *prima facie* wrong with self-love on this view,[13] but, absent practical reason and self-control, this self-love ends up being disordered. In such cases, the offending person becomes "less than human" (i.e., a mere animal), which is why Kant calls these vices the vices of savagery of nature. As I will explain in Part II, because lust demeans human dignity, Kant finds it abhorrent.

The second element of our predisposition to good Kant calls "humanity," which is the predisposition to good when we consider human beings as living, animal and rational beings.[14] As Kant explains it, this element concerns "a self-love which is physical and yet *involves comparison* (for which reason is required); that is, only in comparison with others does one judge oneself to be happy or unhappy. Out of this self-love originates the inclination *to gain worth in the opinion of others*, originally, of course, merely *equal worth*" (R 6:27). According to Kant, our rational capacities allow each of us to judge our own respective situations and compare them to the situations of our fellows, and these comparisons then inform our respective conceptions of happiness. So, human happiness is a social concept, one that cannot be understood apart from one's comparing oneself with others with respect to the satisfaction of one's desires and general ease of living. This predisposition to compare is good, according to Kant, because it is originally directed toward improving oneself so that one is raised in esteem in the eyes of others in an effort to become equal with them. This predisposition, however, can be corrupted, which is why Kant thinks that our comparing ourselves to others with respect to our happiness can lead to vices. These vices entail an "unjust desire to acquire superiority for oneself over others" (R 6:27). Kant identifies these vices as vices of culture, since they can only arise in society (i.e., when human beings compare themselves to others).[15] As I will discuss in Part II, according to Kant, this unjust desire to acquire superiority over others is one of the defining features of the relationship between men and women, and this power dynamic leads Kant to be critical of attempts to use sex to objectify and, thereby, subjugate others.

The final element of the predisposition to good in humans is what Kant calls "personality," which is the predisposition to good when one considers human beings as living, animal, rational, and responsible (i.e., moral) beings (6:26). When Kant

---

[13] Cf. CPrR 5:73: "All the inclinations together (which can be brought into a tolerable system and the satisfaction of which is then called one's own happiness) constitute regard for oneself (*solipsismus*). This is either the self-regard of *love for oneself*, a predominant *benevolence* toward oneself (*Philautia*), or that of *satisfaction with oneself (Arrogantia)*. The former is called, in particular, *self-love;* the latter, *self-conceit*. Pure practical reason merely infringes on self-love, inasmuch as it only restricts it, as natural and active in us even prior to the moral law, to the condition of agreement with this law, and then it is called *rational self-love*." Cf. TP 8:278–279; MM 6:432–434.

[14] This sense of "humanity" is different from the one operative in Kant's second formulation of the categorical imperative, namely, "always act in such a way so that you treat humanity, whether in yourself or another, always at the same time as an end and never merely as a means" (G 4:429). This second, full, sense of "humanity" is more correctly associated with what in the *Religion* Kant calls "personality": "the idea of the moral law alone, together with the respect that is inseparable from it...is personality itself (the idea of humanity considered wholly intellectually)" (R 6:28).

[15] I will have more to say about these vices in Sect. 3.2.3, where I will discuss Kant's account of what he calls "the acquired passions."

writes of our "personality" he does not mean it in the way we do today. That is, he is not talking about the way in which, e.g., one can have an easy-going personality, or a morose personality. Rather, by "personality" he means that human beings are persons, beings endowed with pure practical reason and the capacity to choose who are, therefore, responsible for their choices (Trendelenburg 1910). Kant defines personality as "the susceptibility to respect for the moral law *as of itself a sufficient incentive to the power of choice*" (6:27).[16] It is the capacity human beings have to do what is good *because* reason discerns that it is good (i.e., it is the capacity to be motivated to act by reasons alone rather than also or merely because of one's subjective desires and emotions). Because personality just is the capacity human beings have to respect the moral law, Kant holds that there can be no vices particular to this element of the predisposition to good.

To return to one of the questions I raised at the end of the previous section, how does the preceding account of the predisposition to good in human beings bear on the issue of whether or not Kant dismisses our sensible nature (i.e., our inclinations, desires, appetites, and emotions) as evil? First of all, Kant claims each of these predispositions is negatively good—"they do not resist the moral law"—and they are "predispositions *to the good* (they demand compliance with it)" (R 6:28). Second, and more importantly, Kant explicitly denies that the source of radical evil can "be placed, as is commonly done, in the sensuous nature of the human being, and in the natural inclinations originating from it" (R 6:34–35). In other words, Kant flatly denies that our sensuous natures are evil and insists that our sensuous natures and inclinations "bear no direct relation to evil (they rather give the occasion for what the moral disposition can demonstrate in its power for virtue)" (R 6:35). Actually, Kant goes even further, claiming that when people try to exterminate their sensuous natures (through, for example, mortifications of the flesh[17]), they thereby act immorally (CL 27:379). These points about the goodness of animality shall prove important to my discussion of Kant's account of sexual desire, since Kant's evaluation of animality commits him to thinking that sexual desire, as one feature of animality, is not in principle evil. Instead of locating our propensity to evil in our animality, Kant locates it in a certain predisposition to acts of will, which he distinguishes into three different gradations of the propensity to evil.

The Propensity to Evil[18] Kant defines a propensity as "the predisposition to desire an enjoyment [i.e., physical pleasure] which, when the subject has experienced it,

---

[16] Notice that Kant's way of putting this does not commit him to the view that humans always respect the law, nor does it commit him to the view that humans possess personality only insofar as they respect the law; having personality is a function of being susceptible to respecting the moral law, and this susceptibility is grounded in the capacity human beings have for practical reasoning.

[17] Kant takes mortifications of the flesh to be certain practices of discipline designed to eliminate our susceptibility to bodily pleasure.

[18] Some critics take Kant's discussion of radical evil in human nature as an illicit and not very successful attempt to smuggle a theological account of evil into his purportedly non-theologically grounded ethics. For a discussion of these criticisms and a response to them, see G. Felicitas

3.1 Unsocial Sociability and Radical Evil in Human Nature

arouses an *inclination* to it" (R 6:29). This use of "inclination" is peculiar, since Kant typically intends the term to mean "habitual desire." But Allen Wood (1970, 216) points out that Kant occasionally uses "inclination" to mean a certain kind of choice, namely, one that is motivated primarily by inclinations. Accordingly, one should understand the propensity to evil to be a tendency to act in ways that take one's inclination to be the primary motive for one's actions.[19] As Kant puts it, "the difference, whether the human being is good or evil, must not lie in the difference between incentives that he incorporates into his maxim (not in the material of his maxim) but in their subordination (in the form of the maxim): *which of the two he makes the condition of the other"* (R 6:36).[20] Kant distinguishes three different gradations of such a propensity, moving from least evil to most.

The lowest gradation of the propensity to evil Kant calls "frailty." One is frail when one adopts the moral law as the principle of one's maxim (i.e., one resolves to do what is good because one recognizes it as truly good), but when it comes time to act, one's subjective desires figure more strongly as a motivator and lead one not to do what one took to be good. So, frailty involves knowing what is good and in some sense wanting to do what is good, but inconsistently doing what is good when it comes time to act. As Kant puts it, "it is the general weakness of the human heart in complying with the adopted maxims" (R 6:29). Think here of the college student who knows that she should start her paper well in advance of the deadline and wants to do so but ends up writing the paper the night before because she managed her time poorly and prioritized interests other than writing the paper in a timely manner.

The second grade of the propensity to evil is "impurity." One is impure when one does what morality requires, but only on the basis of one's subjective desires rather than on the recognition that what one takes to be good really is good. The impure person acts in conformity with the moral law, but she does so from a motive or motives other than respect for the law. So, impurity involves doing what is good and wanting to do what is good, but doing it for self-serving reasons (such as, merely for the enjoyment, or merely because doing so is prudential or advantageous) rather than doing what is good because one recognizes it as good. This grade of the propensity to evil, as with each grade (R 6:38), involves some self-deception, since the person who acts impurely, on Kant's view, convinces herself that her motives are pure when they are not. To be impure is, according to Kant, "to adulterate moral incentives with immoral ones" (R 6:29). Here one might imagine someone attending the retirement party of a colleague who says to herself, "I'm going in order to

---

Munzel (1999, 133–183). For a more general discussion of and response to general criticisms of Kant's account of radical evil, see Robert Louden (2010).

[19] According to Wood (1970, 216), we should understand Kant's definition of a propensity to mean the following: "the property of the human will which makes it possible for this will to invert, in accordance with a rule or maxim, the rational and moral order of its incentives, to prefer the incentives of inclination to those of duty, and hence to do *evil*."

[20] Cf. Baxley (2010, 68): "the real obstacle we finite imperfect rational beings must strive to overcome in our efforts to lead morally good lives in accordance with the dictates of pure practical reason is a volitional tendency to treat inclinations as sufficient reasons for action."

honor my colleague," but who is also significantly motivated by her desire to be seen by her supervisors at the party so that they'll think of her as loyal to her company and committed to her team.

The third and final grade of the propensity to evil is "depravity," or what Kant calls "corruption of the human heart" (R 6:30). Depravity is "the propensity of the power of choice to maxims that subordinate the incentives of the moral law to others (not moral ones)" (R 6:30). The depraved person deliberately inverts what Kant takes to be the correct ethical order of incentives. That is, the depraved person deliberately prioritizes her own happiness over and against respect for the moral law, and she makes a policy of this subversion.[21] Unlike impurity, the depraved person is not merely allowing inclinations to compete with moral motives; she actually rejects moral motives in favor of her own happiness. All that she does she does so as to secure her own comfort, satisfaction, and well-being with zero regard for what morality requires of her. For this reason, depravity entails corrupting one's moral disposition. At the level of depravity, thinks Kant, "the mind's attitude is thereby corrupted at its root (so far as the moral disposition is concerned), and hence the human being is designated as evil" (R 6:30). I like to think that a depraved person (in Kant's sense) is someone with whom we all have little experience, but perhaps we can imagine an individual who in some ways recognizes what is genuinely good for humans and, therefore, what is morally required of her. But this person recognizes that following through on these requirements will come at a cost, or she concludes that being concerned with moral goodness gets in the way of her full happiness. So she resolves to prioritize herself and her happiness above all else, as a policy.

I now want to illustrate what the three grades of the propensity to radical evil would look like in one and the same person. I will use the example of Giselle, who has just had a birthday and received a thoughtful present from Kate, her significant other. Were Giselle someone whose disposition is frail, she would resolve to express gratitude to Kate (e.g., by writing her a thank you note) but would end up not following through because of her inclinations (perhaps she is always too tired, or too busy doing other things that she likes). If Giselle's disposition were impure, she would resolve to write a thank you card and would follow through, telling herself that this is the good and proper thing to do, but her primary motive would be more self-serving (e.g., she does it because she knows this is a good way to get another gift next year, or perhaps she knows that Kate would be mad at her if she did not write a note). Giselle would be depraved if, as a policy, she acted only for the sake of her own happiness. In this case, what is key is that her depravity commits her to prioritizing her own happiness, as a policy. It is important to see that depravity, thus understood, might well lead one to act in ways that, on the surface (as it were), look like one is in some way concerned with what is genuinely moral. So, on this example, a depraved Giselle might well write a thank you card, but she would do so because she sees the ways in which not writing one can make her unhappy; she

---

[21] Cf. CPr R 5:25: "The direct opposite of the principle of morality is the principle of *one's own happiness* made the determining ground of the will."

3.1 Unsocial Sociability and Radical Evil in Human Nature

would not write one out of concern for what is genuinely good or out of a concern for Kate. In this circumstance, one then hopes that Kate would be able to see Giselle for who she really is and decide to get out of that relationship.

Although depravity signals the worst that humans are capable of when it comes to their moral dispositions,[22] each of the three levels of evil specify an important aspect of the unsociable component of human nature that Kant articulates in "Idea for a Universal History," namely, the natural drive to prioritize one's own happiness above all else. Most important for my purposes is the fact that Kant locates the source of moral evil in a certain kind of choice, rather than in the sensible natures of human beings (i.e., rather than in the needs and inclinations humans have). And this insight serves as the answer to the second potential criticism I raised at the start of this chapter, namely, does Kant's philosophical anthropology rule out our being able to act morally? In a word, no. Recall that I developed this criticism in terms of two questions: does Kant think that our sensible nature is evil, and does Kant think that we always act from an interest in our own happiness? I already answered the first question in my discussion of Kant's account of our predisposition to goodness. The second question is answered by Kant's understanding of our propensity to evil in terms of a propensity to choosing in a certain way. Nothing about our sensible nature, according to Kant, *determines* us to act one way or another. To be so determined would preclude our being free agents. Rather, being dependent beings means that we have needs and wants that are always looking to be satisfied, as it were, and so addressing these needs and wants is always one possible way for us to act. Sometimes these needs and wants are especially strong, and they pose a significant obstacle to our acting morally, but they do not determine our action. By way of analogy, think of someone who has a genetic predisposition to enjoy sweets in a serious way. Assuming that consuming sweets is not *prima facie* immoral, this predisposition is not bad. But if it is allowed to run free, without the guidance of one's practical reasoning and the exercise of self-control, a person with this predisposition can easily become unhealthy. Does a person with such a predisposition *have to eat sweets?* Is she *destined* to become a diabetic or obese? I think the answer to both of those questions is "no." And I think it is this kind of situation that Kant has in mind when he expounds our propensity to radical evil.

My reading of Kant's philosophical anthropology stands in contrast to the Anscombian reading, which takes Kant to reject sensible nature as a whole as having no positive value.[23] But the Anscombian reading is based in large part on Kant's discussion of inclinations and moral worth in Section I of the *Groundwork*. So, in order to put the Anscombian reading to rest and round out this account of Kant's philosophical anthropology, I want to turn now to what Kant has to say about the inclinations.

---

[22] For someone critical of Kant on evil, see Claudia Card (2010).

[23] For an example of such a reading of Kant, see David Cartwright (1987).

3.2 Desire and Emotion in Kant's Account of Sensible Nature

So far in this chapter I have presented a reading of Kant that takes unsocial sociability to be central to his philosophical anthropology, and I have interpreted this unsociability in terms of the propensity all humans have to prioritize their own respective conceptions of happiness over doing what is objectively good. My claim is that a failure adequately to appreciate Kant's argument for this propensity has led defenders of the Anscombian reading wrongly to conclude that Kant's ethics involves a wholesale rejection of emotions and desires as not having any positive moral value. This misreading of Kant is exacerbated by (a) misreading Kant's discussion of moral worth and feelings[24] in the *Groundwork,* and (b) reading the passages in the *Groundwork* in complete isolation from some other accounts of feelings and desires that Kant provides, especially in later works such as his *Metaphysics of Morals.* Allen Wood (2008, 41) expresses the problem with this approach quite well:

> Most of us who read the First Section of the *Groundwork* do not suspect (or if we do, we find it unacceptable) that at the end of the section, we still have not learned very much at all about Kant's moral philosophy. So we naturally want to draw large conclusions about Kantian ethical theory based solely on what he says there, and once our image of Kantian ethics is fixed on this basis, we try to read everything else he says as a confirmation of it. But in fact the First Section of the *Groundwork* gives us only very limited information about Kantian ethics, and the attempt to force it to tell us more than it does often leads to serious misunderstandings of Kant's ethical theory.

With this position in mind, I want to review Kant's mature exposition of sensible nature from the *Metaphysics of Morals* and use this account, along with the discussion of radial evil from the previous section, to develop a correct reading of the *Groundwork* passages in question.

3.2.1 Sensible Nature in the Metaphysics of Morals

The Introduction to the *Metaphysics of Morals* contains a long, illuminating discussion of some of the basic vocabulary Kant uses in his ethical theory, and one prominent part of this discussion is Kant's analysis of sensible nature. He distinguishes two faculties that comprise sensible nature: desire and feeling. Kant defines the faculty of desire as "the faculty to be, by means of one's representations, the cause of the objects of these representations," and he defines the faculty of feeling as the susceptibility humans have to feel pleasure or displeasure (MM 6:211). The capacity for feeling pleasure or displeasure, according to Kant, "[both] involve what is

---

[24] Up to this point I have written of "emotions" rather than "feelings." This is to distinguish emotions from the feelings that are sensations (e.g., a tickle or a toothache) and the feelings that are perceptions (e.g., feeling the rough stone of the patio or the smooth silk of my sweater). I resort to using "feeling" within my discussion of sensible nature in general in order to be consistent with the texts of Kant that I quote. "Feeling" in this context should be taken as a synonym for "emotion".

merely subjective in the relation of our representation and contain no relation at all to an object for possible cognition of it" (MM 6:211–212).²⁵ That is, feelings do not (and cannot) give us knowledge of objects in the world²⁶; they only tell us how we are responding to the world.²⁷ So, Kant concludes, when it comes to giving an account of feelings, one must start from the fact that they are context-dependent— "one can only specify what results they have in certain circumstances" (MM 6:212). With these features of feeling in mind, Kant explains his understanding of the relationship between feelings and desire.

According to Kant, although it is possible to feel pleasure (or displeasure) without desiring or eschewing the object one finds pleasant or unpleasant (CPJ 5:203–211), desire and aversion are always connected with pleasure and displeasure, respectively (MM 6:211). But, thinks Kant, "pleasure or displeasure in an object of desire does not always precede the desire and need not always be regarded as the cause of the desire but can be regarded as the effect of it" (MM 6:211). In other words, when, e.g., my desire for raspberries is determined by the pleasure I expect from eating them (because, say, I like raspberries and have learned from experience that they taste good to me), then this pleasure, according to Kant, is "an interest of inclination" (MM 6:212). In such instances my will is determined by sensible nature, by concern for *my* pleasure, rather than being determined by pure practical reason (i.e, by what I, as a result of reasoning about what is truly good for me, resolve to do). But when my pleasure in the raspberries follows the determination of my will by pure practical reason (i.e., when the pleasure is the result of my having reasoned practically and judged that eating raspberries is genuinely good for me because, e.g., of their extraordinary anti-oxidant properties), then Kant calls this "an interest of reason." What I hope is clear is that Kant's distinction between an interest of inclination and an interest of reason is just the difference between acting heteronomously and acting autonomously that I discussed in the previous Chap. 2 (Sect. 2.3.1). This understanding of feelings and how they can relate to desire is in part what motivates Kant to draw the conclusions he draws in the *Groundwork* regarding the inability of sensible feelings to produce actions that have what he calls "moral worth."

---

²⁵ On the basis of this passage, some commentators have interpreted Kant's moral psychology of sensible nature as hedonistic. For a recent defense of Kant's hedonism, see Morrison (2008). The classic paper on Kant's hedonism is by Andrews Reath (1989), who challenges the hedonistic reading of Kant. For someone who takes issue with Reath's approach see Herman (2007, Chapter 8). Herman defends Kant's hedonism as playing an important methodological role, namely to show the limits of subjective theories of value and the need for a Kantian account of dignity to correct these limitations.

²⁶ Ido Geiger's (2011) reading of Kant on emotions seems mistakenly to assume that they are disclosive of goodness.

²⁷ I think some critics of Kant erroneously read the foregoing passage as implying that Kant reduced all pathological emotions to sensations. See, for example, John Sabini and Maury Silver (1988). For a response to Sabini and Silver, see Maria de Lourdes Borges (2004), and for another defense of Kant's account of emotions, see Kelly Sorensen (2002).

3.2.2 Moral Worth and Pathological Feelings in the Groundwork

Kant uses "pathological" (*pathologisch*) as a synonym for "sensible" (*sinnlich*) when discussing feelings and desires, and to the contemporary reader, "pathological feelings" and "pathological desires"[28] can come across as wrongheaded, since "pathological" in contemporary English typically connotes sickness, but we should not take Kant to be saying that pathological feelings are essentially illnesses or that they are essentially bad. Rather, Kant uses the term "pathological" to describe those feelings (and desires) that depend on (i.e., have their source in) our sensibility. Such pathological feelings, according to Kant, are to be distinguished from a feeling such as respect for the moral law, which, though it has some effect on our sensibility, finds its source in reason.[29] Whereas respect functions as a moral motivator (i.e., actions done out of respect for the moral law have what Kant calls 'moral worth' or 'moral content'), the pathological cannot function in this way, and because of *this* inability to be moral motivators Kant criticizes pathological feelings (and desires).

Kant's criticisms of the pathological run throughout his ethical writings and are most prominent in those texts where he discusses what, in the *Groundwork*, he calls "pure moral philosophy" (G 4:388–389), and this points to Kant's concerns with the way in which pathological feelings (and desires) pose an alternative motive for acting, one that competes with the motive of acting out of respect for the law. In order properly to understand Kant's reasons for being critical of the moral worth of the pathological, I ought first to clarify what he means by 'moral worth' and distinguish this concept from what can be said to have 'moral value'.

Moral Worth and Moral Value In Section I of the *Groundwork* Kant distinguishes actions that have moral worth (or moral content) and are, therefore, worthy of esteem from those that do not have moral worth and are (merely) worthy of "praise and encouragement" (G 4:398). In making this distinction, Kant is *not* drawing a line between what has moral value and what lacks moral value altogether. Rather, as Allen Wood (2008, 28) argues, "the distinction he is drawing is between what has a special, fundamental, essentially or authentically *moral* value from what is valuable from the moral standpoint but does not have the sort of value that lies right at the heart of *morality*." Along these lines, one might distinguish different kinds of moral (as opposed to merely instrumental) value in Kant's writings. We can find Kant distinguishing between (1) those acts that are consistent with the moral law and are

---

[28] Most of what Kant says about pathological feelings regarding their lack of moral worth applies *mutatis mutandis* to pathological desires, since Kant believes that all inclination (which is habituated sensible desire) and "every sensible impulse is based on feeling" (CPrR 5:72). The one notable difference is that pathological feelings indicate a passive power, whereas pathological desires indicate an active (though sensuous) power.

[29] The feeling of respect as the sole moral motive in Kant's ethics is the subject of much debate in the scholarship. Although I will have some things to say about respect in the next chapter within the context of discussing Kant's account of our duties to others, entering into that debate within the context of this book would take me too far afield. For a summary of some of the main interpretations of Kantian respect, see Iain Morrisson (2008, Chapter 5).

3.2 Desire and Emotion in Kant's Account of Sensible Nature

done out of respect for the moral law, as well as (2) whatever promotes or is conducive to (1). The first class of actions are those that possess moral worth/esteem and, therefore, build moral character, whereas broad moral value (but not moral worth) can be ascribed to the second class.[30] As Robert N. Johnson (2009, 38) observes, Kant "explicitly and repeatedly asserts that many dutiful actions not done from duty, such as those form sympathy and honor, *also* deserve praise and indeed can be morally meritorious.".[31]

Although, as I shall argue below, some pathological feelings can, in fact, have the kind of broad moral value Wood identifies, no pathological feeling (or desire), according to Kant, can have moral worth. Anne Margaret Baxley (2010, 37–38) neatly summarizes Kant's view when she claims that inclination (as well as all pathological feelings and desires that are not governed by moral principle) cannot be the ground of morally worthy actions because "it is always an accidental or contingent matter whether inclination harmonizes with the requirements of duty....when an agent adopts a policy of action on the basis of inclination, the moral rightness of her action has nothing to do with an antecedent commitment on her part to morality (a commitment on her part to do the what is right for its own sake."[32] Because the pathological is contingent in this way, actions that are motivated by pathological feeling and desire, without the guidance of moral principle, can result in actions in conformity with duty, but just as easily can result in actions that are contrary to duty. In order to cash this out, I follow Baxley in distinguishing two ways in which the pathological, according to Kant, is contingent and cannot, therefore, function as a genuine moral motive for Kant (i.e., one that results in morally worthy action).

Contingency and the Inclinations The first way in which pathological feelings and desires are contingent has to do with their being fickle and transient. The concern comes to the fore in the second section of the "Introduction to the metaphysics of morals," where Kant discusses the pathological feeling of pleasure. As I have already noted, Kant claims that "pleasure and displeasure cannot be explained more

---

[30] Cf. Baxley (2010, 32): "Kant distinguishes between an action *accompanied by inclination (mit Neigung)* and an action motivated *from inclination (aus Neigung)*. This means that morally worthy action can be accompanied by inclination and that a person with a good will can act beneficently from duty *with sympathy and love*—she need not do her duty in the absence of sympathy, or in the face of indifference, in order to have a good will." Baxley disagrees with Wood, who reads Kant as holding that authentic moral worth only applies to actions done from duty, where 'done from duty' requires that one act in the face of temptation or adversity. As Wood puts it, 'The action with authentic moral worth is the one where the agent faced with adversity rises to the occasion and does the dutiful thing in spite of adverse circumstances' (Wood 2008, 29). For Wood's reading, also see Wood (2006, 35–36, notes 1 &2). Such interpretive disagreements aside, the main point is that Kant does not reduce all moral value to what he calls "moral worth." If he did, that would be a reason to think that the Anscombian reading is right to accuse Kant of promoting a moral rigorism.

[31] "For any moral theory, including Kant's, whether one *ought* to praise an action is a substantive moral question, since praising is an action and so is itself up for moral evaluation" (Johnson 2009, 37). Cf. Johnson 1996.

[32] The account that follows is indebted to Baxley (2010).

clearly in themselves; instead, one can only specify what results they have in certain circumstances, so as to make them recognizable in practice" (MM 6:212). Kant's point here is fairly straightforward. Due to differences in human physiology, as well as differences in the circumstances in which different human beings find themselves, different objects cause different people to feel pleasure or pain, and at different times. What may seem pleasant to one person at one time may strike another as revolting (e.g., eating raw oysters, or reading the work of Duns Scotus). Indeed, the same person can find an object unpleasant at one time and pleasant at another (as, e.g., when someone as an adult comes to appreciate certain art or music that she disliked in her younger days, such as the music of Tom Waits). Kant thinks this contingency is characteristic not merely of the pleasure and displeasure one can take in an object; it is also characteristic of pathological feelings and desires in general: different objects and events can cause different feelings and motivate different desires in people at different times. What might, for example, be an occasion for compassion in my case may only engender feelings of indignation and anger in another (think, e.g., of the various affective responses people have to the homeless or the unemployed).

Just as our having pathological feelings is a contingent matter, so too is their being in conformity with what duty requires. Even though such transient pathological feelings can and sometimes do give rise to actions that are in conformity with what the moral law requires, these feelings are a mere happy accident, according to Kant, a function of our physical constitution and the situations in which we find ourselves; and so these actions do not properly proceed from our wills (i.e., they do not proceed from a deliberate commitment to and recognition of what the moral law requires). So, actions motivated by pathological feelings may just as well conform with duty as not conform with duty. This is what lies behind Kant's remarks in the *Groundwork* concerning the sympathetic philanthropist (G 4:398). Although the philanthropist's sympathy is amiable and "deserving of praise and encouragement," such sympathetic feelings are a mere accident of the philanthropist's natural disposition. Indeed, the philanthropist may well have been born without a sympathetic disposition, or, as Kant claims, he might find himself "overclouded with grief" such that his sympathy is extinguished. If the ground of his philanthropy is this contingent pathological emotion, then his beneficence is equally contingent and, therefore, the mere product of his circumstances rather than the result of a deliberate choice.[33]

The second way the pathological is contingent is related to the first but is more fundamental to Kant's position. According to him, pathological feelings (and desires) are basically expressive of one's own self-love.[34] More specifically,

---

[33] The literature on Kant's example of the sympathetic philanthropist is vast. For a thorough and well-respected treatment of the issues pertaining to this example, see Baron (1995, 111–226).

[34] Cf. CPrR 5:72: "All the inclinations together (which can be brought into a tolerable system and the satisfaction of which is then called one's own happiness) constitute regard for oneself (*solipsismus*). This is either the self-regard of *love for oneself*, a predominant *benevolence* toward oneself (*Philautia*), or that of *satisfaction with oneself* (*Arrogantia*). The former is called, in particular,

pathological feelings are expressions primarily, if not exclusively, of my needs and wants as opposed to the needs and wants of others. And although self-interest can and sometimes does conform with what the moral law requires, self-interest can just as easily move us to act in ways that are contrary to what the moral law requires of us, since what promotes my individual well-being need not conform with the requirements of morality. Here we see the relevance of Kant's example of the shopkeeper from Section I of the *Groundwork*. The shopkeeper gives each of his customers the same price for his wares, and the customers are thus served honestly, but the shopkeeper's motive (as Kant formulates the example) is one of self-interest, since he knows that "where there is a good deal of trade a prudent merchant does not overcharge" (G 4:397). But this, again, is a matter of contingent circumstances; were the shopkeeper the only merchant available within one hundred miles, self-interest alone would dictate that the shopkeeper charge as much as he can whenever he can, insofar as this would be most conducive to him making the most profit.[35]

As I have been stressing throughout this chapter and a good deal of the previous one, according to Kant, pathological feelings (and their associated desires) often function as motivations for actions that compete with the motivations people have as a result of practical reasoning, and being motivated by inclinations can result in us ignoring our duties, which points to yet another reason Kant tends to be critical of the pathological, namely belief that pathological feelings can impair our ability to think rationally and, therefore, to act autonomously.[36] There are two species of the pathological that Kant picks out as especially dangerous to the moral dispositions of humans: affects (*Affekten*), which are a kind of feeling, and passions (*Leidenschaften*), which are a species of desire.

3.2.3 Affects and Passions as Detriments to Moral Disposition

In *Anthropology from a Pragmatic Point of View,* Kant treats affects and passions together, most likely because they pertain to sensible feeling and sensible desire, respectively. "The feeling of a pleasure or displeasure in the subject's present state that does not let him to rise to *reflection* (the representation by means of reason as to whether he should give himself up to it or refuse it) is *affect*," according to Kant, whereas "inclination that can be conquered only with difficulty or not at all by the subject's reason is *passion*" (A 7:251). Kant claims that being subject to affects and passions is an "illness of the mind" because both of them "shut out the sovereignty

---

self-love; the latter, *self-conceit*" (CPrR, 5:73). This passage speaks only of inclinations, but it is worth recalling that Kant believes that "all inclination and every sensible impulse is based on feeling…" (CPrR 5:72).

[35] Cf. Baxley (2010, 35–36); Wood (1999, 27–33); and Korsgaard (1996, 55–60).

[36] Kant does not think that our capacity to feel renders us causally determined and, therefore, completely unfree to act. Rather, the impairment of freedom due to pathological feelings is akin to the kind of impairment drinking too much alcohol has on one's ability to choose.

of reason"—that is, both preclude autonomous action (A: 7:251). He thinks, however, that in the final estimation, passion is more detrimental to moral disposition than affect.[37] In order to see why, one needs to examine what he says about each in particular.

Affects Kant defines affect (*Affekt*), a particular species of pathological feeling, as "surprise through sensation, by means of which the mind's composure (*animus sui compos*) is suspended....it quickly grows to a degree of feeling which makes reflection impossible (it is thoughtless)" (A 7:252). Affects, on Kant's view, most closely resemble what may be called emotional states of excitement.[38] The spontaneous occurrence of affect is something that inhibits rational activity, which is why Kant claims that someone who is "customarily seized by affect like a fit of madness, no matter how benign these feelings may be, nevertheless resembles a deranged person" (A 7:253). Kant claims that affect "always makes itself incapable of pursuing its own end, and it is therefore unwise to allow it to come into being intentionally" (A 7:253), since affects produce "a momentary damage to freedom and dominion over oneself" (A 7:267). In other words, to be in the grip of pathological feelings such as affects severely inhibits one's ability to think clearly and to choose and to act well (e.g., think of the effects anger, fear, and shame can have on people). "Whoever is seized by affect like a fit of madness, no matter how benign these emotions may be, nevertheless resembles a deranged person" (A 7:253). Affects, in other words, are temporary yet powerful obstacles to autonomous action. Think, for example, of someone who is completely overcome with emotion when told of some bad news, or, alternatively, someone who loses her temper any time a certain politician is mentioned. These cases are cases where people suffer affects.

Passions Kant further elucidates what he takes affects to be by distinguishing them and their effects from passions. Affects are occurrent emotional events that come on suddenly and leave people unable to act reflectively or rationally. Passion, however, "(as a state of mind belonging to the faculty of desire) takes its time and reflects, no matter how fierce it may be, in order to reach its end" (A 7:252). Hence, argues Kant,

> Affect works like water that breaks through a dam; passion, like a river that digs itself deeper and deeper into its bed. Affect works on our health like an apoplectic fit; passion, like consumption or emaciation. Affect is like drunkenness that one sleeps off, although a headache follows afterward; but passion is regarded as a sickness that comes from swallowing poison, or a deformity...Affects are honest and open, passions on the other hand are deceitful and hidden. (A 7:252)

Because passion can coexist with calm reflection, according to Kant, "they do the greatest damage to freedom, and if affect is *drunkenness*, then passion is an *illness* that abhors all medicine" (A 7:265–266). One of the things that makes passions so

---

[37] Cf. Rolf Löchel (2006) who examines the way in which Kant thinks that affects are characteristic of women while passions are more characteristic of men.

[38] Cf. MM 6:407–408: "an affect is called *precipitate* or *rash (animus praeceps)*, and reason says, through the concept of virtue, that one should *get hold of* oneself."

dangerous to moral disposition is that they always involve a maxim, which means that they are connected to reason in a certain way, which is why Kant thinks that non-human animals are not subject to passions (A 7:266). He claims that passions are "cancerous sores for pure practical reason, and for the most part they are incurable because the sick person does not want to be cured and flees from the dominion of principles, by which alone a cure could occur" (A 7:266). In short, according to Kant, passions are "without exception *evil*," since passions abandon freedom and rational self-control "and finds its pleasure and satisfaction in a slavish mind" (A 7:267). Here we might imagine someone who hates one of her colleagues so much that she sets herself the task of doing whatever it takes, however long it takes, to ruin her colleague's career. Such a strong, sensible desire for the professional demise of another is an example of passion.

Kant divides passions into two kinds: those due to natural inclination and those that are due to human culture (i.e., they can be acquired only because humans live socially) (A 7:267–268). Among natural passions he groups the inclination for sex and freedom, the former of which I discuss in Chap. 5.[39] In the latter group, he places "the *manias for honor, dominance,* and *possession,*" which, unlike the natural passions, are not connected to affect but instead involve "the persistence of a maxim established for certain ends" (A 7:268). The cultural passions, according to Kant, all stem from the same inclination, namely, the desire for the capacity to have a general influence over other human beings. One gains such influence, thinks Kant, by getting the inclinations of other human beings into one's power, that is, by being able to know, predict, and control the inclinations of others so that one can get these others to do what one wills. Kant claims that "getting other human beings' inclinations into one's power, so that one can direct and determine them according to one's intentions, is almost the same as *possessing* others as mere tools of one's will" (A 7:271), which, he thinks, constitutes a basic violation of human dignity (G 4:429–435). The cultural passions, then, stem from the inclination to objectify others, to use them as mere instruments for one's own purposes, which is why the cultural passions are of particular interest when it comes to Kant's sexual ethics. As I shall argue, sexual desire and sexual pleasure provide opportunities for manipulating others into serving as mere instruments for one's own gratification and for allowing oneself to be so manipulated.

Of the three particular cultural passions, the one for domination most concerns me, and for two reasons. First, Kant claims that this passion (which he identifies as "intrinsically unjust") starts "from the fear of being dominated by others, and is then soon intent on placing the advantage of force over them" (A 7:273). Second, Kant distinguishes between the ways in which women try to dominate men and the ways men try to dominate women, which reflects his understanding of gender and gender relations, which I examine in Chap. 5. According to Kant, men use physical strength and the fear of this strength to dominate women, but women use charm, which, he thinks, "comprehends an inclination of the other part to be dominated" (A 7:273). As he understands them, gender relations involve women in general being in an

---

[39] Curiously, Kant does not provide an analysis of sexual instinct in his *Anthropology*.

inferior position to men because men in general tend to be physically stronger than women (Wood 2008, 228). The tool women use in order to overcome this discrepancy and have dominion over men, according to Kant, is social grace and charm. As far as Kant is concerned, this "battle of the sexes" is a consequence of the desire humans have to dominate each other, and the particular way in which this desire for domination plays out between men and women is a consequence of the nature of sexual appetite, which is just a drive to objectify another for one's gratification. So, as I shall argue in Chap. 5, sexual drive and sexual relations according to Kant is one area of human existence in which unsocial sociability can have particularly serious and dangerous consequences.

3.3 The Natural Desire for Happiness and Its Place in Kant's Ethics

I spent the last section arguing against the traditional reading of Kant on sensible feelings and desires, which takes him to reject sensible nature wholesale as having no positive moral value whatsoever. Contrary to such a misreading, I have argued that Kant criticizes sensible/pathological emotions and desires only insofar as they function as obstacles to autonomous action and incline us to heteronomy. The next chapter presents Kant's normative virtue ethics as his account of how the development of a virtuous disposition helps humans control the tendency to give themselves over to the pursuit of happiness above all else and, instead, develop into morally good people. But this chapter's account of Kant's philosophical anthropology has yet to address the way in which happiness is, according to Kant, the natural end of human beings. So, what remains to be seen is how he reconciles his rejection of heteronomy and endorsement of autonomy with his belief that happiness is the natural end of human beings. This is important for Kant's sexual ethics, too, since sexual satisfaction, as the most powerful pleasure of which we are capable (according to Kant), will be a part of some people's happiness. Accordingly, I conclude this chapter first by briefly giving an overview of Kant's view of happiness and then explaining how happiness, as the natural end of humans, fits into his moral theory.

3.3.1 The Complete Satisfaction of All of One's Inclinations

Throughout his practical philosophy Kant defines happiness in a number of different ways that are all closely related but not necessarily equivalent.[40] His considered view, though, is that happiness consists in the complete satisfaction of all of one's

---

[40] Sometimes, for example, Kant writes as though happiness is the sum total of the satisfaction of all of one's inclinations (G 4:393). At other times he writes as though happiness is the satisfaction one takes in knowing that all of one's inclinations have been satisfied (CPrR 5:22). Victoria Wike (1994) gives a systematic treatment of the concept of happiness as it functions in Kant's ethics.

3.3 The Natural Desire for Happiness and Its Place in Kant's Ethics

inclination and the pleasure one takes in such complete satisfaction: "A rational being's consciousness of the agreeableness of life uninterruptedly accompanying his whole existence is *happiness*" (CPrR 5:22). Although Kant maintains that it is the natural end of human beings and, as such, constitutes part of the highest good for them, it alone cannot form the sole basis of the good life for human beings nor is it the primary component of our highest good. One reason that it cannot be the sole basis of a good life, according to Kant, is that one's happiness is an empirical matter—that is, it is a matter of one's changing circumstances and desires, both of which are subject to fluctuation over time and from moment to moment and are largely out of one's control. In other words, happiness is very much contingent, as are inclinations on whose satisfaction it is based: Kant expresses this contingency as follows:

> Now, it is impossible for the most insightful and at the same time most powerful but still finite being to frame for himself a determinate concept of what he really wills here. If he wills riches, how much anxiety, envy, and intrigue might he not bring upon himself in this way! If he wills a great deal of cognition and insight, that might become only an eye all the more acute to show him, as all the more dreadful, ills that are now concealed from him and that cannot be avoided, or to burden his desires, which already give him enough to do, with still more needs. If he wills a long life, who will guarantee him that it would not be a long misery? If he at least wills health, how often has not bodily discomfort kept someone from excesses into which unlimited health would have let him fall, and so forth. (G 4:418).[41]

According to Kant, because happiness is an empirical concept (1) each human's happiness is going to be particular to her and, so, be unfit as the basis of an objective ethics, and (2) each person's conception of her own happiness is going to be indeterminate and, so, a poor guide for her action.[42] Actually, in one sense, a single-minded pursuit of happiness, according to Kant, can result in a life that is less satisfying rather than more (G 4:395).[43] This result is possible because, I have already argued, Kant maintains that human beings are not merely embodied animals (to use the language of *Religion*, human beings do not merely possess animality) but are also rational beings (i.e., are also beings endowed with humanity and personality). And as rational beings, thinks Kant, humans are called to another, more important end:

---

[41] Cf. CPJ 5:430; G 4:418.

[42] Kant identifies hypothetical imperatives whose end is happiness as "assertoric imperatives" or "precepts of prudence" (G 4:415–416). Wood (1999, 65–70) gives a helpful exposition of Kant's account of assertoric imperatives and how they relate to other kinds of imperatives.

[43] There is a sense in which for Kant human beings are *condemned* to have happiness as their natural end. It is exactly the same sense in which he writes of human beings as "dependent beings" and identifies this dependency (which takes the form of needs and wants) as the source of our imperfection, morally-speaking: "To be happy is necessarily the demand of every rational but finite being and therefore an unavoidable determining ground of its faculty of desire. For, satisfaction with one's whole existence is not, as it were, an original possession and a beatitude…but is instead a problem imposed upon him by his finite nature itself, because he is needy and this need is directed to the matter of his faculty of desire…" (CPrR 5:25). Cf. Grenberg (2005, 26–28).

> The human being is a being with needs, insofar as he belongs to the sensible world, and to this extent his reason certainly has a commission from the side of his sensibility which it cannot refuse, to attend to its interest and to form practical maxims with a view to happiness in this life and, where possible, in a future life as well. But he is nevertheless not so completely an animal as to be indifferent to all that reason says on its own and to use reason merely as a tool for the satisfaction of his needs as a sensible being. For, that he has reason does not at all raise him in worth above mere animality if reason is to serve him only for the sake of what instinct accomplishes for animals. (CPrR 5:61)

As he puts it in the *Groundwork*, "The true vocation of reason must be to produce a will that is good, not perhaps *as a means* to other purposes, but *good in itself*....This will need not, because of this, be the sole and complete good, but it must still be the highest good and the condition of every other, even of all demands for happiness" (G 4:396). In other words, happiness, as the natural end of human beings, is subordinate to the development of a moral disposition, which is the end of human beings *qua* rational beings. More to Kant's point, "making someone happy is quite different from making him good, or making him prudent and sharp-sighted for his own advantage is quite different from making him virtuous" (G 4:442). The proper relationship between happiness and morality, for Kant, is a matter or subordinating the former to the latter, which is something Kant had to clarify even to critics who were his contemporaries.

3.3.2 Worthiness to Be Happy

Kant's essay, "On the Common Saying: That May Be Correct in Theory, But It is of No Use in Practice" is primarily a response to some criticisms of Kant made by Christian Garve, a philosopher and contemporary of Kant.[44] Garve's criticisms are worth considering here because they anticipate some of the main lines of argument that form the Anscombian reading of Kant's ethics. According to Garve, Kant maintains that "observance of the moral law, without any regard for happiness at all, is the *sole final end* for the human being, that it must be considered the creator's sole end" (TP 8:279). Kant, however, maintains that neither the cultivation of a moral disposition alone nor human happiness alone are the sole and final ends of humans. Rather, he thinks that the final end for humans is "the highest good possible in the world, which consists of the union and harmony of the two" (TP 8:279). In a long passage that deserves to be quoted in full, Kant clearly lays out his view regarding the place of happiness in his ethics:

> I explained morals provisionally as the introduction to a science that teaches, not how we are to become happy, but how we are to become worthy of happiness. In doing so I did not fail to remark that the human being is not thereby required to *renounce* his natural end, happiness, when it is a matter of complying with his duty; for that he cannot do, just as no finite

---

[44] The essay actually contains three separate responses by Kant to three people with whom he disagrees: Garve, Thomas Hobbes, and Moses Mendelssohn. But only his response to Garve is relevant to my purposes.

rational being whatever can; instead, he must *abstract* altogether from this consideration when the command of duty arises; he must on no account make it [happiness] the *condition* of his compliance with the law prescribed to him by reason; indeed, he must, as far as is possible for him, strive to become aware that no *incentive* derived from that gets mixed , unnoticed, into the determination of duty, and this is effected by his representing duty as connected with the sacrifices its observance (virtue) costs us rather than with the advantages it yields, so as to represent the command of duty in all its authority, as requiring unconditional obedience, sufficient in itself and in need of no other influences. (TP 8: 278–279)

In many ways, the preceding passage summarizes many of the points I have been pressing over the course of this chapter and the last. According to Kant, human beings, as dependent rational beings, have two ends that correspond to their being, on the one hand, (embodied) animal beings, and on the other hand, rational beings capable of reflection, deliberation, and choice. Insofar as their capacity for reason endows them with a dignity that distinguishes them from other living beings, humans are called, as it were, to develop moral dispositions as their supreme though not complete good (CPrR 5:110). But they also find themselves, naturally, as it were, called on to secure their own happiness, since they are embodied animal beings. And this latter call to happiness can and always (to some degree) does serve as a "counterweight" to the demands of practical reason when practical reason considers what is genuinely good, not just for the reflecting individual *qua this human being with these particular needs* but for this human being *qua rational being*. So, when a conflict between the demands of one's own happiness and the demands of morality occurs, Kant's ethical theory argues that people ought to comply with the demands of morality, even if that means sacrificing one's happiness to a certain degree (or even completely).[45] This conclusion, of course, does not mean that happiness has no place in Kant's ethics. It just means that happiness, for Kant, must be understood against the backdrop of his philosophical anthropology, which conceives of human beings as dependent beings who by nature are unsocially sociable and, so, have a propensity to act in ways that secure their own happiness at the expense of others and what is genuinely good.

3.4 Looking Ahead

This chapter and a good portion of the last examined Kant's philosophical anthropology as it informs his practical philosophy. I proceeded in this way because my reading of Kant's ethics sees his conception of human beings as dependent (i.e., finite, imperfect, and not self-sufficient) rational beings as the guiding theme running through all of his thinking on ethics, both normative and practical. As I have implied all along, insofar as the Anscombian reading of Kant ignores the way in which Kant's practical philosophy is informed by his philosophical anthropology,

---

[45] Kant famously claims that when, for example, a prince asks a subject to give false testimony on pain of execution, if these are the only two options, the moral thing for the subject to do would be not to lie (CPrR 5:30).

just to that extent is the Anscombian reading mistaken. Despite being mistaken, however, the Anscombian reading has enjoyed, and continues to enjoy, widespread acceptance as a reading of Kant. This dominance is why I have spent so much time trying to argue that it simply misreads Kant on moral obligation and fails to appreciate and understand his conception and evaluation of human nature in general and of human sensible nature in particular.

But criticizing the Anscombian reading of Kant is not my primary end; it is a mere means to my primary end. This primary end is a systematic exposition and evaluation of Kant's practical ethics as it concerns sex and marriage. The issues on which I have thus far focused (the imperfection of humans and its implications for how we experience the demands of genuinely good action as a limit on our pursuit of happiness; the tendency of humans to prioritize our own happiness over what is genuinely good and at the expense of others; the ways in which human needs, desires, and emotions can provide occasions for people to prioritize their happiness over what is genuinely good), these issues are of central importance to understanding Kant's analysis of sex and marriage. This next chapter presents the basics of Kant's normative ethical theory, which is a theory of virtue. But, you will not be surprised to learn, it is a theory of virtue that takes its lead from Kant's account of human beings as dependent beings who are unsocially sociable. So, Kant's conception of virtue is concerned primarily with the development of people's capacities to cultivate and control their desires and emotions, and in presenting his theory, Kant provides a framework for understanding the ways in which people ought to pursue their own goods and the goods of others in ways that, I will argue, will prove important for understanding his prescriptions regarding human sexual behavior and his account of the institution of marriage.

References

Baxley, Anne Margaret. 2010. *Kant's Theory of Virtue: The Value of Autocracy*. Cambridge: Cambridge University Press.
Baron, Marcia. 1995. *Kantian Ethics Almost Without Apology*. Ithaca: Cornell University Press.
Card, Claudia. 2010. Kant's Moral Excluded Middle. In *Kant's Anatomy of Evil*, ed. Sharon Anderson-Gold and Pablo Muchnik, 74–92. Cambridge: Cambridge University Press.
Cartwright, David. 1987. Kant's View of the Moral Significance of the Kindhearted Emotions and the Moral Insignificance of Kant's View. *Journal of Value Inquiry* 2: 291–304.
Cohen, Alix. 2008. Kant's Answer to the Question 'What is Man?' And Its Implications for Anthropology. *Studies in History and Philosophy of Science, Part A* 39 (4): 506–514.
De Montaigne Michel. 1965. *The Complete Essays of Montaigne*. Trans. Donald M. Frame. Stanford: Stanford University Press.
De Lourdes Borges, Maria. 2004. What Can Kant Teach us about Emotions? *Journal of Philosophy* 101 (3): 140–158.
Ferguson, Michaele. 2012. Unsocial Sociability: Perpetual Antagonism in Kant's Political Thought. In *Kant's Political Theory*, ed. Elisabeth Ellis, 150–169. University Park: Penn State University Press.
Geiger, Ido. 2011. Rational Feelings and Moral Agency. *Kantian Review* 16 (2): 283–308.
Grenberg, Jeanine. 2005. *Kant and the Ethics of Humility: A Story of Dependence, Corruption, and Virtue*. Cambridge: Cambridge University Press.

References

———. 2010. Social Dimensions of Kant's Conception of Radical Evil. In *Kant's Anatomy of Evil*, ed. Sharon Anderson-Gold and Pablo Muchnik, 173–194. Cambridge: Cambridge University Press.

Herman, Barbara. 2007. Rethinking Kant's Hedonism. In *Moral Literacy*, 176–202. Cambridge, MA/London: Harvard University Press.

Hobbes, Thomas. 1994 (1668). *Leviathan*. Ed. Edwin Curley. Indianapolis: Hackett Publishing Company.

Johnson, Robert N. 1996. Kant's conception of merit. *Pacific Philosophical Quarterly* 77: 310–344.

———. 2009. Good Will and the Moral Worth of Acting from Duty. In The Blackwell Guide to Kant's Ethics, ed. Thomas E. Hill, Jr., 19–51. Malden: Blackwell Publishing, Ltd.

King, Lily. 2014. *Euphoria*. New York: Atlantic Monthly Press.

Korsgaard, Christine M. 1996. *Creating the kingdom of ends*. Cambridge: Cambridge University Press.

Löchel, Rolf. 2006. Frauen sind ängstlich, Männer sollen mutig sein – Geschlechterdifferenz und Emotionen bei Immanuel Kant. *Kant-Studien* 97: 50–78.

Louden, Robert B. 2000. *Kant's Impure Ethics: From Rational Beings to Human Beings*. New York/Oxford: Oxford University Press.

———. 2010. Evil Everywhere: The Ordinariness of Kantian Radical Evil. In *Kant's Anatomy of Evil*, ed. Sharon Anderson-Gold and Pablo Muchnik, 93–115. Cambridge: Cambridge University Press.

Morrisson, Iain. 2008. *Kant and the Role of Pleasure in Moral Action*. Athens: Ohio University Press.

Munzel, G. Felicitas. 1999. *Kant's Conception of Moral Character: The "Critical" Link of Morality, Anthropology, and Reflective Judgment*. Chicago/London: University of Chicago Press.

O'Neill, Onora. 2008. Historical Trends and Human Futures. *Studies in History and Philosophy of Science, Part A* 39 (4): 529–534.

Reath, Andrews. 1989. Hedonism, Heteronomy, and Kant's Principle of Happiness. *Pacific Philosophical Quarterly* 70: 42–72.

Rousseau, Jean-Jacques. (1992) (1755). *Discourse on the origin of inequality*. Trans. Donald A. Cress. Indianapolis: Hackett Publishing Company

Sabini, John, and Maury Silver. 1988. Emotions, Responsibility, and Character. In *Responsibility, Character, and the Emotions: New Essays in Moral Psychology*, ed. Ferdinand Shoeman, 165–177. Cambridge: Cambridge University Press.

Schneewind, J.B. 2009. Good out of evil: Kant and the idea of unsocial sociability. In *Kant's* Idea for a Universal History with a Cosmopolitan Aim: *A Critical Guide*, ed. Amélie Oksenberg Rorty and James Schmidt, 94–111. Cambridge: Cambridge University Press.

Sorensen, Kelly. 2002. Kant's Taxonomy of the Emotions. *Kantian Review* 6: 109–128.

Trendenenburg, Adolf. 1910. A Contribution to the History of the Word Person, trans. Carl H. Haessler. *The Monist* 20 (3): 336–363.

Wike, Victoria. 1994. *Kant on happiness in ethics*. Albany: State University of New York Press.

Wood, Allen W. 1970. *Kant's moral religion*. Ithaca: Cornell University Press.

———. 1991. Unsocial Sociability: The Anthropological Basis of Kantian Ethics. *Philosophical Topics* 19 (1): 325–351.

———. 1999. *Kant's ethical thought*. Cambridge: Cambridge University Press.

———. 2003. Kant and the Problem of Human Nature. In *Essays on Kant's Anthropology*, ed. Brian Jacobs and Patrick Kain, 38–59. Cambridge: Cambridge University Press.

———. 2006. The Good Without Limitation. In *Groundwork for the Metaphysics of Morals*, ed. Christoph Horn and Dieter Schönecker, 25–44. Berlin/New York: Walter de Gruyter.

———. 2008. *Kantian Ethics*. Cambridge: Cambridge University Press.

———. 2009. Kant's Fourth Proposition: the unsociable sociability of human nature. In *Kant's* Idea for a Universal History with a Cosmopolitan Aim: *A Critical Guide*, ed. Amélie Oksenberg Rorty and James Schmidt, 112–128. Cambridge: Cambridge University Press.

———. 2010. Kant and the Intelligibility of Evil. In *Kant's Anatomy of Evil*, ed. Sharon Anderson-Gold and Pablo Muchnik, 144–172. Cambridge: Cambridge University Press.

Chapter 4
All You Need Is Love, Respect, & Autocracy: Kant's Virtue Ethics

Abstract This chapter completes my response to the Anscombian reading by presenting the main contours of Kant's normative ethical theory, which is a virtue theory, a designation that runs directly counter to the Anscombian reading. I proceed as follows. First, I explain Kant's understanding of his doctrine of virtue in terms of morally obligatory ends, ends that he thinks help us cultivate virtue, which he defines as the capacity for self-constraint we can develop and exercise when it comes to the kinds of obstacles that stand in the way of our acting autonomously, obstacles that have to do with a disordered valuing of our two basic ends (happiness and the development of a moral disposition). Next, informed by the work of Anne Baxley, I discuss some misreadings of Kant's account of virtue and then present what I take to be a cogent reading of Kant's theory of virtue, which takes into account the different aspects of virtue as the "autocracy of practical reason." I close by presenting Kant's account of the two morally obligatory ends of virtue, one's own perfection and the happiness of others, and I explain the ways in which respect and love inform Kant's understanding of how our pursuit of those ends results in virtue.

The previous two chapters have set the stage for this one, insofar as they established that Kant's conception of human beings as dependent, morally imperfect beings is central to his practical philosophy. Both my defense of his understanding of moral obligation (Chap. 2) and my exposition of his philosophical anthropology (Chap. 3) form part of my response to the Anscombian reading of Kant's ethics, which I identified in the Preface as the most significant obstacle to recognizing Kant's writings on ethics as a resource for those engaged in the same-sex marriage debate. I say that they form part of my response because the bulk of the philosophical work of those chapters did not concern Kant's normative ethical theory but instead explained key concepts informing that theory. This chapter completes my response (and, so, Part I) by presenting the main contours of his normative ethical theory, which is a virtue theory, a designation that runs directly counter to the Anscombian reading. The Anscombian reading, you will recall, depicts Kant's ethics as the paradigmatic case of a deontological theory, which is an ethical theory concerned primarily with evaluating human acts in terms of strict, formal rules that apply universally to all people (Chap. 2, Sect. 2.2). The main alternative to a theory such as Kant's, so the

Anscombian reading goes, would be a virtue theory, which focuses on the concrete particulars of human life and conceives of human goodness primarily in terms of the development of certain dispositions or character traits.

The Anscombian reading's understanding of Kant's ethics as deontological and, therefore, as opposed to virtue theories of ethics can only seem correct to someone who ignores Kant's full normative theory, which he presents in his *Metaphysics of Morals,* a work that the Anscombian reading does not take into account. So, one of the aims of this chapter is to present the basics of Kant's theory of virtue as it appears in that work. The other is to draw attention to those aspects of Kant's theory of virtue that bear on his analysis of sex and marriage. Throughout the previous chapter I foreshadowed the way in which Kant's sexual ethics and his concern with sexual objectification are informed by his philosophical anthropology. As I will argue in Part II, part of the reason why sexual objectification figures prominently in Kant's ethics of sex and marriage is because of his conviction that human beings have a tendency to prioritize their own respective happiness over and against what is objectively morally good. Insofar as Kant's account of virtue outlines the ways in which we can develop our characters so that we consistently do not give into this tendency, Kant's account of virtue will be an important part of the way in which contemporary practical ethicists can draw on Kant's ethics as a resource in the debate over-same sex marriage. Hence, my need to present the main features of Kant's account of virtue.

I proceed as follows. First, by drawing on my account of his philosophical anthropology from the previous chapter, I explain Kant's understanding of his doctrine of virtue in terms of morally obligatory ends, ends that he thinks help us cultivate virtue, which he defines as the capacity for self-constraint that we can develop and exercise when it comes to the kinds of obstacles that stand in the way of our acting autonomously. Next, drawing on some of the work of Anne Baxley, I discuss some misreadings of Kant's account of virtue that are consistent with, if not motivated by, the Anscombian reading. I then present what I take to be a cogent reading of Kant's theory of virtue, which takes into account the different aspects of virtue as the "autocracy of practical reason." I close by presenting Kant's account of the two morally obligatory ends of virtue, one's own perfection and the happiness of others, and I explain the ways in which respect and love inform Kant's understanding of how our pursuit of those ends results in virtue, each of which, I will argue, is of the utmost importance when it comes to understanding the implications of Kant's ethics for sex and marriage.

4.1 Kant's Doctrine of Virtue: Morally Obligatory Ends & Strength of Will

As Lara Denis observes (2006), Western European philosophers have conceived of virtue in a variety of ways. Kant's account of virtue, which he presents in the "Doctrine of Virtue" (the second part of his *Metaphysics of Morals*), shares some features with a handful of those earlier theories, but it cannot be reduced to them.[1] More to the point, one cannot accurately compare Kant's theory of virtue to earlier theories without taking into account the way in which his philosophical anthropology informs his understanding of virtue (Wood 2008, 145–146).[2] It should come as no surprise by now that I think one can only come to an adequate understanding of Kant's theory of virtue by seeing the ways in which it follows from his understanding of human beings as finite, imperfect beings possessing two competing ends.

Kant begins the *Doctrine of Virtue* by explaining his understanding of obligation in terms of necessitation or constraint, insisting that such necessitation does not apply to rational beings *per se* but only to human beings. According to Kant, human beings are "rational *natural* beings, who are unholy enough that pleasure can induce them to break the moral law, even though they recognize its authority; and even when they do obey the law, they do it *reluctantly* (in the face of opposition from their inclinations), and it is in this that such *constraint* properly consists" (MM 6:379). Consistent with the reading I have presented thus far, in this passage Kant acknowledges our propensity to pursue happiness (i.e., what pleases and satisfies us) above all else, which can induce us to act immorally. In a note to the text, however, Kant also acknowledges that if we consider human beings in terms of our humanity (i.e., the second element of our predisposition to good and the ground of our dignity), when we act badly, we can also truly be said to break the moral law reluctantly. In other words, he prefaces his account of his theory of virtue by recognizing our propensity to evil and our predisposition to good.

Our propensity to evil, on Kant's telling, involves a tendency to will in certain ways. As I have argued, contrary to the Anscombian reading, Kant does not locate our propensity to evil in our sensible natures; rather, he places it in our propensity to choose in ways that prioritize our happiness over our acting genuinely morally good. The propensity to evil lies in our tendency to prioritize the end we have in virtue of being rational *animals* over and against the end we have as *rational* animals, and that, according to Kant, is disordered. Accordingly, when Kant presents his definition of virtue, he does so by acknowledging the way in which our inclinations (i.e., our sensible desires, which taken together aim at our respective conceptions of happiness), pose ends that can and often do function as alternatives to ends we are morally obligated to pursue. "Impulses of nature, accordingly, involve

---

[1] Nancy Sherman (1997), for example, argues that the respective theories of virtue of Aristotle and Kant share certain similarities, but she stops short of saying that they are basically the same.

[2] Cf. Robert Johnson (2008), who argues against the view that Kant's ethics is a virtue ethics. Johnson's his argument in many ways rests on a constructivist reading of Kant.

obstacles within the human being's mind to his fulfilment of duty and (sometimes powerful) forces opposing it, which he must judge that he is capable of resisting and conquering by reason..." (MM 6:380). This passage appears to support the Anscombian reading, but only if one ignores Kant's careful choice of words. He asserts that the obstacles are "impulses of nature," by which he means the raw, uncultivated desires and feelings human beings have by virtue of being (embodied) animal beings. Some of these uncultivated emotions and desires need to be controlled (e.g., affects and passions, respectively), but others can and should be tamed and cultivated, according to Kant. Indeed, as I will argue (Sect. 4.3 below), part of human virtue consists precisely in this.

Drawing on the distinction he makes between finite beings with imperfect wills, such as ourselves, and beings with holy wills, such as God, Kant makes a closely related distinction between a doctrine of morals and a doctrine of virtue. A doctrine of morals, which holds for all rational beings, articulates what he calls "the autonomy of practical reason," a phrase that Kant uses to describe what reason uninfluenced by inclination, correctly judges to be genuinely good. A doctrine of virtue, however, only applies to imperfect rational beings such as human beings, and articulates the way in which such beings can develop virtue (i.e., can cultivate our disposition to will such that our reflective tendency is to act according to the correct judgments of practical reason). Because virtue constitutes our good precisely insofar as we are dependent, morally imperfect beings in the ways that Kant describes, he defines virtue in terms of the struggle that arises for us because of our imperfection: "the capacity and considered resolve to withstand a strong but unjust opponent is *fortitude (fortitudo)* and, with respect to what opposes the moral disposition *within us*, **virtue** (*virtus, fortitudo, moralis*)" (MM 6:380). Before I elucidate what Kant means by virtue as "fortitude," I want first to explain why Kant conceives of his doctrine of virtue in terms of morally obligatory ends, and this means I need briefly to present his account of human choice.

4.1.1 Choice, Inner Constraint, & Morally Obligatory Ends

Kant defines the faculty of desire as "the faculty to be, by means of one's representations, the cause of the objects of these representations" (MM6:211), but he distinguishes between the way in which this faculty operates with respect to non-human animals and human beings. Kant defines "choice" as the ability to bring about the objects of one's desires, and he distinguishes between animal choice and human choice. According to Kant, animal choice "can be determined only by *inclination*," whereas human choice "can indeed be *affected* but not *determined* by impulses, and is therefore of itself (apart from an acquired proficiency of reason) not pure but can still be determined to actions by pure will" (MM 6:213). Although human beings can act in ways affected by our sensible inclinations, according to Kant, inclinations do not determine our actions (as they do with respect to non-human animals) because our choices can also be informed by reasoned considerations. So, although

4.1 Kant's Doctrine of Virtue: Morally Obligatory Ends & Strength of Will

my pet chicken cannot but eat the clover when it is hungry or drink water when it is thirsty (all things being equal), my being hungry or thirsty (i.e., my sensible appetites), on Kant's view, do not determine my actions—I can, despite even extreme hunger or thirst, refuse food or water. In making this distinction between animal and human choice, Kant is saying that human beings, unlike animals, enjoy freedom of choice, which Kant defines as "independence from being *determined* by sensible impulses" (MM 6:213).[3] Kant thinks that one important consequence of our being capable of human choice is that we can act according to laws, that is, we can freely act in ways that are objectively necessitated (on Kant's understanding of "necessitated" [Chap. 2, Sect. 2.2.2]) by reason. Our capacity to act according to such laws motivates Kant's division of the *Metaphysics of Morals* into two parts, only one of which concerns virtue.

The *Metaphysics of Morals* consists of the "Doctrine of Right" and the "Doctrine of Virtue." This division of the book reflects the distinction Kant makes between the two ways in which legislation—specifically, the way in which laws necessitate/constrain human choice—functions when it comes to human beings. Accordingly, Kant distinguishes between two aspects to lawgiving: "**first,** a law, which represents an action that is to be done as *objectively* necessary, that is, which makes the action a duty; and **second,** an incentive, which connects a ground for determining choice to this action *subjectively* with the representation of the law" (MM 6:218). Kant's point is that we can distinguish between (a) what a law prescribes as being required of us with respect to our actions and omissions, and (b) the reasons why someone chooses to obey (or not obey) a particular law. The "Doctrine of Right" treats "juridical" lawgiving, which is the type of lawgiving that focuses merely on laws as objectively necessary without any concern for the reasons why people follow them (MM 6:219). So, the "Doctrine of Right" deals with what Kant calls "outer freedom" and, accordingly, concerns the ground of the positive laws that a state develops in order to protect the rights of its citizens. For example, as far as juridical laws are concerned, it does not matter why I refrain from stealing your personal property so long as I do not steal it. It is "The Doctrine of Right" that contains Kant's account of marriage (i.e., marriage law). The "Doctrine of Virtue," however, has to do with what Kant calls "inner freedom," which does not merely concern what the law prescribes as objectively required of us; it is also concerned with what Kant calls "ethical" lawgiving, which has to do with our incentives in following these laws. Mary Gregor (1963, 27) explains the difference between outer and inner freedom—and so the different subject matters of the "Doctrine of Right" and the "Doctrine of Virtue"—in the following way:

> We can describe outer freedom as that absence of compulsion which allows the subject of the law to act in pursuit of his own ends, whatever these may be, so long as, in his actions, he leaves a like freedom open to every other subject of the law. This is the sort of freedom which can be realized through the restraining power of legal sanctions and without reference to the subject's virtue or lack of virtue....Ethical laws, on the other hand, are those which arise in the inner legislation of pure practical reason, as conditions of inner freedom.

---

[3] So, a being with a holy will is one that has freedom of choice but not human choice.

> They aim at realizing a condition in which our power of choice is free from the influence of sensuous inclination as such and open to that of pure practical reason with its motive of duty. (MM 6:383–384)

Gregor immediately goes on to note that, for Kant, "what leads us to act contrary to pure practical reason is the ends which we adopt on the basis of our sensuous desires." As Kant himself expresses it,

> since the sensible inclinations of human beings tempt them to ends (the matter of choice) that can be contrary to duty, lawgiving reason can in turn check their influence only by a moral end set up against the ends of inclination, an end that must therefore be given a priori, independently of inclinations. (MM 6:380–381)

This passage is key to understanding why Kant construes of the doctrine of virtue in the way that he does. So, there are a few things worth noting here. First of all, Kant very carefully expresses his point concerning the opposition inclination poses, being sure not to indict sensible inclinations *per se*. What he says is that our sensible desires *can* tempt us to adopt ends that are contrary to our moral obligation. This is just the point I have been pressing for the last two chapters, namely, that our sensible natures make it such that we always can (but need not) act in ways that prioritize our respective conceptions of happiness over and against what is morally required of us. Second, Kant conceives of virtue, and, so, of our capacity to withstand the temptation to prioritize our own happiness over acting well, in terms of our prioritizing certain ends. Since the danger of vice (i.e., of what Kant in *Religion* calls depravity) involves[4] the danger of our acting heteronomously and adopting ends determined solely by our sensible natures, Kant sees the saving grace of virtue in terms of adopting ends determined by reason, ends that help us develop the strength (fortitude) to overcome the temptations of our sensible inclinations. Third, contrary to the Anscombian reading, insofar as Kant conceives of virtue in terms of our adopting certain ends, his theory of virtue is teleological. As Allen Wood (2008, 166) observes, "the theory is not based on the inherent 'rightness' or 'wrongness' of actions but on which actions promote certain obligatory *ends*...."

What kinds of ends, according to Kant, are ends that we are morally obligated to adopt? Ends we have in virtue of our being rational beings. If the only ends we were able to adopt were the ends we have in virtue of being animal beings, then, thinks Kant, there would be no such thing as what is genuinely (i.e., objectively) morally good for human beings. This is because in such a scenario we would only be able to pursue our happiness. Writing about the ends of sensible inclinations, Kant asserts that "if maxims were to be adopted on the basis of those ends (all of which are self-seeking), one could not really speak of the concept of duty" (MM 6:382). As I have already explained (Chap. 3, Sect. 3.3.1), happiness, as Kant construes it, is irreducibly subjective, which means that happiness cannot be the ground of ethics (i.e., we

---

[4] I say that vice "involves" acting heteronomously rather than "vice just is our acting heteronomously" because Kant distinguishes between the different propensities to evil (Chap. 3, Sect. 3.1.2), with only the third degree, depravity, counting as vice, properly speaking. In other words, moral weakness, which is a lack of virtue, is not the same as vice, which is to act contrary to virtue (MM 6:384). Cf. Baxley (2010, 79–83) and Engstrom (2002, 307–308).

cannot develop an account of what is genuinely good for human beings *qua* finite rational beings by merely relying on a concept of human happiness). So, Kant concludes, if there is to be a coherent concept of duty (i.e., if there is to be a genuine ethics), there must be ends that we have in virtue of our rational nature, and our adopting these ends is what results in our developing virtue, that is, our developing the moral strength to overcome our propensity to prioritize ends of inclination. Kant identifies two ends that are morally obligatory for us: our own perfection and the promotion of the happiness of others. Both of these ends he thinks derive from our status as beings possessing dignity. Before I explain how Kant arrives at these two ends and present his explanation of what their pursuit entails, I want to step back and look more closely at Kant's definition of virtue in terms of fortitude or strength in order once again to cut off some basic misunderstandings of his theory of virtue, particularly misunderstandings informed by the Anscombian reading of his ethics.

4.1.2 Kant's Argument Against Virtue as Habit

It would be worth beginning this section by explaining why Kant conceives of virtue in terms of strength of will or resolve rather than as a matter of habit (as, e.g., Aristotle does). Although Kant was most likely unfamiliar with the texts of Aristotle's ethics,[5] he was aware of some then-contemporary theories of virtue as a matter of developing certain habits, and he rejects this understanding of virtue as mistaken:

> Virtue is not to be defined and valued merely as an *aptitude* and (as the prize essay of Cochius, the court-chaplain, puts it) a long-standing *habit* of morally good actions acquired by practice. For unless this aptitude results from considered, firm, and continually purified principles, then, like any other mechanism of technically practical reason, it is neither armed for all situations nor adequately secured against the changes that new temptations could bring about. (MM 3:383–384).

Kant has been criticized for this view. For example, Martha Nussbaum (2001, 172) claims that "Kant thought that virtue must always be a matter of strength, as the will learns to keep a lid on inappropriate inclinations, rather like a good cook holding down the boiling pot" (Cf. Annas 1993). A critic such as Nussbaum seems committed to a version of the Anscombian reading of Kant, since she takes Kant's understanding of virtue as strength to mean that he believes human goodness involves nothing more than (i.e., nothing greater than) merely controlling or extinguishing our inclinations.

This understanding of virtue, however, misrepresents Kant's view. Nussbaum, it seems, fails to acknowledge the way in which Kant's philosophical anthropology informs his critique of virtue as "habit" [*Gewohnheit*] or "aptitude" [*Fertigkeit*]. First of all, Kant rejects the understanding of virtue as a matter of habit because he

---

[5] One of the only times Kant discusses Aristotle is in the "Doctrine of Virtue" (MM 6:404–405), and he seems to misrepresent Aristotle's doctrine of the mean.

understands a habit [*Gewohnheit*], as a tendency to act unthinkingly as a matter of custom. According to him, "if the practice of virtue were to become a habit the subject would suffer loss to that freedom in adopting his maxims which distinguishes an action done from duty" (MM 6:409). For Kant, then, a habit [*Gewohnheit*] is mechanical, something we mindlessly do because we are used to doing it.[6] A habit on his understanding is rather like the tendency to bite one's nails or to smoke cigarettes; it is not what Nussbaum has in mind when she writes of virtue as a habit, which she takes to have the sense it has in Aristotle, namely of *habitus*.[7] According to Aristotle, moral virtue consists in a settled disposition to act whereby the non-rational, desiring part of the soul has been shaped by the rational part and, so, harmonizes with rational choice (Arisototle 2009, Books I and II). For Kant, however, there can be no such harmonizing between the rational and non-rational parts of the soul because the rational and non-rational aspects of human beings each provide us with a respective end to pursue, and these two ends make different and competing claims on us.[8] The reason Kant and Aristotle do not see eye-to-eye on this issue of agreement between the non-rational and rational parts of human beings is because they disagree in their understanding of human nature. Baxley (2010, 80) clearly expresses the consequences of this disagreement for understanding Kant's conception of virtue:

> Kant therefore rejects any conception of human virtue that mistakenly holds that we can bring our sensible nature into full or complete harmony with reason *so that we need not be constrained by duty to act well*. Such a conception of moral excellence conflates human virtue with holiness, and it involves an objectionable and dangerous self-deception as well as a failure to know ourselves as finite imperfect beings, beings that must work hard to cultivate the requisite strength of will to overcome a deep-seated tendency to subordinate moral considerations to considerations based on happiness, and to acquire a moral disposition involving a "moral preparedness to withstand all temptations to evil."

Kant's philosophical anthropology precludes him from understanding virtue in terms of a habit or aptitude for acting in certain ways. This still leaves us with the question, "What does he mean when he defines virtue in terms of strength or resolve?" For those committed to the Anscombian reading of Kant's ethics the strength of virtue just is the strength we need in order to control our wild inclinations. This understanding of virtue as strength is misleadingly narrow and fails to

---

[6] Cf. Engstrom (2002, 292), who says the following about Kant's rejection of virtue as habit: "the habits in question are either altogether 'blind' in that they are regularities of conduct that do not depend for their possibility on the subject's being conscious of the rule that constitutes them, or else at least 'morally blind' in the sense that, even where such consciousness is involved in their establishment (for example, in the case of the clerk who is given instructions based on the shopkeeper's exercise of technically practical reason), they do not depend on the subject's recognition that the rule is in agreement with duty, the recognition on which all morally worthy action is based."

[7] For an understanding of habit indebted to Aristotle see Kenny (1992, 85). For the sense of *habitus* in Aquinas, see Davies (2014, 188–201).

[8] Cf. Wood (2008, 151): "For Kant the agreement of inclination with reason is not a condition of virtuous action in the same way that for Aristotle it is a condition for virtue that nonrational [*sic*] appetite should be guided by reason."

appreciate the way in which Kant believes that the strength of virtue is not merely a matter of self-control but instead entails what Kant calls the "autocracy" of practical reason.

4.2 Misunderstanding Kantian Virtue: Self-Mastery and Sensible Nature

Kant defines the "*autocracy* of practical reason," as involving "consciousness of the *capacity* to master one's inclinations when they rebel against the law" (M 6: 383). As with his definition of virtue in terms of resolve or strength of will, Kant's characterization of autocracy as our capacity for self-mastery, particularly with respect to rebellious inclinations, seems to lend credence to criticisms such as Nussbaum's. But this is how things seem only if one is already committed to the Anscombian reading. That reading reduces Kant's account of virtue as self-mastery to the erroneous view that Kant's theory of virtue calls for the elimination or suppression of inclination (Cf. Baxley 2010, 75–79). Each of these ways of understanding the self-mastery of virtue, however, is demonstrably false.[9]

Regarding the claim that self-mastery involves the elimination of sensible inclinations, I have already presented evidence that Kant does not hold this view. First of all, he explicitly denies that the ground of moral evil lies in our sensible natures (R 6:34–35). He also explicitly states that sensible nature and the inclinations "bear no direct relation to evil (they rather give the occasion for what the moral disposition can demonstrate in its power for virtue)" (R 6:35). He regards the attempt to rid oneself of our sensible feelings and desires as immoral (CL 27:379), and he even criticizes the Stoics, who "mistook their enemy, who is not to be sought in the natural inclinations, which merely lack discipline" (R 6:57). In *Metaphysics of Morals* Kant unambiguously maintains that "depriving oneself (slavishly) of what is essential to the cheerful enjoyment of life, by *avarice*, or depriving oneself (fanatically) of enjoyment of the pleasures of life by exaggerated *discipline* of one's natural inclinations" are both "opposed to a human being's duty to himself" (MM 6:452). Indeed, given that Kant identifies happiness as a natural and good end of human beings, and given that we have this end in virtue of being *natural* rational beings (i.e., in virtue of being rational animals with sensible natures), he would blatantly contradict himself were he committed to an understanding of self-mastery as the elimination of our sensible natures (Cf. Herman 1993, 23–44).

---

[9] Baxley (2010, 75–79) distinguishes between three ways in which critics of Kant misread his account of virtue. She claims that these authors read Kant's theory of virtue as calling for the extirpation, suppression, or silencing of sensible inclinations. I think, however, that what Baxley identifies as silencing (namely, the idea that the virtuous agent pays no mind to the inclinations when she deliberates) is just another way to suppress the inclinations. See, for example, Chap. 3, Sect. 3.3.2 where I discuss Christian Garve's criticisms of Kant.

What about the claim that self-mastery should be understood as the complete suppression of our sensible inclinations and emotions? This might seem to be a difficult criticism to answer, since it seems to be consistent with the conception of human nature I have attributed to Kant. I have argued that Kant takes humans to be morally imperfect, which he understands as entailing our experience of genuine moral goodness as obligatory because we have two competing ends, namely, happiness and the cultivation of a moral disposition. I have also argued that Kant's understanding of our propensity to radical evil is just a tendency we have to prioritize our respective conceptions of happiness over and against what is required of us morally. So, one might understandably conclude that the effort and struggle that Kant sees as characteristic of our moral life just is the effort and struggle we constantly face in suppressing our sensible natures.

This conclusion is understandable but mistaken. The key to avoiding the mistake lies in paying attention to the way in which Kant (and I) have expressed Kant's distinction between finite beings with morally imperfect wills, such as ourselves, and an infinite perfect being with a holy will, such as God. A being with a holy will is one who cannot but do what reason (correctly) judges to be genuinely good. Such a being possesses a rational nature but does not have a sensible nature and, therefore, *cannot* but act well. Imperfect beings, such as ourselves, possess both rational natures and sensible natures. This means that it is possible for us to act in a way other than as reason judges to be genuinely good, since we have sensible inclinations and emotions that are directed to our respective conceptions of happiness. More specifically, we experience genuine moral goodness as obligatory because it is always *possible* for us to act in a way that ignores the correct conclusions of practical reason regarding moral goodness in favor of the objects of our sensible desires. When Kant says that it is possible to opt for the objects of one's sensible desire (and, thereby, for one's own happiness) over and against what one judges to be genuinely morally good, this does not require him to hold the view that there is a constant *felt* conflict between what one wants with respect to one's happiness and what one judges to be genuinely morally good. Such a constant conflict is what the suppression reading of self-mastery takes Kant to be committed to, and that is why it is mistaken. In his discussion of self-mastery in the *Collins Lectures* Kant clearly rejects the suppression reading:

> But if a man rules himself so well that he prevents any rebellion of the rabble in his soul and keeps peace within it (which here, however, is not contentment with everything, but good command and unity in the soul), and if he now conducts so good a government within himself, then no war will arise in him, and where there is no war, no conquest is necessary either. It is therefore far better if a man is so governed that he need gain no victory over himself. (CL 27:368–369)

This preceding passage points to one of the important features of Kant's concept of autocracy correctly understood, namely, that autocracy involves the cultivation of our sensible inclinations and emotions.

4.3 Understanding Kantian Virtue: Controlling and Cultivating Sensible Nature

As Adam Cureton and Thomas Hill (2015, 98) describe Kant's understanding of the virtuous agent, "her will is both autonomous and autocratic; it has legislative power to settle on moral principles independent of inclinations but also executive power to carry out those commands despite inclinations to the contrary." In other words, the virtuous agent according to Kant acts well—that is, she acts autonomously—because she has a virtuous/autocratic character, which is just to say that she has cultivated a character that makes it easier to act autonomously rather than heteronomously. The elements of such an autocratic character are much richer and nuanced than the misreadings I discussed in the previous section. To be sure, *part* of what it means to be autocratic involves controlling certain inclinations and emotions, but this is just a part. More important to autocracy is the cultivation of our sensible natures—of our sensible desires and emotions—so that we develop desires and feelings that are conducive to our acting morally and, so, do not tempt us to act contrary to what is genuinely and objectively good.

With respect to the idea that autocracy involves controlling some aspects of our sensible natures, Kant has a particular subset of emotions and desires in mind, namely, affects and passions. As we have already seen (Chap. 3, Sect. 3.2.3) both affects and passions are unequivocal threats to our moral disposition. Affects are those sensible feelings that come upon us suddenly, without warning, and which leave us unable to think. In other words, affects are occurent emotional episodes that make rational reflection extremely difficult and, so, make acting autonomously almost impossible. Think here of someone who receives a bad diagnosis from a doctor and immediately falls into a bout of uncontrollable crying; while in such a state, this person cannot hear what the doctor says nor reasonably consider her options for treatment. Passions are those deep-seated desires that are untainted by emotions but are, for that very reason, much more dangerous, since they are desires that coexist with calm reflection and are seemingly immune to modification. Think here, again, of the passion one might have to bring about the complete professional ruin of a hated colleague. Such a strong desire pervades this person's every thought and resists all attempts at modification. Since affects and passions, according to Kant, are immune to modification, they constitute the species of sensible feeling and desire, respectively, that we must control or contain in order to achieve self-mastery. This is why Kant praises apathy as the state needed for virtue when it comes to affects, but he recognizes that his contemporaries often misunderstand the term. "The word 'apathy,'" he claims, "has fallen into disrepute, as if it meant lack of feeling and so subjective indifference with respect to objects of choice; it is taken for weakness" (MM 6:408). Instead of this false view of apathy, Kant proposes that virtue (i.e., self-mastery) presupposes what he calls "moral apathy," which he defines as the "absence of affect" (MM 6:408).[10]

---

[10] Maria Bourges (2008, 47 & 53–59) emphasizes this aspect of Kantian virtue in light of Kant's physiological understanding of emotions. She understates the extent to which Kant thinks we can

Kant's embrace of apathy speaks to the second, even more important, aspect of autocracy, namely the need to cultivate our sensible desires and emotions so that they are consistent with and help us to act autonomously. According to Kant, virtue "contains a positive command to a human being, namely, to bring all his capacities and inclinations under his (reason's) control and so to rule over himself, *which goes beyond forbidding him to let himself be governed by his feelings and inclinations (the duty of apathy)*" (MM 6:408, emphasis added). In other words, according to Kant, virtue requires more than the control of affects and passions. For example, Kant identifies what he calls four "moral endowments" that "lie at the basis of morality, as *subjective* conditions of receptiveness to the concept of duty" (MM 6:399). They are moral feeling, "the susceptibility to feel pleasure or displeasure merely from being aware that our actions are consistent with or contrary to the law of duty" (MM 6:399); conscience, "practical reason holding the human being's duty before him for his acquittal or condemnation in every case that comes under a law" (MM 6:400); love of human beings, "an aptitude of the inclination to beneficence in general" (MM 6:402); and respect, "a feeling of a special kind" that is directed toward human beings as beings with personality (MM 6:402–403). Below I will discuss the roles love and respect play in Kant's doctrine of virtue. For now, and with an eye on self-mastery as entailing a cultivation of certain emotions, I want to note that each of these four moral endowments, according to Kant, are predispositions we have in virtue of being human and concern the ways in which we can be (positively) emotionally affected by the concept of moral duty. In other words, we have these moral endowments naturally, and Kant thinks that they help make it easier for us to act in ways that are genuinely morally good, which is why we need to cultivate them.

In addition to the four moral endowments, Kant claims that autocracy also involves cultivating our sensible natures such that we develop what Kant calls "practical feelings" that can help us as we strive to act autonomously. One can see Kant's reasons for this in some of what I have already argued. First of all, in my critique of the misreading of self-mastery in terms of the suppression of our sensible natures (Sect. 4.1.2 above), I quoted Kant as saying that it is better *not* to have recalcitrant sensible feelings and desires. And since he thinks whether we have such sensible feelings and desires is not merely a matter of luck, he is committed to the view that we can and should cultivate our sensible natures so that our sensible feelings and desires become practical rather than pathological. Second, Kant distinguishes practical feelings of pleasure, which follow our choosing according to what practical reason concludes is good, from pathological feelings of pleasure, which arise in us prior to and independent of any process of practical reasoning and end up determining our choices (Chap. 3, Sect. 3.2.1).[11] A virtuous person, according to Kant, is someone who actively works to develop her practical feelings so that it

---

cultivate emotions, but this is because she understands "cultivation" of the emotions in the way that Aristotle does.

[11] Cf. Katrin Flikschuh (2002, 202–204).

becomes easier to fulfill her moral obligation. Indeed, the virtuous agent, according to Kant, is someone who comes to *enjoy* doing what the moral law requires of her:

> The rules for practicing virtue (*exercitiorum virtutis*) aim at a frame of mind that is both *valiant* and *cheerful* [*fröhlichen*] in fulfilling its duties (*animus strenuus et hilaris*). For, virtue not only has to muster all its forces to overcome the obstacles it must contend with; it also involves sacrificing many of the joys of life, the loss of which can sometimes make one's mind gloomy and sullen. But what is not done with pleasure but merely as compulsory service has no inner worth for one who attends to his duty in this way and such service is not loved by him; instead he shirks as much as possible occasions for practicing virtue. (MM 6:484)

Lest all this talk of cultivating virtuous feelings mislead readers into forgetting the importance of Kant's philosophical anthropology and his rejection of the idea that virtue is a matter of habit, I want to emphasize that, for Kant, the work of cultivating our sensible natures is never done and can never be done.[12] Because we are finite, dependent beings, and because human nature contains what Kant calls a propensity to evil, the work of becoming virtuous can never be achieved perfectly, which is to say that the work of being virtuous is never done. As Kant explains,

> Virtue is always *in progress* and yet always starts *from the beginning.* – It is always in progress because considered *objectively*, it is an ideal and unattainable, while yet constant approximation to it is a duty. That it always starts from the beginning has a *subjective* basis in human nature, which is affected by inclinations because of which virtue can never settle down in peace and quiet with its maxims adopted once and for all but, if it is not rising, is unavoidably sinking. (MM 6:409)

4.4 Kant's Doctrine of Virtue: Self-Perfection and the Happiness of Others

With the preceding correct understanding of Kantian virtue in mind, I can now explain why Kant thinks that the way we become virtuous (i.e., the way in which we become autocratic) is by adopting the two morally obligatory ends he identifies, namely, one's self-perfection and the promotion of the happiness of other people. According to Kant, the way in which we avoid vice, which entails the adoption and prioritization of ends of sensible inclinations, is by adopting morally obligatory ends, which, I have argued, are ends that all human beings should hold in virtue of being rational beings, that is, beings who possess dignity in virtue of our capacity for freely setting ends that are the result of our reasoning practically G 4:427–429). Drawing on this conception of rational beings Kant identifies the supreme principle

---

[12] Baxley (2010, 126) distinguishes between maintaining certain inclinations and feelings that are in agreement with duty and cultivating inclinations and feelings so that they are in accord with duty. I do not make this distinction because I think it can mislead readers into forgetting that human beings, as imperfect rational beings, have what Kant calls a "propensity to evil." I think Kant's claim that we have, by nature, a propensity to evil means that any cultivation of practical desires and emotions also involves the continued maintenance of them.

of the doctrine of virtue, which is the principle he uses to determine which ends we are morally obligated to adopt:

> The supreme principle of the doctrine of virtue is: act in accordance with a maxim of *ends* that it can be a universal law for everyone to have. – In accordance with this principle a human being is an end for himself as well as for others, and it is not enough that he is not authorized to use either himself or others merely as a means (since he could then still be indifferent to them); it is in itself his duty to make the human being as such his end. (MM 6:395)

According to this principle, the only kind of ends that are morally obligatory are ends that each of us should have. Kant thinks that such ends, as I have argued, are ones we possess in virtue of being rational beings, beings that are "ends in themselves." Kant's thinking seems to be that insofar as human beings are ends in themselves, we possess dignity. As beings who possess dignity, morally good behavior for human beings consists in more than merely refraining from treating other people as mere instruments for one's purposes. Kant also thinks that being endowed with dignity enjoins us more positively to make humanity an end for our actions. It may seem odd to write of making humanity an end, since we think of ends as objects to be achieved or attained. But we should understand taking humanity as an end in light of Kant's understanding of what grounds our dignity, namely, our capacity to act freely in pursuit of what practical reason discerns to be genuinely good. With this feature of Kant's understanding of dignity in mind, we can make sense of making humanity an end in terms of making it our end to develop the capacity that grants us dignity. With respect to developing this capacity in myself, according to Kant, making humanity and end translates into perfecting myself. With respect to developing this capacity in others, making humanity my end amounts to promoting their (morally acceptable) conceptions of happiness.

In saying that self-perfection and the promotion of the happiness of others are our most basic ends, I am trying to get at two features of the doctrine of virtue that I have yet to discuss but that are essential to understanding what Kant is trying to do in articulating this doctrine. The first feature is that the doctrine of virtue—and, so, Kant's ethics—does not prescribe laws for *actions* but only for maxims (MM 6:388–389). The point here is pretty straightforward. Kant's doctrine of virtue does not prescribe a list of moral actions or a rulebook for virtue (Hill 2008, 51–53). Instead, it is about our motivation in pursuing certain morally obligatory ends: his doctrine of virtue articulates the ways in which we can cultivate fortitude with respect to prioritizing the development of our moral character over the pursuit of our respective conceptions of happiness, and it does this by identifying the ends we should adopt in developing this fortitude.

This first feature of his doctrine of virtue, leads to the second, namely, that duties of virtue are "wide" duties (i.e., they are what he calls "imperfect" duties) rather than "narrow" duties (i.e., they are not what he calls "perfect" duties) (MM 6:390).[13]

---

[13] Cf. Wood (2008, 168): A duty is wide or imperfect (or, if toward others, a duty of love) if the action promotes a duty of virtue (that is, an end it is a duty to set); an act is required by a strict, narrow, or perfect duty (or a duty of respect to others) if the failure to perform it would amount to

A perfect duty, according to Kant, is one that entails what he calls a narrow obligation, which means that it "admits no exception in favor of inclination" (G 4:422). So, to fail to fulfill a perfect duty is to act immorally. It is telling that all of the perfect duties that Kant specifies are ones that *prohibit* acting in certain ways (e.g., not to lie, not to commit suicide, not to defile oneself by lust). An imperfect duty, by contrast, is one that puts us under what Kant calls a "wide obligation" to pursue a certain end, but "the law cannot specify precisely in what way one is to act and how much one is to do by the action for an end that is also a duty" (MM 6:390). Were we never to act in pursuit of those ends prescribed by imperfect duties, then, thinks Kant, we would be morally blameworthy. But imperfect duties leave us with a lot of "playroom" or latitude in how, when, where, and to what extent we should pursue our obligatory ends (MM 6:390). Insofar as Kant takes ethical duties (i.e., duties of virtue) to be imperfect duties of wide obligation, his account of virtue undermines the Anscombian reading's claim that Kant is committed to rigorism in ethics. Kant leaves quite a bit of latitude for how, where, and when one pursues one's own perfection and the promotion of the happiness of others. Nonetheless, Kant provides some specifics on what the successful pursuit of each of these morally obligatory ends entails.

4.4.1 Self-Perfection and the Happiness of Others as Ends of Virtue

When Kant presents his exposition of each of the ends of virtue he distinguishes between the ways we can pursue each end with respect to our being natural, sensible beings and with respect to our being finite rational, and, so, moral beings, and this approach further underscores my claim that Kant's philosophical anthropology is the *leitmotif* of his practical philosophy.

With respect to our natural perfection, Kant argues that this involves "the *cultivation* of any *capacities* whatever for furthering ends set forth by reason" (MM 6:391). Since our capacity for setting ends in the first place is due to our possessing humanity, Kant concludes that self-perfection involves making ourselves "worthy of humanity by culture in general," by which he simply means that we procure and promote "the *capacity* to realize all sorts of possible ends, so far as this is to be found in the human being himself" (MM 6:392). What Kant has in mind here seems readily understandable. One of the ways in which we can and should perfect ourselves is by developing those talents and abilities that we have that would allow us to pursue ends that we correctly reason to be good for us. For example, if Jessica comes to realize that she has a talent for and interest in being a poet, then the morally obligatory end to perfect herself can be pursued by developing those abilities that are conducive to her becoming a good poet. Notice that this kind of self-perfection

---

a failure to set this obligatory end at all, or a failure to respect humanity as an end in someone's person. Cf. Herman 1993 (63, note 27).

involves self-mastery insofar as (a) the resolve, e.g., to pursue activities conducive to being a poet is something that results from a process of practical reasoning (as opposed to mere sensible inclination, and (b) pursuing and perfecting these abilities requires work and discipline, both of which, thinks Kant, will entail the controlling of affects and passions and the cultivation of emotions and inclinations conducive to the pursuit of this end. But this raises, the question, "How far should one go in pursuing and developing these capacities?" Here again we see evidence of Kant's commitment to latitude and practical wisdom in concrete situations in which we may find ourselves: "the different situations in which human beings may find themselves make a human being's choice of the occupation for which he should cultivate his talents very much a matter for him to decide as he chooses" (MM 6:392).[14]

With respect to our perfection of ourselves as moral agents, Kant claims that we each have a duty to cultivate our capacity to do what is genuinely good because we recognize it as such, since "the greatest perfection of a human being is to do his duty *from duty*" (MM 6:392). Kant's idea here is that we each should cultivate our dispositions so that we become the kind of people who recognize the dignity each person (including ourselves) possesses and, in light of such recognition, are motivated to do what is good out of respect for this dignity. True to his view of human nature, Kant recognizes that we can never perfectly cultivate our moral dispositions, since we cannot be holy (Cf. Chap. 2, Sect. 2.2.1). Nor can we know the extent to which we have been successful in cultivating our moral dispositions, since "a human being cannot see into the depths of his own heart so as to be quite certain, in even a *single* action, of the purity of his moral intention and the sincerity of his disposition, even when he has no doubt about the legality of the action" (MM 6:392).[15] Nonetheless, "the way to acquire it [virtue] is to enhance the moral *incentive* (the thought of the law), both by contemplating the dignity of the pure rational law in us (*contemplatione*) and by *practicing* virtue (*exercitio*)" (MM 6:397).

Kant's discussion of our duty to promote the happiness of others is also expressed in terms of the way in which we can and should promote this duty with respect to others *qua* animal, sensible being and *qua* rational, moral agent. With respect to the latter, Kant claims that we have a duty to promote the moral well-being of others, but that this duty is merely a negative one. That is, "it is my duty to refrain from

---

[14] Cf. Wood (2008, 169): "Kant does not mean to say that we have a duty to *maximize* our own perfection or the happiness of others. The ends are not conceived as summable quantities at all. The duties we have regarding them are not duties regarding anyone's happiness or perfection regarded as collective totalities. Rather, they are duties to include all the instances of our own perfection and the happiness of others among our ends, but they allow us to set our own priorities among these instances and to pursue some rather than others if they fit better into our lives."

[15] Cf. G (4:407): "In fact, it is absolutely impossible by means of experience to make out with complete certainty a single case in which the maxim of an action otherwise in conformity with duty rested simply on moral grounds and on the representation of one's duty....we like to flatter ourselves by falsely attributing to ourselves a nobler motive, whereas in fact we can never, even by the most strenuous self-examination, get entirely behind our covert incentives, since, when moral worth is at issue, what counts is not actions, which one sees, but those inner principles of action that one does not see." Cf. Fingarette (1969/2000).

doing anything that, considering the nature of a human being, could tempt him to do something for which his conscience could afterwards pain him, to refrain from what is called giving scandal" (MM 6:394). With respect to the former, Kant argues that we have an obligation to promote the natural welfare of others, which takes the form of beneficence (i.e., doing, and not merely wishing, the welfare of others). His argument draws on his understanding of humans as unsocially social beings:

> Since our self-love cannot be separated from our need to be loved (helped in the case of need) by others as well, we therefore make ourselves an end for others; and the only way this maxim can be binding is through its qualification as a universal law, hence through our will to make others our ends as well. (MM 6:393)

Kant acknowledges that we are social beings who depend on each other in various ways for our well-being, but he also points out that our propensity for prioritizing our self-love cannot be separated completely from the need we each have to be loved. In other words, Kant maintains that our love for others, which is the affective component of our motivation for promoting their welfare, is in some way informed by our natural capacity for self-love. This is why, unlike the duty to perfect oneself (which Kant defends on the basis of his notion of respect for the dignity of human beings) the duty to promote the natural welfare of others is one that rests both on love and respect.

In the "Doctrine of the elements of ethics," Kant goes on to identify specific duties that he believes fall under the wide obligations to perfect oneself and to promote the happiness of others, and I will have occasion in Part II to look more closely at some of those, particularly the ones that bear on Kant's ethics of sex and marriage.[16] I want to conclude this chapter, and Part I, by giving overviews of the two main affective components to Kantian virtue, namely respect and love, since respect motivates Kant's account of the ways we ought to perfect ourselves, and both respect and love figure into Kant's account of how we ought to treat others with respect to promoting their own happiness. As I shall argue in Part II, Kant's account of the role of respect and love in the development of virtuous character is the main resource in his ethical theory for developing a successful solution to the moral problem of sexual objectification.

4.4.2 Kant's Account of Respect for the Moral Law

As I have already noted (Chap. 3, Sect. 3.2.2), Kant maintains that respect for the moral law (i.e., for human beings as representatives of that law) is the sole moral motivator, that is, it is the only kind of motivation that can result in morally worthy action. I also noted that there is a great deal of scholarly disagreement over the most accurate interpretation of Kantian respect and how he takes it to function as a moral

---

[16] Wood (2009) gives an overview of the duties that concern our self-perfection, while Baron and Fahmy (2009) discuss the duties Kant thinks we have to promote the happiness of others.

motivator. As Iain Morrisson (2008, 134–135) points out, some interpreters (e.g., Paul Guyer [1993], Karl Ameriks [1987], Andrews Reath [1989] and Nancy Sherman [1990]) argue that respect does not play a positive motivational role but is, instead the effect of our having chosen morally; but other Kant scholars, such as Erica Holberg (2016), Richard McCarty (1993) and A.T. Nuyen (1991) argue that the feeling of respect plays a positive, affective role in motivating moral action; and yet one other school of interpretation, of which A. Murray MacBeath (1973) is a representative, Kant's account of respect and its motivational role is hopelessly confused. For my purposes I need not get into the interpretive weeds of these debates, though I will note that my reading of Kantian respect largely follows Morrisson's, which explains respect's positive motivational function as largely analogous to the way in which sensible emotions and inclinations can motivate non-morally worthy action. In addition to substantial textual evidence in its favor (Morrisson 2008, 135–159), this reading has the benefit of being consistent with Kant's philosophical anthropology as I have presented it.

Kant's most extensive discussion of respect as a moral motivator occurs in Chapter Three of his *Critique of Practical Reason*. Within this context, he is concerned to distinguish respect from all merely sensible feelings and desires, since he is trying to establish that respect is the only genuine motivator of morally worthy action. So, Kant identifies two functions of respect: a negative and a positive. The negative function concerns the way in which respect affects our sensible feelings and inclinations, which are competing with respect insofar as they present themselves to us as alternative motivations for action. According to Kant, all of our inclinations (the satisfaction of which constitutes our happiness) "constitute regard for oneself" (CPrR 5:73). Kant distinguishes two forms that this self-regard can take: "either the self-regard of *love for oneself,* a predominant *benevolence* toward oneself (*Philautia*), or that of *satisfaction with oneself* (*Arrogantia*). The former is called, in particular, *self-love*; the latter, *self-conceit*" (CPrR 5:73). The negative function of respect comes into play when the moral law thwarts our inclinations and produces a feeling of pain, but here the distinction between self-love and self-conceit is important. Respect for the law is an emotion that "merely *infringes upon* self-love, inasmuch as it only restricts it, as natural and active in us even prior to the moral law" (CPrR 5:73). In other words, respect curbs the self-love that is natural to us in virtue of being sensible beings whose natural end is happiness. Self-love, then, is not evil and can be transformed into something morally good, so long as it is made subservient to the demands of the moral law (i.e., so long as it takes second-place to what is genuinely morally good for us when there is a question of competition between the two), and then Kant calls it "rational self-love." When it comes to self-conceit, however, respect "strikes it down," "since all claims to esteem for oneself that precede accord with the moral law are null and quite unwarranted" (CPrR 5:73). In other words, self-conceit is self-love that has been perverted by depravity; according to Kant, it is the form self-love takes when one resolves to prioritize one's own happiness over and against the demands of morality. No wonder that Kant insists that respect strikes this sensible feeling down.

4.4 Kant's Doctrine of Virtue: Self-Perfection and the Happiness of Others

The positive function of respect is where much of the scholarly disagreement lies. Nonetheless, it seems fair to say that in addition to the curbing of self-love and striking down of self-conceit, the moral law can also produce a positive feeling in us, a peculiar kind of pleasure we take in acknowledging "the majesty of this [moral] law" (CPrR 5:77). The feeling is peculiar because, Kant argues, unlike sensible feelings and inclinations, the positive feeling of respect is "produced solely by reason" (CPrR 5:76). In a seldom quoted passage from *Religion* (Morrisson 2008, 153), Kant explains the way in which respect functions as a positive moral feeling:

> This susceptibility to simple respect for the moral law within us would thus be the moral feeling, which by itself does not yet constitute an end of the natural predisposition but only insofar as it is an incentive of the power of choice. But now this is possible only because the free power of choice incorporates moral feeling into its maxim: so a power of choice so constituted is a good character, and this character, as in general every character of the free power of choice, is something that can only be acquired. (R 6:27).

The virtuous person, according to Kant, is someone who is motivated to pursue her genuinely morally good ends out of a feeling of respect, that is, out of the esteem she feels for human dignity.[17]

I can illustrate how respect functions, according to this reading of Kant, by way of an example. Recall our couple from Chap. 3, Giselle and Kate. Let's presume that their neighbor, Dan, just broke his leg. Let's stipulate that Dan is elderly, lives alone, and has no extended family. And let's stipulate that both Giselle and Kate know these things because of their acquaintance with Dan over the few years they have been neighbors. Giselle and Kate deliberate about whether they should go visit Dan. There are all sorts of reasons, both for and against, that might arise in the course of their deliberations. If, however, Giselle and Kant are virtuous, then it would be fair to say that their deliberation might not take very long. They would understand that it is genuinely good for them to visit Dan and help him, and, just as importantly, they would do so cheerfully. On this telling of the story, Giselle and Kate would still act from respect, but there is nothing in Kant's account that precludes them also acting for other emotions that have been cultivated by autocratic reason (Cf. Baron 1995, Chapter 6).[18]

But let us suppose that Giselle and Kate are not virtuous, since such a scenario would make it easier to see how respect functions in light of Kant's account from his *Critique of Practical Reason*. On this scenario their sensible inclinations may be especially strong and run counter to the genuinely good thing to do: for example, they might feel disinclined to go because they had planned to spend the day in bed

---

[17] Cf. Erica Holberg (2016, 242): "Respect as pleasurable feeling produced through dutiful willing demonstrates that our sensibility is responsive to and informed by the subjective willing of the moral law. The fact that respect as a moral pleasure is a necessary feature of dutiful actions means that simply in acting from pure practical reason for the sake of duty (something all of us can always freely do, regardless of the constitution of our sensibility), sensibility is brought along to love the law. Each dutiful action builds upon previous dutiful actions and supports future dutiful actions, and the pleasurable feeling of respect is a necessary feature of how this happens."

[18] Critics of Kant, such as Michael Stocker (1997) and Bernard Williams (1981) fail to appreciate those aspects of Kant's moral theory that allow for this scenario.

watching Netflix, or because they had plans to go out to see a play together, or because they find Dan boring, though they tolerate him in small doses. If, in addition to the demands of their sensible inclinations, they ask themselves, "What is the genuinely morally good thing to do here?", then they might consider what Dan deserves as a matter of being a person with dignity. And this thought, according to Kant's account of moral reasoning, should elicit from them a feeling of respect for the moral law (or, more specifically, for the dignity Dan possesses), which would help them see that their sensible inclinations should take a backseat to what Dan deserves (the negative function of respect), and it would also bring about a feeling of esteem for Dan *as a human being*, which is a positive feeling that they could then act upon in going to visit Dan in the hospital.

The feeling of respect, according to Kant, is the main motivation for perfecting oneself, and I do not think it is difficult to see why Kant holds this view. Given that self-perfection requires dedication and hard work, perfecting ourselves out of respect for our own status as beings possessing dignity helps us overcome those sensible feelings and inclinations that stand in the way of such perfection and moves us to develop our talents out of a sense of esteem for our own worth.

4.4.3 Kant's Account of the Emotion of Love

Although respect for the moral law figures prominently throughout Kant's practical philosophy, his remarks about love are sparser and harder to find. Kant identifies a number of different kinds of love, and it is not always clear which kinds are emotions or how the different kinds of love are related.[19] Kant uses the term "love" (*Liebe*) in a number of different ways, not all of which denote emotions. Kant's broadest distinction concerning love is the distinction he makes between pathological love (*pathologische Liebe*) and practical love (*praktische Liebe*) (G 4:399). Pathological love is a sensible feeling (or desire, as I will argue), whereas practical love is not a feeling at all but a willing of the good of others. For this reason, practical love, according to Kant, is "very inappropriately" called love (MM 6:401). Strictly speaking, practical love is a maxim, a principle of action whereby one wills the good of others by adopting as one's own end the promotion of their happiness. Practical love, therefore, can be commanded; it is also, according to Kant, a duty, namely the duty of benevolence (*Wohlwollen*).

When examining the emotion of love in Kant's writings, then, one must focus on pathological love, since it is the only kind of love that is felt. Kant distinguishes between two kinds of pathological love. First, Kant seems to equate pathological love, the feeling of love, with the "love that delights" (*Liebe des Wohlgefallens*). This is particularly true of his discussions of the emotion of love in the "Doctrine of

---

[19] Indeed, the incongruity between Kant's seeming dismissal of pathological love and certain intuitions about the moral worth of love as an emotion have even led some defenders of Kant's moral theory to criticize his views on the subject. See, for example, Baron (2002: 391–407).

4.4 Kant's Doctrine of Virtue: Self-Perfection and the Happiness of Others

Virtue." The love that delights involves taking "pleasure in the perfection of others" (MM 6:449).[20] It is, according to Kant, "a pleasure joined immediately to the representation of an object's existence" (MM 6:402). Second, Kant identifies the "love that wishes well" (*Liebe des Wohlwollens*) as pathological love. Then there is the odd case of a third kind of love in Kant's writings, namely "love of human beings" (*Menschenliebe*). Kant's understanding of the love of human beings is particularly vexing because, in the "Doctrine of Virtue," it seems as though this species of love is a *special kind* of feeling of love, one that has closer affinities with the feeling of respect than it does with pathological feelings. I will argue that love of human beings is what results when we autocratically cultivate our unreflective, natural pathological feeling of love and transform it into the kind of sensible, practical feeling that characterizes the virtuous agent, according to Kant. First, though, I want to explain what Kant means by the love that wishes well and explain its relationship to the love that delights.

The Love That Wishes Well & the Love That Delights Kant's account of the love that wishes well occurs in the notes taken by Georg Ludwig Collins for lectures Kant delivered *circa* 1775[21] and the lecture notes taken by Johann Friedrich Vigilantius in 1793–1794. In the Collins notes, one finds the following distinction, which seems to support the view that the love that wishes well is a species of pathological love: "All love is either love that wishes well [*Wohlwollens*] or love that delights [*Wohlgefallens*]. Well-wishing love consists in the wish and inclination to promote the happiness of others. The love that delights is the pleasure we take in showing approval of another's perfections" (CL 27:417, translation modified). Whereas the love that delights is a sensible, pathological *emotion*, the love that wishes well is a sensible, pathological *desire* to benefit another person by promoting her or his happiness. Given the preceding description of Kant's account of the way in which the will can be pathologically determined, one can deduce an interesting relationship between the love that wishes well and the love that delights. Since, according to Kant, all inclination is based on feeling, one can conclude that the pleasure that precedes desire and determines the faculty of one's will in the case of the love that wishes well is the pleasure one takes in the perfection of others. In other words, in the case of the pathological love that wishes well (*Liebe des Wohlwollens*), one's will is determined by the love that delights (*Liebe des Wohlgefallens*). The relationship between the love that delights (in the perfections of the object of love) as the basis for the love that wishes well comes across in a short passage from the Vigilantius Lectures:

> No duty, and hence, not the duty of love either, can be founded on inclination; for example, inclination towards nature's products, the perfection of structure in a spider or an insect, can

---

[20] Kant seems to think that the love that delights can only take living beings as its object (see, e.g., CPrR 5:76). Given the definitions I quote, I think this is an unnecessary restriction. I don't think his definitions of the love that delights preclude one from loving (in this sense) one's home or a well-made martini.

[21] Manfred Kuehn (2015), drawing on the work of Werner Stark, convincingly argues that the Collins lecture notes are based on a purchased set of notes dating from lectures given *circa* 1775.

> bring it about that through knowing the object we love it—not, however, from duty, but by virtue of the attraction of natural impulses, *per stimulos*. This is the basis of love in all those cases where, in exercising the act of love, we have our own welfare in view.... We call this love from inclination kindness (*favor*), when it has the intention of laying upon the other an obligation towards us, and is thus coupled with an interest. (VL 27:670)

Despite the use of a non-human example, the preceding passage supports my reading of the relationship between the two kinds of pathological love. The pleasure taken in the perfection of the object is "the basis of love" when it comes to *acts* of love motivated by a personal interest. The love that delights and the love that wishes well are two sides of the same moral psychological coin.[22] The former is a species of the sensible *feeling* of pleasure in the perfection of others; the latter is a species of the sensible *desire* to promote the happiness of others. The following passage nicely illustrates Kant's evaluation of pathological love in the life of an individual moral agent:

> If we now, on the other hand, take well-doing (*Wohltätigkeit*) from love, and consider a man who loves from inclination, we find that such a man has a need of other folk, to whom he can show his kindness. He is not content if he does not find people to whom he can do good. A loving heart has an immediate pleasure and satisfaction in well-doing, and finds more pleasure in that than in its own enjoyment. This inclination must be satisfied, for it is a need. This is a kindness of heart and temper, but no moralist should seek to cultivate such a thing; it is benevolence from principle that must be cultivated, for the other is based on a man's inclination and need, which gives rise to an irregular sort of behavior. (CL 27:414)[23]

The love that delights and the love that wishes well are pathological forms of love, expressions of love that are not guided by rational moral principles but by one's own self-love (i.e., a concern for one's own good).

Love of Human Beings There is, however, another form of love, according to Kant. His discussion of love of human beings [*Menschenliebe*] appears in subsection "c" of Section XII of the "Introduction" to the "Doctrine of Virtue." It consists of four relatively short paragraphs. Kant begins by saying that love is a matter of feeling (*Empfindung*) and not willing so that "a duty to love is an absurdity." This is a familiar claim, as is his next claim that benevolence (*Wohlwollens*) is "very inappropriately" called "love." The second paragraph of the subsection elaborates what Kant takes to be the duty we all have to do good to others. Although he does not say

---

[22] I am not claiming that every desire to promote the happiness of others is a case of the (pathological) love that wishes well, and, so, I am not claiming that every case of desire to promote the happiness of others is motivated by the love that delights. What I am claiming is that cases of the *pathological* desire to promote the happiness of others are cases of the love that wishes well, which is a desire, and this desire is associated with the *pathological feeling* of the love that delights. Kant thinks that we can develop inclinations to love on the basis of "the good disposition of benevolence" (CL 27:417–419), but here he seems to be thinking of the capacity we have to develop dispositions for certain desires and emotions on the basis of a moral disposition (rather than merely, unreflective, natural impulses): "if I love others from obligation, I thereby acquire a taste for loving, and by practice it becomes love from inclination" (CL 27:419).

[23] Coincidentally, this passage makes the same point about actions motivated by pathological feelings as Kant's example of the sympathetic benefactor in the *Groundwork* (4:398–399).

4.4 Kant's Doctrine of Virtue: Self-Perfection and the Happiness of Others

so explicitly, in this paragraph Kant relies on a distinction he makes between "benevolence" (*Wohlwollen*) and "beneficence" (*Wohltun*). Kant explains the difference later in the text, within the context of his discussion of the duties of love. "Benevolence is satisfaction in the happiness (well-being) of others; but beneficence is the maxim of making others' happiness one's end, and the duty to it consists in the subject's being constrained by this reason to adopt this maxim as a universal law" (MM 6:452).

The third paragraph of the subsection holds the key to understanding *Menschenliebe*, though this is concealed by Mary Gregor's translation of the text.[24] The paragraph begins with a seemingly unrelated observation about the feelings of aversion one may have toward vice and then quickly returns to the topic of beneficence. Gregor translates the key passage as follows:

> *Beneficence* is a duty. If someone practices it often and succeeds in realizing his beneficent intention, he eventually comes actually to love the person he has helped. So the saying "you ought to *love* your neighbor as yourself" does not mean that you ought immediately (first) to love him and (afterwards) by means of this love do good to him. It means, rather, *do good* to your fellow human beings, and your beneficence will produce love of them in you (as an aptitude of the inclination to beneficence in general). (MM 6:402)

Here is the original German:

> Wohltun ist Pflicht. Wer diese oft ausübt und es gelingt ihm mit seiner wohltätigen Absicht, kommt endlich wohl gar dahin, den, welchem er wohl getan hat, wirklich zu lieben. Wenn es also heißt das nicht: du sollst unmittelbar (zuerst) lieben und vermittelst dieser Liebe (nachher) wohltun, sondern: tue deinem Nebenmenschen wohl, und dieses Wohltun wird Menschenliebe (als Fertigkeit der Neigung zum Wohltun überhaupt) in dir bewirken!

In the second and third sentences of the passage Kant uses the verb "*zu lieben*" and the substantive "*Liebe*," which Gregor translates as "to love" and "love," respectively. With these words Kant clearly means to denote a feeling, since he juxtaposes "love" in these contexts to duty (just as he did in the first two paragraphs in the subsection). Gregor's translation misleads, however, insofar as she does not clearly indicate that "love of them" in the last sentence is a translation of "*Menschenliebe*." So her translation does not distinguish clearly enough between the two earlier uses of "love," which denote feelings, and Kant's use of "*Menschenliebe*," which is not a feeling but an aptitude of the inclination to do good to others.

As I translate and understand this passage, *Menschenliebe* is a pathological inclination to do good to others that has been transformed and cultivated by fulfilling one's duty of beneficence. In other words, doing good to others from a sense of moral duty has certain effects on our sensible natures, and there is a receptivity (*Empfänglichkeit*) to this on the part of our sensibility. In the case of beneficence, the result is a training of our pathological desires so as to produce a practical desire (Cf. Chap. 3, Sect. 3.2.1) to do good to others, and this is what Kant calls *Menschenliebe*. Remember that Kantian virtue requires one to use reason "to bring all his capacities and inclinations under his (reason's) control," and if, as I argued

---

[24] My reading of this passage differs, for example, from Christoph Horn's (2008), which reduces all love to a pathological affect. Cf. Arroyo (2016).

above, this is to mean something more than just the self-control of Kantian apathy, it has to entail the rational cultivation of one's feelings and inclinations so that they more readily and easily comply with the rational requirements of morality.[25] *Menschenliebe* lies at the basis of morality as a subjective condition to the receptiveness of duty on the part of our sensibility (i.e., "on the side of feeling"), as a necessary precondition of our capacity for virtue. Were our sensible natures not receptive and responsive to the governing of reason, we would be incapable of being virtuous, which is a duty. Our developing a capacity to feel love of human beings is part of what it means to become virtuous.

4.4.4 Respect, Love, & Our Relations with Others

In the first Chapter of the second Part of the "Doctrine of the elements of ethics," Kant explains our duties of virtues to others in terms of a duty to love other people. He maintains that "*love* and *respect* are the feelings that accompany the carrying out of these duties" (MM 6:448), which is why I have spent so much time explaining how Kant understands these feelings. He goes on to explain the relationship between love and respect by drawing an analogy between these two emotions and physical forces of attraction (love) and repulsion (respect), which "bind together rational beings (on earth)." He continues,

> The principle of **mutual love** admonishes them constantly to *come closer* to one another; that of the **respect** they owe one another, to keep themselves *at a distance* from one another; and should one of these great moral forces fail, "then nothingness (immorality), with gaping throat, would drink up the whole kingdom of (moral) beings like a drop of water." (MM 6:449).

Some interpreters of Kant, such as Marcia Baron (2002, 392), claim that Kant's way of explaining the relationship between love and respect "is intuitively odd." Perhaps, but only if one ignores Kant's philosophical anthropology. I think the preceding analogy makes a great deal of sense in light of Kant's view of human beings. The principle of mutual love demands that we adopt the promotion of the happiness of others as our end. This requires us to work with others (1) in order find out what constitutes their happiness, and (2) in order to help them attain happiness as best we can—hence love as a force of attraction. But there is a danger here, a danger due to our unsocial sociability. The danger is our propensity to assume that we know what is best for other people, regardless of what they may think. The tendency, in other words, is to disrespect the autonomous agency of other people by treating them as

---

[25] An instructive example of Kantian virtue and what it means rationally to cultivate one's feelings and inclinations is Kant's account of the duty to cultivate a sympathetic disposition (MM 6:456–457). Cf. Baron (1995). Although Kant acknowledges that there is what might be called a "natural receptivity" to feelings of sympathy (such as in the case of the sympathetic philanthropist from the *Groundwork*), he also claims that using these sympathetic feelings "as a means to promoting active and rational benevolence is still a particular, though conditional, duty" (MM 6:456).

children (in effect, by acting as their 'guardians', to borrow Kant's phrase from "What is Enlightenment?"). What keeps us from doing this? The principle of respect, which limits our self-esteem and requires us to acknowledge the dignity of other people, dignity grounded in their capacity to exercise choice—hence respect as a force of repulsion. If the principle of love were to fail, then the principle of respect would demand that we leave each person to her or his own business, which would entail the impossibility of moral community. If the principle of respect were to fail, we would all try to control the lives of our fellow human beings, which would entail the impossibility of moral community, too (insofar as the idea of moral community entails a community among equals).[26]

4.5 Looking Ahead

In this chapter I presented a reading of Kant's normative ethical theory, which is a theory of virtue, though one that conceives of virtue differently than some earlier theories. I have argued that Kant's understanding of the virtuous agent is much richer than the picture one would develop by merely drawing on the traditional reading of Kant. Indeed, as I have argued throughout Part I, Kant's ethics is through and through informed by his philosophical anthropology, and his account of virtue is no different. The virtuous agent, according to Kant, is someone who works on achieving self-mastery, a task that can never be fully perfected or completed, since we are dependent, finite rational beings. Such self-mastery just is the autocracy of practical reason, according to Kant, and it involves more than the bare self-control or suppression or extermination of one's unruly sensible feelings and inclinations. Kantian autocracy, properly understood, entails the full moral development of our characters, which involves the maintenance and cultivation of our sensible natures as well as our capacities to will autonomously.

Throughout Part I have repeatedly drawn attention to some of the ways in which features of Kant's understanding of moral obligation, or his view of human nature, or his account of virtue inform what he will have to say about sex and marriage. As I conclude this Chapter and Part I, I am finally in a position to make good on my claim that Kant's ethics is particularly suited to work as a resource for those engaged in the contemporary debate over same-sex marriage. Virtue, according to Kant, is the self-mastery needed to withstand a strong but unjust opponent, one that "opposes the moral disposition *within us*" (MM 6:380). This opponent is our uncultivated sensible feelings and inclinations, which tempt us and sometimes lead us to prioritize our own respective conceptions of happiness over and against what is genuinely morally good. As I have argued, these unreflective and uncultivated sensible feelings and inclinations are what Kant calls affects and passions. They are particularly dangerous and tempting because they aim at those objects of our will that seem to

---

[26] Cf. Melissa Seymour Fahmy (2011) who argues that it is sometimes morally required of us to convince someone to change her ends on the grounds of our duty of beneficence.

be most important to our happiness, that seem to be most pleasant. It is significant, then, that Kant claims that sexual inclination

> is, in fact, the strongest possible sensible pleasure in an object. – It is not merely *sensitive* pleasure, as in objects that are pleasing in mere reflection on them (receptivity to which is called taste). It is rather pleasure from the *enjoyment* of another person, which therefore belongs to the *faculty of desire* and, indeed, to its highest stage, passion. But it cannot be classed with either the love that is delight or the love of benevolence (for both of these, instead, deter one from carnal enjoyment). It is a unique kind of pleasure (*sui generis*), and this ardor has nothing in common with moral love properly speaking, though it can enter into close union with it under the limiting conditions of practical reason. (MM 6:426)

Kant's analysis of this strongest and *sui generis* passion and his account of how it can be tamed by practical reason, is the subject of Part II.

References

Annas, Julia. 1993. *The Morality of Happiness*. New York: Oxford University Press.
Aristotle. 2009. *The Nicomachean Ethics*. Trans. David Ross, rev. and ed. Lesley Brown. Oxford: Oxford University Press.
Arroyo, Christopher. 2016. Kant on the Emotion of Love. *European Journal of Philosophy* 24 (3): 580–606.
Baron, Marcia W. 1995. *Kantian Ethics Almost Without Apology*. Ithaca: Cornell University Press.
———. 2002. Love and Respect in the *Doctrine of Virtue*. In *Kant's* Metaphysics of Morals: Interpretive Essays, ed. Mark Timmons, 391–407. Oxford/New York: Oxford University Press.
Baron, Marcia, and Melissa Seymour Fahmy. 2009. Beneficence and Other Duties of Love in *The Metaphysics of Morals*. In *The Blackwell Guide to Kant's Ethics*, ed. Thomas E. Hill Jr., 211–228. Malden/Oxford: Wiley-Blackwell.
Baxley, Anne Margaret. 2010. *Kant's Theory of Virtue: The Value of Autocracy*. Cambridge: Cambridge University Press.
Bourges, Maria. 2008. Physiology and the Controlling of Affects in Kant's Philosophy. *Kantian Review* 13 (2): 46–66.
Cureton, Adam, and Thomas E. Hill. 2015. Kant on Virtue and the Virtues. In *Cultivating Virtue: Perspectives from Philosophy, Theology, and Psychology*, ed. Nancy E. Snow, 87–109. Oxford/New York: Oxford University Press.
Davies, Brian. 2014. *Thomas Aquinas'* Summa Theologiae: *A Guide and Commentary*. Oxford: Oxford University Press.
Denis, Lara. 2006. Kant's Conception of Virtue. In *The Cambridge Companion to Kant and Modern Philosophy*, ed. Paul Guyer, 505–537. Cambridge: Cambridge University Press.
Engstrom, Stephen. 2002. The Inner Freedom of Virtue. In *Kant's* Metaphysics of Morals: Interpretive Essays, ed. Mark Timmons, 289–315. Oxford/New York: Oxford University Press.
Fahmey, Melissa Seymour. 2011. Love, Respect, and Interfering with Others. *Pacific Philosophical Quarterly* 92: 174–192.
Fingarette, Herbert. 1969. *Self-Deception*. Berkley/Los Angeles: University of California Press.
Flikschuh, Katrin. 2002. Kantian Desires: Freedom of Choice and Action in the *Rechslehre*. In *Kant's* Metaphysics of Morals: Interpretive Essays, ed. Mark Timmons, 185–207. Oxford/New York: Oxford University Press.
Gregor, Mary J. 1963. *Laws of Freedom: A Study of Kant's Method of Applying the Categorical Imperative in the Metaphysik der Sitten*. New York: Barnes & Noble, Inc..
Herman, Barbara. 1993. *The Practice of Moral Judgment*. Cambridge, MA/London: Harvard University Press.

References

Hill, Thomas E. 2008. Kantian Virtue and "Virtue Ethics.". In *Kant's Ethics of Virtue*, ed. Monika Betzler, 29–59. Berlin: Walter de Gruyter.

Holberg, Erika A. 2016. The Importance of Pleasure in the Moral for Kant's Ethics. *The Southern Journal of Philosophy* 54 (2): 226–246.

Horn, Christoph. 2008. The Concept of Love in Kant's Virtue Ethics. In *Kant's Ethics of Virtue*, ed. Monika Betzler, 147–173. Berlin: Walter de Gruyter.

Johnson, Robert N. 2008. Was Kant a Virtue Ethicist? In *Kant's Ethics of Virtue*, ed. Monika Betzler, 61–75. Berlin: Walter de Gruyter.

Kenny, Anthony. 1992. *The Metaphysics of Mind*. Oxford: Oxford University Press.

Kuehn, Manfred. 2015. Collins: Kant's Proto-critical Position. In *Kant's Lectures on Ethics: A Critical Guide*, ed. Lara Denis and Oliver Sensen, 51–67. Cambridge: Cambridge University Press.

Macbeth, A. Murray. 1973. Kant on moral feeling. *Kant-Studien* 64 (1–4): 283–314.

McCarty, Richard. 1993. Kantian Moral Motivation and the Feeling of Respect. *Journal of the History of Philosophy* 31 (3): 421–435.

Morrisson, Iain P. 2008. *Kant and the Role of Pleasure in Moral Action*. Athens: Ohio University Press.

Nussbaum, Martha C. 2001. *Upheavals of Thought: The Intelligence of Emotions*. Cambridge: Cambridge University Press.

Nuyen, A.T. 1991. Sense, Passions, and Morals in Hume and Kant. *Kant-Studien* 82 (1): 29–41.

Sherman, Nancy. 1997. *Making a Necessity of Virtue: Aristotle and Kant on Virtue*. Cambridge: Cambridge University Press.

Stocker, Michael. 1997. The Schizophrenia of Modern Ethical Theories. In *Roger Crisp and Michael Slote*, ed. Virtue Ethics, 66–78. Oxford/New York: Oxford University Press.

Williams, Bernard. 1981. Persons, character, and morality. In *Moral Luck: Philosophical Papers, 1973–1980*, 1–19. Cambridge: Cambridge University Press.

Wood, Allen W. 2008. *Kantian Ethics*. Cambridge: Cambridge University Press.

———. 2009. Duties to Oneself, Duties of Respect to Others. In *The Blackwell Guide to Kant's Ethics*, ed. Thomas E. Hill Jr., 229–251. Malden/Oxford: Wiley-Blackwell.

Part II
Gender, Sex, and Marriage in Kant's Ethics

Chapter 5
Dependency & Domination: Gender & Kant's Practical Sexual Ethic

Abstract This chapter provides an overview of Kant's practical sexual ethic, drawing attention to the way in which his views are informed by both his philosophical anthropology and his understanding of gender. I begin by examining what Kant says about "the character of the sexes," which is the phrase he uses to describe what we would call "gender." Specifically, I present the way in which Kant characterizes women and analyze the implications of his account for (a) his understanding of the moral agency of women, and (b) his understanding of gender relations. Next, I examine Kant's understanding of sexual appetite and explain the ways in which he thinks it involves the objectification of the object of one's sexual desire. I conclude the chapter with a detailed examination of Kant's treatment of various sexual vices in order to bring to light the moral reasoning that informs his practical sexual ethic. In this way I hope to identify how and why Kant finds sex problematic, which will allow me in the next chapter to explain why and to what extent he thinks marriage is the solution to this problem.

Although Kant never composed a single, sustained treatise on practical sexual ethics, he writes about the topic quite a bit throughout his practical philosophy, particularly in the lecture notes we have from Georg Ludwig Collins (which date from around 1775) and Johann Friedrich Vigilantius (which date from 1793). Unfortunately, these aspects of his writings have not received nearly the same amount of scholarly attention as some other topics in his practical philosophy, especially in his normative ethical theory. This is likely due in part to the influence Kant's normative ethical theory has had on Western European philosophy and the controversies his theory has engendered, including the ways in which the Anscombian reading presents a Kant who is unfit to offer a cogent practical ethics—sexual or otherwise. But it is also due to the fact that much of what Kant has to say about sex and gender would *prima facie* (i.e., apart from the context I supply in Part I) strike most contemporary readers of Kant as obviously false, old-fashioned, and misogynistic. So, for example, we find Barbara Herman (2002, 55) admitting that Kant's views about sex are "outrageous—appropriate objects of derision, not discussion. Kant has dreadful things to say about women; his hostility toward sex, the body, and our affective lives generally is famous; and he has strongly conventional views about marriage, children, and the family." Herman, though, goes on to argue that despite these flaws, in certain respects Kant's sexual ethic is consistent with certain feminist critiques of sexuality.[1] So, she thinks that we can learn from what Kant has to say on the subject of sex—though she does not think there is much to learn from his views on women, except, perhaps, how to avoid certain forms of misogyny and mistakes about gender (Herman 2002, 55–56).

Of course, I agree with Herman that Kant's sexual ethic contains important insights that can be of value to us today, despite the ways in which some of what he says, and the way in which he says it, can strike us as offensive and embarrassingly close-minded. I disagree with her, however, in her estimation of the value of Kant's remarks on women. To be clear, I think that most of what he has to say about women is subject to serious criticism for being sexist, if not misogynistic. But I think that his remarks hold value apart from the lessons we can learn from them about how *not* to think of women.

First, Kant's view of women largely informs what he has to say about sexual relations, particularly his worry about the way in which sex can objectify the object of one's desire. More specifically, part of Kant's motivation in criticizing our sexual appetite as objectifying is a worry about the way in which men use sex and the threat of sex to subjugate and oppress women. So, one cannot mine his practical sexual ethic for philosophical gems without also working through the ways in which it is informed by certain views about women and their allegedly natural relationship to men. Second, and equally important for my purposes of arguing that Kant is relevant to the contemporary debate over same-sex marriage, is Kant's account of women, particularly his conception of the ways in which women and men complement each other. His account speaks to the ways in which the status of women in his society (and in general) was and to a certain extent remains precarious, and how, as far as he is concerned, marriage can be a source of liberation in an otherwise oppressive social structure. So, I will argue, we can read Kant's account of gender relations as his (admittedly misguided) attempt to empower women, given his understanding of the natural relations between women and men; and *at the same time* we can criticize him for taking these relations as natural (i.e., simply given and unchangeable through human agency) and in so criticizing him draw attention to some ways in which such social relations can still be, and for some still are, a source of oppression for women.

My aim in this chapter is to provide an overview of Kant's practical sexual ethic, drawing attention to the way in which his views are informed by both his philosophical anthropology and his understanding of gender. I begin by examining what Kant says about "the character of the sexes," which is the phrase he uses to describe what we would call "gender." Specifically, I present the way in which Kant characterizes women and analyze the implications of his account for (a) his understanding of the moral agency of women, and (b) his understanding of gender relations. Next, I examine Kant's understanding of sexual appetite and explain the ways in which he thinks it involves the objectification of the object of one's sexual desire. I conclude the chapter with a detailed examination of Kant's treatment of various sexual vices

---

[1] Elizabeth Brake (2005, 83–88) disagrees with Herman on this point.

in order to bring to light the moral reasoning that informs his practical sexual ethic. In this way I hope to identify how and why Kant finds sex problematic, which will allow me in the next chapter to explain why and to what extent he thinks marriage is the solution to this problem.

5.1 Kant on the Character of the Sexes

It would be helpful to preface my exposition of Kant's characterization of the sexes with an explanation of how contemporary theorists understand the difference between "sex" and "gender." Alison Stone (2007) provides definitions of each term, which will prove useful in evaluating Kant. Sex, according to Stone (2007, 33), has to do with the condition of being biologically male or female. So,

- A human being is biologically male if they have XY chromosomes, testes, "male" internal and external genitalia, a relatively high proportion of androgens, and "male" secondary sex characteristics.
- A human being is biologically female if they have XX chromosomes, ovaries, "female" internal and external genitalia, relatively high proportions of oestrogen and progesterone, and "female" secondary sex characteristics.

Gender, according to Stone (2007, 30), is social and consists of

- Social expectations and assumptions about what behaviors and traits are appropriate for male and female individuals. For example, it is commonly expected that males will relish confrontation while females will try to avoid it.
- The psychological traits, and the understandings of themselves, that individuals tend to develop under the influence of these social expectations. For instance, males often do come to relish confrontation more than females.

Kant, like most men writing throughout the history of Western European philosophy, did not distinguish between sex and gender. (Of course, he also did not understand human biology in terms of genes, chromosomes, and hormones.) As a result, he tends to conflate sex and gender, uncritically accepting that what we would call gender traits (in his parlance, "characteristics of the sexes") are caused by what we would call sex traits (in his parlance, feminine or masculine "nature"). To continue with Stone's example, Kant would claim that the tendency of men to relish confrontation is a function of masculine nature, while the tendency to avoid it is a consequence of feminine nature. Writing about what he takes to be the essential traits of women, Kant claims that "culture does not introduce these feminine qualities, it only allows them to develop and become recognizable under favorable conditions" (A 7:303).

Kant's most extended discussion of the character of the sexes appears in two places: *Anthropology from a Pragmatic Point of View* (1798), and an early work called, *Observations on the Feeling of the Beautiful and Sublime* (1764). *Observations* is a very early work, which raises a question as to how well this work reflects Kant's mature view. As Mari Mikkola (2011, 92) convincingly argues, though, "Kant's claims in the *Observations* and *Anthropology* are sufficiently similar to undermine the suggestion that he substantially altered his view of women over time." Nonetheless, I rely more heavily on Kant's *Anthropology*, which has a more extensive treatment of the character of the sexes.[2]

I want to say from the start that it is very difficult to write about Kant's account of the character of the sexes and about his understanding of women in particular.[3] Much of what he says strikes me as false and offensive, and the temptation is merely to dismiss it as such. What keeps me from doing so is that it is not merely an antiquated view that we can observe and dismiss from the comfort of the twenty-first century. Kant's view of women—unlike, say, Aristotle's view of the planetary orbits—is still alive and with us today, and it is not merely a view held by people we might want to dismiss as stupid or as grossly bigoted. For example, Pope John Paul II (2006), in his "theology of the body" defends an understanding of the complementarity of the sexes that shares some important features with Kant's understanding of the masculine and feminine genders.[4] Along these lines, the contemporary philosopher, J. Budziszewski (2012, 40) claims that it is so difficult for us contemporaries to discuss sexual difference because we fail to grasp four essential truths about sexual difference, one of which he calls the "duality of path":

> The developmental trajectories of men and women are different at both ends—not only in what they start with, the susceptibilities and tendencies that each sex must discipline and prune, but in what they end with, what each sex ripens into when all goes as it should.

Such a passage could have been written by Kant. But what Budziszewski and Pope John Paul II and Kant each fail to understand (or perhaps don't want to understand) is that the sexual differences they identify are due to gender, that is, they are due to the way in which we socialize individuals with respect to the sex we identify for them. More to the point, as Cordelia Fine (2010) painstakingly argues and documents, largely because of the persistence of belief in the kind of natural sexual differences and complementarity Budziszewski discusses, gender bias against women remains a pervasive problem in Western society. So, in dealing with the rest of the material in this first section, I am trying to walk a fine line between (a) acknowledging the real and significant errors in Kant's thinking on women and (b) gleaning

---

[2] Kurt Mosser (1999) raises questions about the sources some feminist critics use in their evaluations of Kant, including Kant's *Anthropology*. So, we find Mosser observing that "the Anthropology lectures were given, as we have seen, as early as the 1770s, and it is unclear how much, if any [*sic.*] revision they underwent" (350). Mosser, also, however, acknowledges that Kant approved the publication of the *Anthropology* (344). To my mind, Kant's approval indicates that the content of the work accurately reflects his mature view.

[3] It is worth acknowledging that a similar issue arises with respect to Kant's discussion of race, particularly, though not exclusively, in his *Anthropology* (A 7:311–320). Bernasconi (2001), for example, is very critical of Kant's treatment of race. For an example of a thinker who is critical of Kant's racism and yet finds some value in his moral and political philosophy for developing an ethics of race, see Naomi Zack (2011, 141–145).

[4] Helga Varden (2015, 18) draws some helpful comparisons between Kant's views and the views expressed by conservative interpretations of some religions. Cf. Daly (1985).

from his account (despite its errors) some insights that will help us both understand his sexual ethic and perhaps better prepare us for engaging and criticizing the kind of gender bias and sexism that we see today, particularly as it appears in some of the positions and arguments of those engaged in the same-sex marriage debate.

5.1.1 Kant on Feminine Nature

More often than not, Kant presents what he takes to be the traits characteristic of women within the context of a comparison with men, and his opening observation in his *Anthropology* begins with just such a comparison. Kant compares men and women to natural machines, and he claims, "in all machines that are supposed to accomplish with little power just as much as those with great power, **art** must be put in. Consequently, we can already assume that the provision of nature put more art into the organization of the female part than of the male" (A 7:303).[5] Contemporary readers may not quite understand what Kant means when he writes that nature has put more "art" (*Kunst*) into females than it has in men. In the eighteenth century, *Kunst* meant "the 'ability' or 'skill' of a human being 'to bring into existence a different thing outside of itself'" (Caygill 1995, 85). Although this term was typically used to indicate the ability to create a work of art such as a painting or a poem, in this context Kant uses it to indicate that woman *qua* females are more sophisticated and developed than men, at least with respect to their initial natural endowments. Here Kant foreshadows what he takes to be one of the natural, essential functions of femininity, namely, to civilize men. Indeed, the passage just cited continues: "for [nature] furnished the man with greater power than the woman in order to bring both into the most intimate *physical* union, which, insofar as they are nevertheless also *rational* beings, it orders to the end most important to it, the preservation of the species" (A 7:303).

There are a few things to note with respect to this opening passage from the discussion of the character of the sexes. First, although Kant identifies women as being more sophisticated naturally, he designates a subsidiary position for them when it comes to relations between women and men, since he thinks that they are not nearly as physically strong as men. Second, Kant hints at the way in which he understands the natural sexual function between men and women, namely, as an activity in which men use their greater strength in order to satiate their sexual desires. In other words, nature makes men physically stronger so that they can have their way with women and thereby fulfill nature's purpose with respect to sexual intercourse: procreation. Third, Kant identifies both women and men as rational beings. This might seem to imply that Kant takes women and men to be equal, but this would be mistaken (Kleingeld 1993). As Nancy Tuana (1993, ix, 163) observes, Kant belongs to

---

[5] Holly Wilson (1998, 289–290) takes this metaphor to indicate that Kant believed that sexual difference is something that is in the process of evolving, due in part to the way our unsocial sociability motivates our general evolution from a crude state to a more cultured one.

a long tradition in Western European philosophy, dating back to Aristotle, where "[woman] was depicted as an underdeveloped male, different not in kind but in degree from man. Woman's difference was defined in terms of lack: she was less rational, less moral, less evolved."

Kant asserts that "one can only come to the characterization of this sex [females] if one uses as one's principle not what we *make* our end, but what *nature's end* was in establishing womankind" (A 7:305). In a move inconsistent with his approach to practical philosophy overall (Chap. 3, Sect. 3.1), Kant defers to "nature's end," that is, a natural teleology (Wood 2008, 224).[6] Such natural teleology, "can also serve to indicate the principle for characterizing woman—a principle that does not depend on our choice but on a higher purpose for the human race" (A 7: 305). According to Kant, we can identify two ends as natural to females *qua* females: "(1) the preservation of the species, (2) the cultivation of society and its refinement by womankind" (7:306). He goes on to explain each of these aims in turn.

With respect to the preservation of the species, when nature "decided" that women would bear children and carry fetuses to term, it placed the burden of propagating the species on women. As a result, and in order to protect women during the times they are pregnant, Kant believes that nature implanted a fear of physical injury and timidity in women. The idea seems to be that by fleeing danger there is less of a chance that a woman, and her offspring, would be harmed. And it is by this natural fear and timidity that woman's nature "rightfully demands male protection for itself" (A 7:306). With respect to the cultivation of society (i.e., men), Kant claims that nature made women "man's ruler" through their "modesty and eloquence in speech and expression" (A 7:306). This allows women to instill in men the "finer feelings that belong to culture—namely those of sociability and propriety" (A 7:306). Men, according to Kant, are naturally crude beings who need to be tamed and civilized by women, which is why nature made a woman "clever while still young in claiming gentle and courteous treatment by the male, so that he would find himself imperceptibly fettered by a child through his own magnanimity, and led by her, if not to morality itself, to that which is its cloak, moral decency, which is the preparation for morality and its recommendation" (A 7:306).

I will have more to say about these alleged ends of women when I discuss Kant's account of domestic relationships between men and women. At this point I want to emphasize the way in which these ends "indicate a principle for characterizing women" that leads Kant to depict them as less than fully rational. For example, in one of his more revealing remarks, Kant claims that an upper-class woman "appears demure only by compulsion and makes no secret of wishing that she might rather be a man so that she could give her inclinations larger and freer latitude; no man, however, would want to be a woman" (A 7:307). Part of the reason why no man would want to be a woman has to do with what Kant takes to be the social station of women, which he believes to be a function of feminine nature.[7] But it also has to do

---

[6] The notion of natural teleology also plays an important role in Kant's account of sexual vices, which I discuss below (Sect. 5.3).

[7] Kant claims that women are merely "passive citizens," since they depend on another to manage their affairs (MM 6:314; TP 8:294–296). See Sect. 5.1.3 below.

with the fact that Kant believes women to be less capable when it comes to the exercise of their rational capacities. For example, in the opening page of his essay, "What is Enlightenment?",[8] Kant discusses the various obstacles to achieving enlightenment, which Kant defines as "the human being's emergence from his self-incurred minority" (WIE 8:35). After identifying laziness and cowardice as the two chief impediments to enlightenment, on which the guardians capitalize, Kant remarks that "by far the greatest part of humankind (*including the entire fair sex*)" believes "the step toward majority not only troublesome but also highly dangerous" (WIE 8:35, emphasis added).[9] Perhaps this is why Kant claims that scholarly women "use their *book* somewhat like their *watch*, that is, they carry one so that it will be seen that they have one; though it is usually not running or not set by the sun" (A 7:307), and that women are not fit for "deep reflection and a long drawn out consideration" (OBS 2:229).

5.1.2 Feminine Virtue, Masculine Virtue, and the Moral Agency of Women

Feminist scholarship over the past seventy years has firmly established that "the meanings that we find in our male and female bodies are given by the cultures in which we live—by the symbolic associations that these cultures attach to maleness and femaleness" (Stone 2007, 112).[10] So, not only is Kant mistaken for thinking that the traits he ascribes to women are caused by their natures *qua* women; we also have good reason to think that the traits he ascribes to women do not apply to a significant portion of them, and where they do apply, we have equally good reason for thinking that these traits have been socialized in ways that further the interests of men. With such interests of men in mind, one serious implication for Kant's view of women concerns the way in which his characterization of them seems to preclude women

---

[8] Robin May Schott (1997, 333) challenges what she takes to be the essay's "fundamental conception of rationality, autonomy, and freedom."

[9] Helga Varden (2015, 28–30) argues that Kant believes woman can become enlightened and engage in public reason no less than men can. On Varden's reading of the long passage from which I quote, "Kant condemns men for being ever so willing to make women their 'dumb domesticated animals,' for 'carefully prevent[ing]…these placid creatures from daring to take a single step without the walking cart which they have confined them,' and for presenting the world as a dangerous place that women should be deeply afraid of" (29). Although I am sympathetic with Varden's attempt to defend Kant from certain feminist criticisms, I see no evidence in the text to indicate that Kant writes specifically of the way men treat women. Rather, in the text Varden quotes, Kant is remarking on the way guardians (all of whom would have been men) treat those who remain in minority (which would include men and women).

[10] Cf. Simone de Beauvoir (1952, 267): "One is not born, but rather becomes, a woman. No biological, psychological, or economic fate determines the figure that the human female presents in society; it is civilization as a whole that produces this creature, intermediate between male and eunuch, which is described as feminine." Varden (2015, 15–19) provides an extended comparison of Kant and Beauvoir on gender.

from being full moral agents. Women, as Kant depicts them, are dominated by their sensible natures, which is one reason why Kant approvingly quotes Alexander Pope, saying that one can characterize females by two points: "the inclination to *dominate* and the inclination to *enjoyment*" (A 7:305). In other words, whereas men are ruled by reason, women are ruled by their inclinations, and this is so even in the case of virtuous women. In a revealing passage from his *Anthropology*, Kant summarizes the differences between feminine and masculine virtue:

> Feminine virtue or lack of virtue is very different from masculine virtue or lack of virtue, not only in kind but also as regards incentive. – She should be *patient*; he must be *tolerant*. She is *sensitive*; he is *sentimental*. – Man's economic activity consists in *acquiring,* woman's in *saving*. – The man is jealous *when he loves*; the woman is jealous even when she does not love, because every lover won by another woman is one lost from her circle of admirers. – The man has his *own* taste; the woman makes herself the object of *everyone's* taste. – "What the world says is *true,* and what it does, *good,*" is a feminine principle that is hard to unite with a *character* in the narrow sense of the term. However, there have still been heroic women who, in connection with their own household, have upheld with glory a character suitable to their vocation. (A 7:307–308)

The preceding passage helps explain Kant's distinction between the "beautiful virtue" of women and the "noble virtue" of men (OBS 2:231–233). According to this distinction in types of virtue, Kant judges that "women will avoid evil, not because it is unjust but because it is ugly, and for them virtuous actions mean those that are ethically beautiful. Nothing of ought, nothing of must, nothing of obligation" (OBS 2:231).

For Kant to say that there is no "ought" for women when it comes to virtue is just for him to say that women are ruled by inclination rather than by reason, that they apparently are incapable of acting autonomously. And in case that were not obvious from the preceding remarks, Kant makes the following confession in the *Observations*: "It is difficult for me to believe that the fair sex is capable of principles....In place of these, however, providence has implanted goodly and benevolent sentiments in their bosom, a fine feeling for propriety and a complaisant soul" (OBS 2:232). The implications of these remarks for his estimation of the moral agency of women should be immediately apparent in light of what I argued in Part I. First of all, insofar as Kant characterizes dependent rational beings such as ourselves in terms of our experience of moral obligation, the fact that there is "nothing of obligation" for women in his estimation means that he holds women to be less than fully human. Second, and just as importantly, insofar as he claims that women are incapable of principles and are dominated by their sensible feelings and inclinations, they are also incapable of virtue, genuine (male, noble) virtue. You recall that Kant conceives of virtue in terms of the autocracy of practical reason, which involves not just the control, maintenance, and cultivation of our sensible natures but also the principled development of our capacity to will autonomously. Given the preceding understanding of women, Kant would have to conclude that they are incapable of genuine virtue.

It is no surprise, then, to find philosophers critically dismissive of Kant's account of gender and its influence on his understanding of moral agency. For example, Inder S. Marwah (2013, 557) argues that "Kant's account of gender is in the simplest and most banal way entirely androcentric, pervaded by a masculinist bias that both directly and indirectly relegates women to a subordinate moral and political status." Jean P. Rumsey (1997, 131) observes that women, according to Kant, are rational animals and, therefore have a *kind* of reason, but it is "pragmatic, shrewd, and subject to being overridden by the emotions. Lacking a basis in principle, it falls short of the practical reason demanded by the predisposition to morality." Robert Louden (2000, 82) understandably confesses, "it is particularly depressing that someone who believes he is writing in 'the genuine [*eigentliche*] age of criticism, to which everything must submit' says some of the things he says."

On the other hand, some scholars have argued that Kant's remarks should not be read as committing him to the view that women are incapable of full moral agency. For example, Kurt Mosser (1999, 344–345) argues that Kant's *Observations* and *Anthropology* do not accurately reflect Kant's mature, considered view of women because both date from Kant's pre-critical period. Mari Mikkola (2011, 99) has argued that "Kant never explicitly claims in the *Observations* or the *Anthropology* that women are not rational." And she convincingly points out that if Kant believed women to be incapable of autonomous action—and, therefore, without dignity as persons—then it would make no sense that Kant clearly "thinks we are prohibited from treating women in ways that violate such worth and make them mere means to be used for men's ends" (106). Helga Varden (2015, 3) takes Mikkola's argument further and argues that "what Kant was uncertain about was their [women's] ability to partake in public reason" and that Kant "never denies women the right to work themselves into an active condition."[11]

Although I sympathize with Mosser, Mikkola, and Varden in their attempts to defend Kant from certain feminist criticisms, when one takes all of Kant's remarks into account, it is hard not to see some merit in the criticisms scholars such as Marwah, Rumsey, and Louden make. In general, I think it is fair to say that Kant's evaluation of women is sexist, which is why thinkers such as Herman argue that the value of Kant's writings on women is negative, that is, we can learn from Kant how *not* to talk about women. Despite this, I think Mikkola and Varden in particular are right to point out that Kant's sexist characterization of women is inconsistent with central tenets of his normative ethical theory.[12] In light of these considerations, I want to suggest that one way to understand Kant's characterization of women is to read it as a reflection of Kant's recognition that in general women occupy a precarious social position. Granted, he thinks that the social position of women can be traced back to their natures, which is an error he makes in part because of his not having a distinction between sex and gender. Leaving the mistaken causal ascription

---

[11] I examine Varden's argument regarding active citizenship in the next section.
[12] Cf. Varden (2015, 30): "I tend to think that if he could come back from the dead and see what has happened, including how many female philosophers first proved him wrong precisely by furthering his philosophy, he would smile."

aside, Kant's recognition of the inferior social status of women is a significant influence on his sexual ethics and, I maintain, something from which we can learn when trying to discern the ways in which society continues to subjugate and oppress women.

5.1.3 Kant on Gender Relations and the Precarious Status of Women

I think that it is fair to say that Kant's characterization of the traits of women and their relationship with men is largely informed by what he takes to be their natural ends *as* women. In particular, his assertion that nature intends women to preserve the species through pregnancy seems to frame his whole account of women. In this respect, Kant appears to agree with Beauvoir, who also locates the reproductive role of women as the central cause of their oppression, at least historically (Beauvoir 1952). As she expresses the point:

> Man's superior strength must have been of tremendous importance in the age of the club and the wild beast. In any case, however strong the women were, the bondage of reproduction was a terrible handicap in the struggle against a hostile world. Pregnancy, childbirth, and menstruation reduced their capacity for work and made them at times wholly dependent upon the men for protection and food. As there was obviously no birth control…closely spaced [*sic*] maternities must have absorbed most of their strength and their time, so that they were incapable of providing for the children they brought into the world. (62)

Kant tells a similar, if chauvinistically expressed, story when he contrasts the state of marriage in a civil society with what he thinks must be the case regarding the relationship between men and women who are lovers in a state of nature. In the state of nature (i.e., a state outside of a genuine civil society), according to Kant, "superiority is simply on the side of the man" (A 7:303). By "superiority" Kant means brute physical strength. Because men are able to overpower women, Kant claims that a woman in the state of nature "is a domestic animal" (A 7:304). As Kant imagines this scenario, "The man leads the way with weapons in hand and the woman follows him loaded down with his household belongings" (A 7:304). As we will see, his construal of gender relations in the state of nature is one reason why Kant thinks that the institution of marriage is a good institution. This point about the relationship between Kant's understanding of gender relations and his account of marriage connects with the second end Kant identifies for the female sex, namely the cultivation of society. Interestingly, and consistent with my presentation of Kant in Part I, it is our unsocial sociability that motivates the domestic arrangement between women and men and leads, Kant thinks, to the cultivation of society.

Women are able to achieve their second natural end within civil society because the domestic context allows women to rule over men: "Women want to dominate, man to be dominated" (A 7:306).[13] But the sense of "dominate" needs to be

---

[13] Cf. Beauvoir (1952, 61): "I have already stated that when two human categories are together, each aspires to impose its sovereignty upon the other. If both are able to resist this imposition, there

5.1 Kant on the Character of the Sexes

explained, lest we misunderstand Kant's remark to indicate that women are superior to men. Women, according to Kant, naturally want to procreate—it is the first of their natural ends. Men, on his account of things, use their strength in order to make sexual unions possible. So each in their own way and for their own reasons wants to live in community with the other (sociability). But at the same time, at least with respect to men, the same drive that wants to bring them together with women also wants to treat them as mere objects (unsociability). In society, however, men are not allowed simply to take whichever woman they want whenever they want. There are laws and rules of social decorum and courtship. These rules of social decorum and courtship, thinks Kant, are the means women use to domesticate men, to cultivate them and form them into civilized individuals. Men play along—that is, they want to be dominated—because, according to Kant, only by being dominated will they be able successfully to navigate the social norms and rules of decorum that women have regarding courtship and finding a mate. Here men *want* to be dominated in the same sense as I *want* a root canal if I have a tooth abscess. To put the matter bluntly, the only (socially acceptable) way men are going to find someone with whom to have sex is if they successfully navigate the rules of courtship women have developed. But in the process of playing this game, men are "forced" to behave in certain ways and develop certain character traits (e.g., manners and self-control), and these modifications of their behavior and character have a moralizing effect: it makes men into less crude and more sophisticated moral agents (this is similar to the way in professors often offer extra credit to students for attending public lectures in the hopes that these students eventually develop characters that motivate them to attend without such incentives). Men, though, are not the only ones who benefit from this arrangement. "Woman becomes free by marriage; man loses his freedom by it" (A 7:309). As Kant understands domestic relations between the sexes, women benefit by being free of the tyranny of men in the state of nature and, therefore, get to exercise some control, even if it is limited and allegedly motivated by inclination.

Kant thinks that the terms of the marriage contract largely concern the rightful governance of sexual relations between spouses. Consequently, on his view, the domestic partnership of married couples is driven by self-love (insofar as Kant construes sexual appetite as the desire to use another for my own sexual gratification). This helps explain why Kant maintains that "in the *equality* of claims of two people who cannot do without each other, self-love produces nothing but squabbling (A 7:303). In other words, Kant reasons that were the domestic relationship between men and women a relationship of equals, their respective need for each other (which is driven by self-interest) would create a situation that is essentially unsociable. Kant, therefore, concludes that "one [spouse] must be superior to the other in some way, in order to rule over or govern him" (A 7:303). So the physical inequality that characterized gender relations in the state of nature gets transformed into a kind of

---

is created between them a reciprocal relation, sometimes in enmity, sometimes in amity, always in a state of tension. If one of the two is in some way privileged, has some advantage, this one prevails over the other and undertakes to keep it in subjection."

"moral inequality" in the household, to use a phrase of Jean-Jacques Rousseau (1992), which explains Kant's claim that women gain freedom in marriage while men lose it. Actually, the influence of Rousseau is apparent in Kant's characterization of domestic relations and the ways in which women and men complement each other (Tuana 1992, 61–63; Varden 2015, 4).[14] When it comes to what Kant calls the "progress of culture," he says that men are superior to women with respect to "physical power and courage," while women are superior to men with respect to their "natural talent for mastering his desire for her" (A 7:303; Cf. Rousseau 1979, especially Book V). So, men still tend to exert their superiority through brute force, but culture provides women an opportunity to exert their wills within the context of the domestic relationship. In the household, "the woman should *dominate* and the man should *govern*, for inclination dominates, and understanding governs" (A 7:309).[15]

Specifically, women "dominate" through what Kant calls "feminine ways." These feminine ways, according to him, are "weaknesses," but reasonable people are able to see that these feminine ways are the means women use "for governing men and using them for their own purposes" (A 7:303–304). Kant then illustrates what he means by "feminine ways" by giving a side-by-side comparison of what he takes to be typical masculine and feminine traits: men are easy to study, since men are forthright; women do not betray their own secrets, though they cannot keep the secrets of others because they are so gossipy. Men love domestic peace and will do whatever a woman wants in order to get it; women do not shy away from "domestic warfare" which is something a woman wages "with her tongue," with what Kant describes as a woman's "loquacity and eloquence full of affect, which disarms the man" (A 7:304). Men rely on the right of the stronger at home, which is a right they have as protectors of the household; women rely on the right of the weaker, which is a right they have to be protected by men, and a woman exercises this right by disarming her man "by tears of exasperation while reproaching him with his lack of generosity" (A 7:304). "The husband's behavior must show that to him the welfare of his wife is closest to his heart. But since the man must know best how he stands and how far he can go, he will be like a minister to his monarch who is mindful only of enjoyment" (A 7:309–310).

Even though Kant agrees with Pope's estimation that women can be characterized by the inclination to dominate, he corrects Pope by saying that the inclination to dominate "is not suitable for characterizing a class of human beings in general in their conduct toward others. For inclination toward what is advantageous to us is common to all human beings, and so too is the inclination to dominate, so far as this is possible for us; therefore it does not *characterize* a class" (A 7:305). This tendency to dominate, according to Kant, just is the way our unsocial sociability expresses itself within the context of the domestic relationship of a married couple.

---

[14] Cf. Rousseau (1992, 39): "Now it is easy to see that the moral aspect of love is an artificial sentiment born of social custom, and extolled by women with so much skill and care in order to establish their hegemony and make dominant the sex that ought to obey."

[15] Jane Kneller (2006, 468) takes this remark to be a "desperate attempt to paper over" the authoritarian assumptions motivating Kant's understanding of domestic relations.

5.1 Kant on the Character of the Sexes

If this tendency is indulged in a vicious way, it turns into the passion for dominance, which Kant judges as "intrinsically unjust." Interestingly, Kant explicitly states that the kinds of "charms" that women allegedly use to exert power over their husbands are *not* what he means by "dominance" with respect to a passion for dominance. Rather, by the passion for dominance he means domination through "the advantage of *strength*" (A 7:273). It is not that women are incapable of developing an inclination to dominate, according to Kant; it is just that they use different means. This distinction between the respective means men and women use to exert their wills in a household points to another way in which, when it comes to romantic and sexual relationships, Kant thinks the situation of women is precarious: women cannot be full (i.e., active) citizens and, therefore, are in need of financial support and legal protection.

Citizens, according to Kant, are "the members of such a society who are united for giving law" (MM 6:314). To be a citizen is to enjoy three essential rights:

> lawful *freedom*, the attribute of obeying no other law than that to which he has given his consent; civil *equality*, that of not recognizing among the people any superior with the moral capacity to bind him as a matter of right in a way that he could not in turn bind the other; and third, the attribute of civil *independence*, of owning his own existence and preservation to his own rights and powers as a member of the commonwealth, not to the choice of another among the people. (MM 6:314)

Insofar as all women (and all children) do not possess financial independence and, so, "have to be under the direction or protection of other individuals" (MM 6:315), they are merely "passive citizens."[16] This means, then, that women are at the mercy of men for their livelihood: first their fathers but then their husbands. And given what Kant takes to be the natural inferiority of women with respect to men's superior physical strength, on his account of things, the condition of women is doubly bad. Not only are they unable to provide for themselves, but they also are physically at the mercy of the men in their lives. Hence, we find Kant observing that "even in marriage [a woman] will be generally seeking to please" (A 7:310). And should she ever find herself divorced or widowed, a woman is in serious danger unless she can secure another husband. No wonder Kant claims that no man would want to be a woman.

Given Kant's account of the inability of women in his day to be active citizens,[17] I would like to suggest that Kant's remarks about the domestic relationship between

---

[16] Although passive citizens are dependent on the wills of others, Kant thinks that "this inequality is, however, in no way opposed to their freedom and equality *as human beings*, who together make up a people" (MM 6:315).

[17] Varden (2015, 3) argues that Kant believed women to be capable working their way into "an active condition," thereby being capable of active citizenship, at least in principle. Her argument turns on her reading of MM 6:315, where Kant claims that a state's laws must "not be contrary to the natural laws of freedom and of the equality of everyone in the people corresponding to this freedom, namely that anyone can work his way up from this passive condition to an active one." Varden (2015, 26; 40, note 30) translates the relevant portion of the text as "anyone can work one's way up," since Kant uses the gender-neutral word *Volk* for "people." Although her translation is defensible, I do not think that it warrants her conclusion that Kant believed women to be capable

women and men be understood in terms of the precarious situation of women. His chauvinism and sexism notwithstanding, one way to interpret Kant's depiction of what he takes to be typical female behavior within marital relationships is that it grows out of a felt insecurity about her own well-being and is tied to an anxiety about the need always to be thinking about ways to guarantee her own welfare. Moreover, insofar as women on Kant's account are financial dependents and barred from active citizenship, there is a seriously restricted range of ways in which a woman can assert what little agency and independence she has.

A number of his remarks seem to suggest this reading of Kant's account of the domestic relationship between women and men. For example, in his account of the character of the sexes he has this odd and interesting interlude about gallantry, that is, the practice of a woman openly having lovers other than her husband (A 7:304–305). Kant condemns this practice as a vice of a luxurious culture/society, but he also says that when women extend favors toward men who are potential lovers, they engage in a justified practice (despite the practice being in ill-repute), since a woman is always in danger of becoming a widow and, so, she always needs to be on the lookout for suitors who might step in to take the place of her husband should he divorce her or be killed.[18] One might give a similar interpretation to the following remark: "In marriage the man woos only his *own* wife, but the woman has an inclination for *all* men; out of jealousy she *dresses up* only for the eyes of her own sex, in order to outdo other women in charm or fashionableness" (7:307). Although it is tempting to dismiss this passage as Kant merely painting women as catty and superficial, one way to read it is as a reflection of his awareness that, given their lack of financial independence, all women are potential competition for each other with respect to finding a husband—this holds true even for married women.

In claiming that some of Kant's representation of female traits can be understood as an acknowledgment of their precarious position in relation to men, I do not mean to excuse those remarks or to justify them as an accurate picture of how women behave. Rather, I am trying to draw attention to the fact that Kant' account of the allegedly typical traits of wives regarding their husbands is in some way reflective of his awareness that women are by and large at the mercy of men—or at least they were during his time. In this way, Kant's account of the typical traits of women can be instructive because it reflects the "art" [*Kunst*] that he believes nature has instilled in women. That is to say, however offensive we may find his ascription of these traits to women, however inaccurately they depict women, and however misguided Kant's belief that they are caused by nature rather than socialization, it is important that we recognize that Kant understood these traits to be nature's way of preparing women to pursue their natural ends in the face of obstacles, and the single greatest

---

of active citizenship. Immediately prior to the passage in question (MM 6:314–315), Kant gives several examples of passive citizens, all of whom are males who make their respective living by working for another: a woodcutter, a blacksmith in India, a carpenter or a blacksmith in Europe, a private tutor, and a tenant farmer. So, it stands to reason that the "anyone" to whom Kant refers means "anyone of these men who are passive citizens."

[18] Cf. Beauvoir (1952, Volume II, Chapter 12) for a similar point of view.

obstacle to women is men. This means that however gendered Kant's account is, it is also an implicit indictment of men, the alleged natures of men, and the way in which men treat women. Insofar as his account of gender relations implies that men systematically oppress women, Kant seems to me to be right, even if he is wrong to attribute the causes of such oppression to our natures. With this kind of reasoning in mind, Allen Wood (2008, 228) suggests that

> in applying the concept of unsocial sociability to sex, Kant especially emphasizes the fact, which he appears to regard as an irremediable feature of human life, that men systematically stand in a decisively superior relation of power—physical, social, economic—over women. This is for him the chief determinant of the fact (as he sees it) that sexual desire is degrading to our humanity and its satisfaction a threat to human rights and dignity.

I think Wood's estimation here is on target. In order to elaborate on it, I turn now to Kant's account of sexual appetite.

5.2 Kant's Account of Bodily Discipline and the Sexual Impulse

Kant's most extended treatment of sex appears in the lecture notes we have from his ethics courses. As I anticipated earlier in this chapter, quite a bit of Kant's writings on the subject will strike many contemporary readers as Draconian. For example, Kant believed that "the sexual impulse is not an inclination that one human has for another, *qua* human, but an inclination for their sex," and "it is therefore a *principium* of the debasement of humanity" (CL 27:385). And he believed that when people engage in same-sex sexual activity they degrade themselves "below the beasts" and "dishonor humanity" (CL 27:391), so much so that he deemed same-sex sexual activity more contemptible than suicide (VL 27:642). In light of pronouncements such as these, Eric Schwitzgebel (2010; Cf. Scruton 1986) has drawn two conclusions regarding Kant's writings on sex: (1) what Kant says about these topics is gobbeldy-gook, and (2) "Kant's moral reasoning appears mainly to have confirmed his prejudices and the ideas inherited from his culture." Although Schwitzgebel's evaluation of Kant gives voice to a certain indignation that many feel when first reading Kant's remarks about sex and sexual ethics, he is too quick to dismiss Kant's thinking on these subjects as merely the product of Kant's prejudices. If one approaches this material charitably, with Kant's philosophical anthropology, his normative ethics, and his historical context in mind, there is quite a bit of value in what he says, even in those texts one may find offensive. To start, remarks such as the ones Schwitzgebel finds offensive should be understood within the context of Kant's views regarding the duties we have to ourselves as bodily beings, duties that he discusses under the heading of "bodily discipline."

5.2.1 Self-Perfection and Bodily Discipline

As I explained in Chap. 4, Kant identifies two wide/imperfect duties of virtue: one's self-perfection and the promotion of the happiness of others. When Kant elucidates what one's self-perfection involves, he further distinguishes between perfect duties one has to oneself and imperfect duties one has towards oneself. Our perfect duties to ourselves involve avoiding those acts that violate our dignity *as* animal beings and *as* moral beings (I will discuss the former in Sect. 5.3 below with respect to Kant's discussion of lust). Our imperfect duties to ourselves concern the positive ways in which we pursue our natural and moral perfection (i.e., the ways in which we positively pursue cultivating those talents and dispositions we have in virtue of our humanity and personality, respectively). With respect to our natural perfection, Kant maintains that each person "owes it to himself (as a rational being) not to leave idle and, as it were, rusting away the natural predispositions and capacities that his reason can someday use" (MM 6: 444). Among those natural predispositions and capacities that Kant discusses, he identifies certain powers of the body. Cultivating the powers of the body "is looking after the *basic stuff* (the matter) in a human being, without which he could not realize his ends" (MM 6:445). In other words, cultivation of the powers of the body involves promoting our physical health and well-being, what Kant describes as "the continuing and purposive invigoration of the animal" in each of us (MM 6:445).

In the "Doctrine of Virtue" he cites gymnastics as the way to accomplish this cultivation of bodily powers. But in the Collins Lecture Notes, Kant has a more extensive treatment of our wide duties towards ourselves with respect to our bodies.[19] If the discussion of the "Doctrine of Virtue" focuses on one element of autocracy with respect to our bodies, namely, the cultivation of bodily strength and vigor, the discussion in the Collins Lectures focuses on the other, equally necessary, component of bodily autocracy, namely the disciplining of our bodies in order to control those appetites, inclinations, and feelings that are unruly (or potentially unruly) (Chap. 4, Sect. 4.3). Kant begins his discussion in the Collins Lecture notes of our duties regarding our bodies by observing that "the body is entrusted to us, and our duty in regard to it is that the human mind should first of all discipline the body, and then take care of it" (CL 27:378). Kant goes on to discuss what he means by "discipline," which he defines in terms of autocracy. He says that discipline is necessary because in the body "there are *principia* by which the mind is affected, and through which the body alters the state of the mind" (CL 27:378). We must, therefore, "guide [the body] according to moral and pragmatic *principia* and maxims." According to Kant, autocracy with regard to our bodies concerns the power the mind (or, more strictly speaking, the person[20]) has for disciplining the body in such a way that the

---

[19] To adapt Mika Mikkola's phrase from earlier, I think there are sufficient similarities between the positions Kant defends in the Collins Lecture Notes and the positions he defends in his *Metaphysics of Morals* to take the notes as consistent with Kant's considered view.

[20] Cf. MM 6:419: "The subject that is bound, as well as the subject that binds, is always the *human being only*; and though we may, in a theoretical respect, distinguish soul and body from each other,

5.2 Kant's Account of Bodily Discipline and the Sexual Impulse

body does not have undue influence over our minds. In this respect, Kant's reasons for promoting autocracy of the body is similar to his reasons for saying that we have an indirect duty to promote our own respective happiness: it is a way of avoiding unnecessary temptations to acting heteronomously.

Bodily discipline, according to Kant, consists in two broad duties: "moderation in its diversions, and sufficiency in regards to its genuine needs" (CL 27: 380). Regarding the latter, he conceives of bodily sufficiency in terms of promoting the body's "vigour, activity, strength, and courage" (CL 27:380). Regarding the former, Kant describes the duty of bodily moderation as "a merely negative kind; the mind has only to prevent the body from being able to necessitate it to anything" (CL 27:378). This discipline should not be understood as total domination or control, in the sense of negating the influence of the body (Chap. 4, Sect. 4.2). As Kant goes on to say, it is impossible to prevent the body from influencing the mind, and, more importantly, "much depends on the body, in regard to our faculties of knowledge, desire and aversion, and appetite" (CL 27:378–379). Therefore, autocracy of the body, understood as the discipline of the mind over the body, has the primary function of preventing the development of unruly inclinations that can impair our rational capacities, broadly understood. "If the mind has no proper control over the body, the habits that we allow to the body become necessities, and if the mind does not repress bodily inclination, the result is the predominance of the body over the mind" (CL 27:379).

Bodily discipline, thinks Kant, is perfected by living "in accordance with our vocation," which is "to produce a will that is good" (G 4:396). So, the body "must certainly be subjected to discipline, but it must not be destroyed by men, nor must its forces be impaired" (CL 27:379).[21] I have already discussed this line of thought in Kant's practical philosophy, specifically, with respect to the full and correct sense in which the autocracy of practical reason, according to Kant, involves the containment of certain sensible inclinations and feelings (Chap. 4, Sect. 4.3). Kant's thinking seems to be that were one to allow the body free reign, as it were, in pursuing the objects of sensual pleasure that we desire, these desires would very quickly turn into inclinations (i.e., habitual sensual desires), which would subsequently threaten our ability to reason well about what is good, at least insofar as any such practical deliberations would be impaired by the constant intrusions of the inclinations. Here it would be helpful to think of the way in which a smoker's inclination can impair her ability to concentrate and focus on the task at hand. As Kant puts it, it is essential

---

as natural characteristics of a human being, we may not think of them as different substances putting him under obligation, so as to justify a division of duties to the *body* and duties to the *soul*."

[21] Cf. CL 27:379: "Many visionary moralists think, by weakening and removing all the body's sensuality, to renounce everything that its sensuous enjoyment promotes, so that thereby the animal nature of the body would be suppressed, and the spiritual life, which they hope one day to attain, might already be anticipated here, and the body approached ever nearer it by a gradual divestment of all sensuality. Such practices may be called mortification of the flesh, though that term was unknown to the pagan world….But all such practices, which include, for example, fasting and chastisements, are fanatical and monkish virtues, which merely emaciate the body."

to virtue that we discipline the human body, and achieve autocracy with respect to our bodily desires, so that we

> let none of the body's enjoyments become entrenched, but endeavor so to train it, that it is capable of doing without everything except necessities, of putting up with a poor diet, and of bearing up cheerfully under all exertions and mishaps. Man feels his life the more, the less need he has to sustain his vital forces. (CL 27:379)

There is no question that Kant's understanding of bodily discipline is gendered. His preference for describing this discipline in terms of "toughening" the body, or "strengthening" it against sensual impulses no doubt carries with it a typically male understanding of the body as lower and unruly, in need of control, with the mind or reason being higher and in need of controlling. But in light of my reading of Kant's account of virtue as self-mastery, and insofar as Kant identifies our animality as good, rejects mortifications of the flesh, and encourages us to cultivate certain bodily powers, I think one can express the need for bodily discipline in ways that avoid being so gendered.

Relatedly, when reading about Kant's injunctions to toughen up and strengthen ourselves to face difficult times (e.g., a poor diet), we ought to remember that he wrote as a person of ill health who was living in eighteenth-century Prussia (Kuehn 2002, 153). For people living in the United States in 2017 with the leisure to read a philosophy book on Kant's ethics and the contemporary same-sex marriage debate, such precautions may seem overwrought, but that is because we occupy a fairly comfortable position. Kant and his contemporaries did not, for example, have indoor plumbing, or heating and air conditioning, or supermarkets that make all manner of produce and meats available year round; they did not have antibiotics and over-the-counter analgesics for purchase at the local 24-hour pharmacy; nor did they enjoy the kind of sanitation we do. So, the kinds of issues that many of us do not think about (because we do not have to) occupied a central place of concern for Kant and his contemporaries. Keeping such material concerns in mind can help us better understand Kant's preoccupation with bodily discipline. This discipline is perhaps most necessary when it comes to the most powerful of sensible pleasures, namely those connected with our sexual appetite.

5.2.2 Kant on Sexual Appetite

The discussion of sex in the Collins Lecture Notes begins as follows: "Man has an impulse directed to others, not so that he may enjoy their works and circumstances, but immediately to others as objects of his enjoyment" (CL 27:384). Kant calls this inclination to enjoy another the "sexual appetite" or "the sexual impulse." He thinks of sexual impulse as a *sui generis* inclination, since it alone makes another human being the object of enjoyment. "Man can certainly enjoy the other as an instrument for his service; he can utilize the other's hands or feet to serve him, though by the

5.2 Kant's Account of Bodily Discipline and the Sexual Impulse

latter's free choice. But we never find that a human being can be the object of another's enjoyment, save through sexual impulse" (CL 27:384).

According to Kant, when we consider the sexual impulse in and of itself, "there lies in this inclination a degradation of man; for as soon as anyone becomes an object of another's appetite, all motives of moral relationship fall away; as object of the other's appetite, that person is in fact a thing, whereby the other's appetite is sated, and can be misused as such a thing by anybody" (CL 27:384–385). As far as Kant is concerned, "there is no case where a human being would already be determined by nature to be the object of another's enjoyment, save this, of which sexual inclination is the basis" (CL 27:385). In other words, it seems as though Kant believes that the natural, physical constitution of human sexual desire is such that mere sexual appetite involves offering oneself up to one's sexual partner as a mere thing for her or his enjoyment. The tendency to objectify people, according to Kant, is what sets sexual appetite apart from all other inclinations. "Since the sexual impulse is not an inclination that one human has for another, *qua* human, but an inclination for their sex, it is therefore a *principium* of the debasement of humanity, a source for the preference of one sex over the other, and the dishonouring of that sex by satisfying the inclination" (CL 27:385).

If we consider Kant's account of the sexual impulse in general, engaging in sexual activity motivated by mere sexual impulse can be immoral in at least two basic ways. On the one hand, the sexual impulse motivates me to objectify myself and, thereby, to fail to respect the humanity in my own person. Kant claims that any man or woman caught up in the sexual impulse "will endeavor to lend attraction, not to their humanity, but to their sex, and to direct all actions and desires entirely towards it" (CL 27:385). Moreover, according to Kant, we tend to feel shameful about sex, and this is because "in presenting ourselves to the other as an object of enjoyment we feel that we are demeaning humanity in our own person and making ourselves similar to the beasts" (VL 27:638). In other words, by giving oneself over to another as a mere object of enjoyment, one thereby fails to respect the humanity in one's own person.

On the other hand, sexual impulse makes the object of desire out to be a thing rather than a being capable of practical reasoning and agency and, so, involves one ignoring the humanity of the object of one's sexual desire. "Each partner dishonours the humanity of the other. Thus humanity becomes an instrument for satisfying desires and inclinations; but by this it is dishonoured and put on par with animal nature. So the sexual impulse puts humanity in peril of being equated with animality" (CL 27:385). In Kant's own words, "those who merely have sexual inclination love the person from none of the…motives of true human affection, are quite unconcerned for their happiness, and will even plunge them into the greatest unhappiness simply to satisfy their own appetite" (CL 27:384). To drive his point home, Kant claims that as soon as the object of desire is possessed and the sexual appetite sated by "consuming" the object of desire she is "thrown away, as one throws away a lemon after sucking the juice from it" (CL 27:384). By desiring the sexual organs of another for one's enjoyment, one thereby reduces the other person to a mere object, a mere means for one's end. And this constitutes a violation of Kant's basic moral principle, namely, that one should always act in such a way so that one "use humanity, whether in your own person or in the person of any other, always at the same time as an end, never merely as a means" (G 4:429).

Given this analysis of sexual appetite, the trick for Kant is going to be explaining how engaging in sexual intercourse can be good:

> Since man, after all, possesses this impulse by nature, the question arises: To what extent is anyone entitled to make use of their sexual impulse, without impairing their humanity? How far can a person allow another person of the opposite sex to satisfy his or her inclination upon them? Can people sell or hire themselves out, or by any kind of contract allow use to be made of their *facultates sexuales*? (CL 27:385–386)

He goes on to say that philosophers tend to censure sexual impulse because of the consequences that result from indulging our sexual appetites, but they do not criticize the act as such. Kant sees a problem with this, namely, that "anyone who could simply obviate these ill-effects might make use of his impulse in any way conceivable" (27:386). In other words, what Kant finds morally objectionable about sex concerns more than just harmful consequences of indulging in the act. There seems to be something about sexual intercourse itself that is the source of his condemnation.[22] So, it will be helpful to look more closely at Kant's reasons for thinking that "there is something contemptible in the [sexual] act itself, which runs counter to morality" (27:386), which is why I now turn to Kant's discussion of sexual vices, which will help us to see that Kant's condemnation of at least some sexual activity is more nuanced and context-dependent than may appear at first glance.

5.3 Kant on Lust and the *Crimina Carnis*

The only sustained discussion of sex in the "Doctrine of Virtue" is Kant's discussion of our perfect duty to ourselves with respect to lust. This duty, according to Kant, is one we have toward ourselves in virtue of our being animal beings (i.e., in virtue of our possessing animality) rather than in virtue of our being moral beings. He begins his discussion by noting that we can understand a natural end—what he also calls "an end of nature"—as a "connection of a cause with an effect in which, although

---

[22] Cf. Christine Korsgaard (1996, 94): "It is important to understand that what bothers him is *not* that one is using another person as a means to one's own pleasure. That would be an incorrect view of sexual relations, and, in any case any difficulty about it, would, by Kant's own theory, be alleviated by the other's simple act of free consent." I think, however, that Korsgaard misreads Kant here. First of all, I do not think that there is relevant difference between treating someone merely as a means and treating a person as an object. Second, Kant explicitly condemns violations of one's own dignity regardless of consent. See, for example, Kant's criticisms of the practice of selling one's own tooth or castrating oneself in order to be a better singer (MM 6:423). In such cases the person clearly consents to these acts, and yet Kant condemns them as immoral. Consent alone, on Kant's view, does not mitigate concerns about using oneself or another merely as a means. I will return to this idea in Chap. 7 when I develop a view of right sexual relations informed by Kant's thinking.

no understanding is ascribed to the cause, it is still thought by analogy with an intelligent cause, and so as if it produced human beings on purpose" (MM 6:424). The natural end of sexual appetite is the preservation of the species. When it comes to the vice of lust, the question for Kant is whether we are free to determine the use of our respective sexual capacities in the pursuit of "mere animal pleasure" as we see fit or "whether the human being is subject to a duty to himself with regard to this enjoyment, violation of which is a *defiling* (not merely a debasing) of the humanity in his own person" (MM 6:424).

Kant identifies lust as the impetus toward sexual pleasure. "Lewdness" is the vice associated with this pleasure, while "chastity" is the virtue. "Unnatural lust," according to Kant, is sexual impulse or appetite that is directed to a fantasy object rather than a real one (MM 6:424). In case it is not clear, in discussing unnatural lust, Kant is talking about masturbation, which he is reluctant to name outright because "it is considered indecent even to call this vice by its proper name" (MM 6:425). Kant thinks masturbation is unnatural because the fantasizing brings about a desire that is contrapurposive to nature's end, namely, procreation (MM 6:425), which is an end that is "more important than that of love of life itself, since it aims at the preservation of the whole species and not only of the individual" (MM 6:425).[23] On Kant's view, someone who masturbates ignores nature's end and instead just wants to satisfy his (and Kant was concerned here with men) sexual appetite.

Kant presumes that "everyone immediately" sees that masturbation is a violation of a duty to oneself. He goes so far as to say that masturbation is more shameful than suicide, since it "debases [humans] beneath the beasts." According to Kant, there is a sense in which suicide requires a certain degree of courage, and he thinks that "in this disposition there is still always room for respect for the humanity in one's own person" (MM 6:425). But when we masturbate we do not merely make ourselves objects; we do so in a way that is contrary to nature, since he believes, even non-human animals do not engage in such conduct. So, the moral offense here seems to be twofold. On the one hand, when one engages in sex merely in order to gratify oneself in light of a sexual fantasy, according to Kant, "the human being surrenders his personality (throwing it away), since he uses himself merely as a means to satisfy an animal impulse" (MM 6:425). This would be a violation of the moral law, which requires us to respect the humanity in our own person by never treating it as a mere means, as a mere tool for achieving some purpose (G 4:429). On the other hand, to use one's sexual organs merely to satisfy one's unnatural lust involves an even worse transgression of our own dignity, since giving in to such appetite reduces us, beings capable of autocracy and acting autonomously, to beings beneath nonhuman animals. In reducing us thusly, unnatural lust is especially damning of our dignity as persons, which is why he points out that such unnatural lust is always shameful (MM 6:425; VL 27:638).

As Joshua Schulz (2007) has observed, the conclusions Kant draws about sex are no doubt due to the definition of sexual appetite with which he starts (Cf. Alan Soble

---

[23] Vincent Cooke (1991) was one of the first commentators to draw attention to the role of teleology in Kant's arguments about practical sexual ethics.

2001). And Lara Denis (1999, 235–237) has raised serious concerns about the way in which Kant invokes nature's end in his arguments regarding unnatural lust, since (1) Kant does not think that the ends of nature are obligatory for us, (2) we can act immorally in promoting the ends of nature, (3) merely designating an act unnatural does not, on Kant's normative ethics, tell us if it is bad or why it is bad, and (4) there are other natural ends deriving from our animality besides the narrow one of preserving the species.

Criticisms such as Denis' notwithstanding, I think there are additional reasons for being suspicious about Kant's moral condemnation of masturbation, reasons that can be found in Kant's own writings on sex. First of all, Kant acknowledges that "it is not so easy to produce a rational proof that unnatural, and even merely unpurposive, use of one's sexual attribute is inadmissible as being a violation of duty to oneself" (MM 6:425). Second of all, even though Kant asserts that "one may not, at least, act contrary to that end [procreation]" (MM 6:426) when it comes to sexual activity between men and women, it is not at all clear what he means by "acting contrary to the end of procreation." More to the point, Kant actually suggests that it is morally permissible for a husband to have sex with his wife even if she is pregnant or sterile (MM 6:426). But if a woman is pregnant or sterile, then a man cannot impregnate her, and, so, they cannot (one would think) act consistently with nature's end for sexual activity. In such circumstances, whatever their reasons for having sex, a wife and husband cannot have sex in order to pursue nature's end, and yet Kant thinks that sex in these circumstances can be morally permissible. Third, in the Vigilantius lecture notes, Kant argues that having sex merely for the purpose of procreation is immoral:

> For though nature, in implanting the sexual impulse in man, has assuredly had this end in view, it does not follow from that, that man is also required to direct his attention solely to this purpose. For to pursue it exclusively can occur no otherwise than by attending not at all to the worth of our humanity; the impulse would be satisfied just like the appetite in eating; this makes it a natural urge on par with every other inclination that nature has ordained in the bodily mechanism. (VL 27:639)

The implication of this line of reasoning is that one needs to do more than merely act in accordance with the end of nature in order to act well regarding our sexual activity, and that means, according to Kant, that acting consistently with nature's end is not a sufficient condition for morally good sex.

So, Kant's reasoning about masturbation as a species of unnatural lust, at least in the "Doctrine of Virtue," leaves us with a conflicting account of morally good sexual activity. On the one hand, Kant explicitly condemns masturbation on the grounds that it is unnatural, i.e., that it runs counter to nature's end of procreation. On the other hand, he also argues in ways that indicate that the moral transgression in masturbation has less to do with it's being contrary to nature's end and more to do with the way in which engaging in so-called unnatural sex acts precludes self-respect. In order to see whether there is more determinate evidence in Kant's writings regarding the grounds on which masturbation in particular and sex more generally can be immoral, I want to look more closely at his discussion of sexual vice, which he distinguishes into *crimina carnis secundum naturam* and *crimina carnis contra naturam.*

5.3.1 Crimina Carnis Secundum Naturam

Kant defines a *crimen carnis* as "the misuse of the sexual impulse." According to Kant, *crimina carnis,* which can be rendered into English as "carnal crimes," are misuses of the sexual impulses insofar as they are contrary to duties to oneself, and they are contrary to our duties to ourselves, according to Kant, because they "run counter to the ends of humanity" CL (27:390). The reference here to duties to ourselves is a reference to the line of thinking that motivates Kant's discussion of lust in the "Doctrine of Virtue." Within that context, I raised the question of whether we should understand Kant's reasoning about the unnatural lust motivating people to masturbate primarily in terms of violations of nature's ends or whether we should understand it in terms of a violation of our dignity as persons. Kant's framing of *crimina carnis* as violations of the ends of humanity indicates that while his reasoning about sexual matters relies on a certain understanding of nature and of ourselves as natural, animal beings, his reasoning primarily concerns our status as finite rational beings who possess dignity.

Why does Kant's framing of the morality or immorality of sex acts in terms of "the ends of humanity" indicate that his reasoning primarily relies on his account of us as beings possessing dignity (rather than on the ends nature sets for us)? Humanity, as Denis (1999, 226) describes it, "here refers to rational nature as a whole, which includes not only the capacity to set and organize ends ('humanity' strictly construed), but also the capacity to determine one's will from respect for the moral law (sometimes called 'personality')." Denis' explanation of the sense of "humanity" operative in Kant's practical sexual ethics actually underscores a point I argued in my discussion of the three elements of our predisposition to good in Chap. 3 (Sect. 3.1.2). In distinguishing the three elements of the predisposition to good (animality, humanity, personality), I stressed that we should not understand these distinctions as committing Kant to a dualistic understanding of human beings, since these distinctions are meant to pick out aspects of the whole person, the whole human being. My reading of the elements of our predisposition to goodness is confirmed by Kant's account of the ends of humanity as they function in his account of our perfect duty to ourselves *qua* animal beings. Kant identifies three ends connected with our animality: "a) his self-preservation, b) the preservation of the species, and c) the preservation of the subject's capacity to use his powers purposefully and to enjoy life" (MM 6:420). Even though these are ends Kant ascribes to us in virtue of our animality, he does not conceive of animality as divorced from humanity, as the language of using our "powers purposively" indicated. Denis (1999, 228) explains Kant's thinking in this portion of the "Doctrine of Virtue" in the following way: "When she [the agent] thinks of herself as a moral being with an animal nature, she will recognize other maxims that threaten the free, moral, and effective use of her humanity." In other words, the perfect duties concerning our animal natures, such as the duties regarding our sexual behavior, are duties we should understand in light of our being *human* animals. Denis again explains why this is the most cogent way to understand ends of humanity as, in this context, tied to our animality: "our animal nature is an integral part of our nature as human beings....because we cannot exist apart from our bodies and because we depend on them for carrying out all our plans, how we treat our bodies reflects how we value our rational nature" (1999, 228–229; Cf. Denis 2007, 43–44).

With this understanding of Kant's reasoning about sex in mind, I can now turn back to Kant's treatment of *crimina* carnis. Kant divides *crimina carnis* into those that are *secundum naturam* and those that are *contra naturam*. *Crimina carnis secundum naturam* are "carnal crimes that accord with nature," whereas *crimina carnis contra naturam* are "carnal crimes that are contrary to nature." The former, according to Kant, are sexual acts that are contrary to sound reason, whereas the latter are sexual acts that are contrary to our animal nature. Kant's explanation of the difference between the two kinds of *crimina carnis* helps to understand the kind of arguments he uses to establish his conclusions concerning these different sex acts. On the one hand, to say that *crimina carnis secundum naturam* run counter to sound reason means that these sexual acts are immoral because they are inconsistent with correct reasoning about our sexual good. Another way to phrase this is to say that *crimina carnis secundum naturam* involve violations of our dignity *qua* rational beings. It is important to note that each of the cases of *crimina carnis secundum naturam* that Kant discusses are species of sex acts where the two people engaged are of different sexes, one male and one female. Kant identifies four such species of *crimina carnis secundum naturam*: incest, adultery, prostitution, and concubinism.

Incest Kant's discussion of lust in the "Doctrine of Virtue" left unresolved the question of whether unnatural lust is immoral because of the way in which it purportedly violated the end of nature regarding sex (i.e., procreation) or whether it is immoral because sexual activity motivated by unnatural lust violates our dignity as rational beings. Kant's discussion of the wrongness of incest provides an interesting case study of his reasoning concerning practical sexual ethics, reasoning that is consistent throughout his lectures and ethics and, therefore, can help illuminate the discussion in the "Doctrine of Virtue." In the Collins Lecture Notes he asks whether there are moral grounds (as opposed merely to a natural ground) that "tell against *incestus*" in all forms of sexual activity. With respect to incestuous relations between siblings, Kant says that the badness of such relations is merely conditional, that is, it depends on the circumstances. He thinks that there is no incest in the state of nature, since "the first men must have married among their sisters" (CL 27:389). In other words, there is nothing about incest that runs counter to our animal natures, even though Kant thinks that nature "implanted a natural resistance to it" (CL 27:389).

Incest is forbidden in civil society, however, and Kant claims that in society incest counts as *crimina carnis contra naturam,* but he does not explain how this is the case (Cl 27:391). That is, Kant does not explain how it is possible that outside of civil society, sexual relations between siblings is morally permissible but within civil society it becomes a perversion, something that runs counter to our animal natures. Whatever his reasoning might be, one thing is clear: moral condemnation of at least some sexual activity is context-dependent. The theme of the context-dependency of the moral goodness or badness of sexual activity is, I shall argue, a recurring, central theme in Kant's practical sexual ethics.

The one unconditional case of the immorality of incest (i.e., the one kind of incest that is immoral both in civil society and in the state of nature) is incestuous relations between parents and children. Kant's reasoning here is revealing. Parent-child incestuous relations are morally prohibited because "in regard to these two [a parent and a child] a respect is necessary that also has to endure throughout life; but this respect rules out equality" (CL 27:389). According to Kant, a healthy parent-child relationship is one where the child respects her or his parent, and the nature of this respect—as opposed to the basic recognition respect that we are each owed as a function of our dignity (Darwall 1977)—is one where the child ought to remain a subordinate to the parent. This rules out morally permissible incest between them because the inequality that characterizes the respect appropriate to the parent-child relationship would only exacerbate the inequality that is possible between an individual and the object of her or his sexual desire, since such desire, according to Kant, already inclines us to treat the objects of our sexual desire as mere things (and, so, treat them as not equal to us). This is why Kant claims that between a parent and child "there is no true intercourse" (CL 27: 390). But even in this case, Kant's reasoning concerns the way in which an incestuous relationship between a parent and child precludes equality and, so, precludes respecting the dignity of the child, which is a different kind of argument than one that relies on the ends of nature setting normative parameters on what we may and may not do.

Adultery Kant rather quickly dismisses adultery as a genuine case of *crimina carnis secundum naturam,* and once again his reasoning here does not rely on the ends of nature but on considerations concerning our status as beings who possess dignity. He defines adultery as the breaking of the marriage vow by engaging in intercourse with someone who is not your spouse, and he explains that the wrongness of this act has to do with the violation of the vow: "Just as betrothal is the greatest of pledges between two persons, lasting for life, and is therefore the most inviolable, so, of all betrayals and breaches of faith, *adulterium* is the greatest, since there is no promise more important than this" (CL 27:390). Hence, concludes Kant, adultery provides a legitimate ground for divorce.

Prostitution and Concubinage Kant asserts that prostitution and concubinism are species of *vaga libido* (indiscriminate lust). He condemns prostitution as immoral, which he says can be engaged in by both sexes. According to Kant, "nothing is more vile than to take money for yielding to another so that his inclination may be satisfied and to let one's own person out for hire" (27:387). Once again, we see Kant's reasoning focus on the question of whether a sexual practice is consistent with our own dignity as persons, and in the case of prostitution his conclusion is that it is not, since a person who engages in prostitution sells his or her body out merely as an instrument: "one cannot make one's person a thing, though this is what happens in *vaga libido*" (CL 27:387).

Concubinage is a different form of *vaga libido*, according to Kant. Whereas prostitution involves the selling of one's own body to another in order for the other to satisfy his sexual impulse, concubinage is the condition under which "the persons mutually satisfy their desires, and have no thought of monetary gain, the one merely serving to gratify the inclination of the other" (CL 27:387). At first, according to Kant, concubinage appears to be a promising candidate for a morally permissible sexual relationship, since the concubine surrenders to another "merely to satisfy inclination, but retains freedom and rights in regard to other circumstances affecting their person" (CL 27:387). Nonetheless, according to him, the concubine still allows her person to be used as a mere thing, since "the impulse is still always directed to sex, merely, and not to humanity" (CL 27:387). More specifically, the concubine contracts out her sexual organ (i.e., a part of herself), and anyone who contracts out a part of herself thereby contracts out her whole person, thereby allowing herself to be used as a mere means. So, according to Kant, in concubinage, there is an inequality that renders the condition ill-suited for the permissible exercising of the sexual impulse, since the agreement "relates only to enjoyment of one part of the person, not to the total state thereof" (CL 27:387). To put it crudely, it is a no-strings-attached contract for the person who takes on the concubine, which results in the concubine being treated as a mere thing. According to Kant, concubinage "is indeed a *pactum,* but *inaequale;* the rights are not reciprocal; in such a pact, the person of the woman is wholly subordinated to the man in sexual matters" (CL 27:390).[24]

5.3.2 Crimina Carnis Contra Naturam

Kant defines *crimina carnis contra naturum* as involving "the use of the sexual impulse that is contrary to natural instinct and to animal nature" (CL 27:391). To say that *crimina carnis contra naturam* are contrary to our animal nature means, for Kant, that non-human animals do not engage in this behavior. According to Kant, "all *crimina carnis contra naturum* debase the human condition below that of the animal, and make man unworthy of his humanity; he then no longer deserves to be a person, and such conduct is the most ignoble and degraded that a man can engage in, with regard to the duties he has towards himself" (CL 27:391). These acts put us below the animals, according to Kant, because no non-human animals stoop to such

---

[24] Kant's condemnation of concubinage confirms my interpretation of his sexual ethic as informed by his conviction that women suffer from inequality with respect to men. So does his condemnation of morganatic marriages (marriages between individuals of different social rank or class): "a morganatic marriage does not fully accord with the right of humanity. For the wife is not put in possession of all the husband's rights, and so does not have total possession of him, though he has absolute possession of her" (VL 27:641).

5.3 Kant on Lust and the *Crimina Carnis*

activities in order to satiate their sexual impulses ("no animal is capable of any such *crimina carnis contra naturum*" [CL 27:392]). It is worth pausing to underscore Kant's reasoning here. His reference to animals is not an attempt to condemn *crimina carnis contra naturum* as contrary to natural teleology. Rather, Kant's point is that these crimes against nature are wrong insofar as they debase our dignity. He identifies three *crimina carnis contra* naturam: masturbation, beastiality, and homosexuality.

Masturbation Masturbation, according to Kant, "is the misuse of the sexual faculty without any object, occurring, that is, when the object of our sexual impulse is totally absent, and yet even without any object the use of our sexual faculty by no means lapses, but is exercised" (CL 27:391). His condemnation in the Collins Lecture Notes is basically the same as the one he makes in the "Doctrine of Virtue." Masturbation runs counter to the ends of humanity, insofar as it violates our dignity and our duty to preserve the species (one is not procreating when one masturbates), and insofar as it conflicts with animal nature, since Kant believed non-human animals do not masturbate. Kant's moral argument against masturbation has been criticized as flawed (Soble 2003; Cf. Gregor 1963,139–142). Additionally, we now know that he was wrong about the behavior of non-human animals. Scientists have observed a number of different species engage in masturbation, and some of that behavior appears to be positively adaptive—that is, it is good for the animal in question (de Waal 1995; Soble 1996). And there is good evidence that masturbating can be beneficial (physically and psychologically) for both women (Nagoski 2015) and men (Leitzmann et al. 2004).

Same-Sex Sexual Activity The next kind of *crimina carnis contra naturum* is *sexus homogenii*, "where the object of sexual inclination continues, indeed, to be human, but is changed since the sexual congress is not heterogeneous but homogeneous, i.e., when a woman satisfies her sexual impulse on a woman, or a man on a man" (CL 27:391). Kant thinks that this impulse runs counter to our humanity because the end of our sexual impulse is the propagation of the species without forfeiture of the person. In violating nature's end in this way, I forfeit my person, insofar as I "degrade myself below the beasts, and dishonor humanity" (CL 27:391). Interestingly, Kant's thinking here seems to be quite similar to the thinking of some of the natural law and new natural law theorists I discussed in Chap. 1 (Soble 2003; Lee and George 1997). Since same-sex couples cannot procreate as a result of their same-sex sexual activity, Kant seems to conclude that their activity can only be an attempt to satisfy their sexual appetite and experience pleasure, and to engage in sex for this reason is to treat oneself (and one's sexual partner) as a mere instrument of one's sexual pleasure. Hence, according to Kant, such behavior forfeits one's person and runs contrary to the ends of humanity. I will have more to say about Kant's argument concerning same-sex sexual activity in the Conclusion of the book (Chap. 7). For now, I want merely to note that, as with masturbation, Kant was wrong to think that non-human animals do not engage in same-sex sexual activity. Joan Roughgarden (2004/2009) has documented many species of non-human animal that engage in same-sex sexual behavior, and a good deal of that behavior is positively adaptive for those animals and, so, good for them.

Bestiality The third and final class of *crimina carnis contra naturum* is bestiality, which Kant defines as sexual intercourse with a member of the "opposite sex" that is not human.[25] His argument, to the extent that he offers one, turns on the same reasoning that motivates his condemnation of masturbation and same-sex sexual activity. To engage in bestiality is to forfeit your own personhood insofar as you treat yourself merely as a means of satisfying your sexual desire, and it lowers you below the beasts, since "no animal turns away from his own species" (CL 27: 392). Here, once again, it is worth noting that Kant's knowledge of non-human animal behavior is mistaken, since scientists have observed non-human animals engaging in sexual behavior with animals of other species (Grönig and Hochkirch 2008).

As I noted in Sect. 5.2 above, a number of scholars have found much to criticize in Kant's practical sexual ethics, and this is especially true of what Kant has to say about so-called *criminal carnis* such as masturbation and same-sex sexual activity. I will have more to say about these criticisms, and I will make my own evaluation of Kant's arguments and what we can draw from them, in the Conclusion to this book. At this stage, however, I want to make two observations about Kant's account of the *crimina carnis,* particularly his evaluation of same-sex sexual activity. First of all, his condemnation of same-sex sexual activity and the *crimina carnis* more generally rest on arguments having to do with the way in which these sexual activities allegedly degrade our personhood and, so, our dignity *qua* rational beings. Second, insofar as Kant's condemnation of same-sex sexual activity and the *crimina carnis contra naturam* in general rely in part on Kant's understanding of the way in which such acts are inconsistent with the behavior of non-human animals, this means that, contrary to the claims of the traditional reading, Kant's practical sexual ethic is informed by empirical assumptions, a feature of his thinking that will be of significance when it comes time to evaluate Kant's potential contribution to the same-sex marriage debate.

5.4 Looking Ahead

In this Chapter I presented Kant's views on gender and sex, and I have argued that the former significantly inform the latter. Although Kant's account of women is offensive and misinformed, his analysis is telling, for at least two reasons. First, Kant's understanding of our unsocial sociability informs his account of domestic life between wives and husbands and his depiction of the characteristics of women; insofar as we are social, wives and husbands need each other in order to thrive

---

[25] Kant makes no mention of someone having sexual intercourse with a member of the same-sex that is not human. Presumably he would also find this to be a case of bestiality. And, regardless, such sexual activity would be immoral, on his view, because it involves two beings of the same sex.

5.4 Looking Ahead

within the domestic relationship of a shared household, but insofar as we are unsocial, Kant believes that wives and husbands vie, in their own gender-specific ways, to exert their respective wills. Second, the relationship between wives and husbands with respect to what Kant sees as the domestic power struggle reflects the greater dynamic he sees between women and men, namely, one where women are at the mercy of men—both physically and with respect to their social position—and are, therefore, in general oppressed by men. Remember, Kant thinks that the passion for dominance concerns the use of physical force by men, especially over women, and the use of physical force includes the use of sex as a way to dominate and control women.

Kant construes sexual appetite as the desire to use the sexual organs of another for one's own gratification. There can be no doubt that there is something grossly reductive in this view of sexual appetite (surely there are reasons to desire someone sexually other than "I want to use that person to have an orgasm"). Kant seems to miss much of the complexity of sexual desire and the ways in which it can be fulfilling for humans, and not merely in the sense of satisfying an appetite. At the same time, for all the ways in which his comments about sexual desire may offend our sexually liberated sensibilities, Kant seems to capture something important and perhaps essential to human sexuality, namely, the way in which its power and significance in our lives can and often does lead to the objectification and subjection of the objects of our sexual desire—and this especially with respect to the way heterosexual men are inclined and socialized to view the objects of their sexual desire. This is why Barbara Herman (2002) argues that Kant's critical views of sex share certain similarities with some contemporary feminist thinkers, such as Andrea Dworkin (1987) and Catherine MacKinnon (1989).[26] Of course, Kant's critical observations about the way sex can objectify people is not quite motivated by the same feminist concerns and insights of Dworkin and MacKinnon, but it is driven by his philosophical anthropology and his conviction that we are inclined to be unsocial, to prioritize our own respective conceptions of happiness over and against what is morally good.

There is a sense, then, that Kant's practical sexual ethics serves as a kind of paradigmatic case study in evaluating the merits of Kant's ethics, particularly with respect to the traditional reading. Remember that one of the key features of the traditional reading is the view that Kant's ethics devalues the empirical as a source of moral evil, which, according to the traditional reading, is why he rejects our sensible/bodily nature as a source of immorality to be controlled and suppressed. I have

---

[26] According to Dworkin (1987), sex between men and women, by its very nature, is objectifying. During the act of coitus, "this physical relation to her—over her and inside her—is his possession of her. He has her, or, when he is done, he has had her. By thrusting into her, he takes her over. His thrusting into her is taken to be her capitulation to him as a conqueror; it is a physical surrender of herself to him; he occupies and rules her, expresses his elemental dominance over her, by his possession of her in the fuck" (79). Although she does not share Dworkins view that sexual relations between men and women cannot but be objectifying, Catherine MacKinnon (1989, 128) takes sexuality to be "a social construct of male power: defined by men, forced on women, and constitutive of the meaning of gender."

already addressed these aspects of the traditional reading within the context of my discussion of Kant's philosophical anthropology (Chap. 3) and his normative virtue theory (Chap. 4). It looks, however, as though Kant's practical sexual ethics might speak against the reading of Kant I have presented thus far, since Kant's understanding of our sexual impulse leaves him with a significant problem. On the one hand, his characterization of sexual desire picks up on the way in which people, especially men, can and do use sex to objectify their sexual partners and thereby to oppress them. On the other hand, human beings possess sexual desire by nature, which means this desire must be in some basic sense good. So, thinks Kant, we are led to ask, "To what extent is anyone entitled to make use of their sexual impulse, without impairing their humanity? How far can a person allow another person of the opposite sex to satisfy his or her inclination upon them" (CL 27:385)? I have already presented Kant's account of sexual vices and the ways in which he thinks the *crimina carnis* violate our dignity and the ends of humanity. Those arguments, insofar as they are moral arguments that draw on Kant's understanding of what it means to respect human dignity, really only serve to underscore the problem I am presently discussing. More specifically, Kant's arguments about *crimina carnis* and his general worries about sexual desire are not merely worries about the harmful consequences sex can have for people (though he thinks that is the case, too). I have already quoted Kant expressing his concern directly in the Collins Lecture Notes:

> All philosophers censure this inclination only for its pernicious effects, and the ruin it brings, partly to the body, and partly to the general welfare, and [they] see nothing reprehensible in the acts as such; but if this were so, if there were no inner abhorrency and damage to morality in employing the inclination, then anyone who could simply obviate these ill-effects might make use of his impulse in any way conceivable....Yet here there is something contemptible in the act itself, which runs counter to morality. (CL 27:386)

This is as close as Kant gets in his writings to condemning sexual desire as *in principle* immoral. But it is important to stress that he never actually makes such a condemnation (Denis 1999, 231).

In fact, for all of his criticisms of mere sexual impulse as the inclination to objectify another for one's own enjoyment, Kant explicitly insists that these remarks concern **mere** sexual impulse. Mere sexual impulse, on Kant's understanding, is the inclination that nature has implanted in us for the purpose of getting humans to procreate; it is the sexual impulse in humans as it is "naturally" implanted in us, that is, prior to and free from the autocratic work of practical reason. But, according to Kant, human virtue consists in part of our cultivating emotions and desires that are consistent with human goodness, and, therefore, we are not merely beholden to nature. This points to the way in which Kant's ethics must allow for morally permissible sexual relations, that is, sexual relations wherein the people involved do not treat each other as mere means for their respective gratification.

In the Collins Lecture Notes Kant claims that "conditions must be possible, under which alone the use of the *facultates sexuales* is compatible with morality" (CL 27:386). In other words, there must be some context that mitigates not merely the allegedly pernicious effects of sexual desire but also its objectifying tendency. As Kant puts it in the Vigilantius Lecture Notes, "if the sexual inclination is to be recognized on the side permitted by morality, it must be able to co-exist with the freedom sanctified by humanity" (VL 27:638). As I will argue in the next chapter, such co-existence is made possible in part by a cultivation of our sexual impulse, but it is also made possible in part by the context in which we choose to engage in sexual activity. More specifically, in order for sexual activity to be morally permissible, it must take place within a context that guarantees that the sexual partners respect each other as ends in themselves. I think Kant's acknowledgment of the way in which the moral goodness of our sexual activity is context-dependent holds the key to answering the Anscombian reading's critique of Kant with respect to his practical sexual ethics, and I think it is the central insight on which contemporary thinkers can draw when participating in the contemporary debate over same-sex marriage. According to Kant, there is but one context in which we can have rightful sexual relations: marriage.

References

Bernasconi, Robert. 2001. Who Invented the Concpet of Race? Kant's Role in the Enlightenment Construction of Race. In *Race*, ed. Robert Bernasconi, 11–36. Malden/Oxford: Blackwell.
Brake, Elizabeth. 2005. Justice and Virtue in Kant's Account of Marriage. *Kantian Review* 9: 58–94.
Budziszewski, J. 2012. *On the Meaning of Sex*. Wilmington: ISI Books.
Caygill, Howard. 1995. *A Kant Dictionary*. Oxford: Blackwell Publishers.
Cooke, Vincent M. 1991. Kant, Teleology, and Sexual Ethics. *International Philosophical Quarterly* 31 (1): 3–13.
Daly, Mary. 1985. *The Church and the Second Sex, with the Feminist Postchristian Introduction and New Archaid Afterwords by the Author*. Boston: Beacon Press.
Darwall, Stephen L. 1977. Two Kinds of Respect. *Ethics* 88 (1): 36–49.
de Beauvoir, Simone. (1952). *The Second Sex*. Trans. H.M. Parshley. New York: Vintage Books.
De Waal, Frans B.M. 1995. Sex as an Alternative to Aggression in the Bonobo. In *Sexual Nature, Sexual Culture*, ed. Paul Abramson and Steven Pinkerton, 37–56. Chicago: University of Chicago Press.
Denis, Lara. 1999. Kant on the Wrongness of "Unnatural" Sex. *History of Philosophy Quarterly* 16 (2): 225–248.
———. 2007. Sex and the Virtuous Kantian Agent. In *Sex and Ethics: Essays on Sexuality, Virtue, and the Good Life*, ed. Raja Halwani, 37–48. New York: Palgrave MacMillan.
Dworkin, Andrea. 1987. *Intercourse*. New York: Free Press.
Fine, Cordelia. 2010. *Delusions of Gender: How Our Minds, Society, and Neurosexism Create Difference*. New York/London: W.W. Norton & Company.
Gregor, Mary J. 1963. *Laws of Freedom: A Study of Kant's Method of Applying the Categorical Imperative in the Metaphysik der Sitten*. New York: Barnes & Noble, Inc..
Grönig, Julia, and Alex Hochkirk. 2008. Reproductive Interference Between Animal Species. *The Quarterly Review of Biology* 83 (3): 257–282.
Herman, Barbara. 2002. Could It Be Worth Thinking About Kant on Sex and Marriage? In *A Mind of One's Own: Feminist Essays on Reason and Objectivity*, ed. Louise M. Antony and Charlotte E. Witt, 53–72. Boulder: Westview Press.
Kleingeld, Pauline. 1993. The Problematic Status of Gender-Neutral Language in the History of Philosophy: The Case of Kant. *Philosophical Forum* 25: 134–150.
Kneller, Jane. 2006. Kant on sex and marriage right. In *The Cambridge Companion to Kant and Modern Philosophy*, ed. Paul Guyer, 447–476. Cambridge: Cambridge University Press.

Korsgaard, Christine M. 1996. *Creating the Kingdom of Ends*. Cambridge: Cambridge University Press.
Kuehn, Manfred. 2002. *Kant: A Biography*. Cambridge: Cambridge University Press.
Lee, Patrick, and Robert P. George. 1997. What Sex can be: Self-Alienation, Illusion, or One-Flesh Union. *American Journal of Jurisprudence* 42 (1): 135–157.
Leitzmann, M.F., E.A. Platz, M.J. Stampfler, et al. 2004. Ejaculation Frequency and Subsequent Risk of Prostate Cancer. *Journal of the American Medical Association* 291: 1578–1586.
Louden, Robert B. 2000. *Kant's Impure Ethics: From Rational Beings to Human Beings*. New York/Oxford: Oxford University Press.
MacKinnon, Catherine A. 1989. *Towards a Feminist Theory of the State*. Cambridge, MA: Harvard University Press.
Marwah, Inder S. 2013. What Nature Makes of Her: Kant's Gendered Metaphysics. *Hypatia* 28 (3): 551–567.
Mikkola, Mari. 2011. Kant on Moral Agency and Women's Nature. *Kantian Review* 16 (1): 89–111.
Mosser, Kurt. 1999. Kant and Feminism. *Kant-Studien* 90: 322–353.
Nagoski, Emily. 2015. *Come as You Are: The Surprising New Science that Will transform Your Sex Life*. New York: Simon & Schuster.
Pope John Paul II. 2006. *Man and Woman He Created Them: A Theology of the Body*. Trans. Michael Waldstein. Boston: Pauline Books & Media.
Roughgarden, Joan. 2004/2009. *Evolution's Rainbow: Diversity, Gender, and Sexuality in Nature and People, with a New Preface*. Berkley/Los Angeles/London: University of California Press.
Rousseau, Jean-Jacques. 1979 (1762). *Émile, or On Education*. Trans. Allan Bloom. New York: Basic Books, Inc., Publishers.
———. 1992 (1755). *Discourse on the Origin of Inequality*. Trans. Donald A. Cress. Indianapolis: Hackett Publishing Company.
Rumsey, Jean P. 1997. Re-Visions of Agency in Kant's Moral Theory. In *Feminist Interpretations of Immanuel Kant*, ed. Robin May Schott, 125–144. University Park: The Pennsylvania State University Press.
Schott, Robin May. 1997. The Gender of Enlightenment. In *Feminist Interpretations of Immanuel Kant*, ed. Robin May Schott, 319–333. University Park: The Pennsylvania State University Press.
Schultz, Joshua. 2007. Good Sex on Kantian Grounds, or a Reply to Alan Soble. *Essays in Philosophy* 8.2: Article 1.
Schwitzgebel, Eric. 2010. Kant on Killing Bastards, on Masturbation, on Wives and Servants, on Organ Donation, Homosexuality, and Tyrants. http://schwitzsplinters.blogspot.com/2010/03/kant-on-killing-bastards-on.htmll
Scruton, Roger. 1986. *Sexual Desire: A Philosophical Investigation*. London: Weidenfeld and Nicolson.
Soble, Alan. 1996. *Sexual Investigations*. New York/London: New York University Press.
———. 2001. Sexual Use and What to Do About It: Internalist and Externalist Sexual Ethics. *Essays in Philosophy* 2.2: Article 2.
———. 2003. Kant and Sexual Perversion. *The Monist* 86 (1): 55–89.
Stone, Alison. 2007. *An Introduction to Feminist Philosophy*. Malden: Polity Press.
Tuana, Nancy. 1992. *Woman and the History of Philosophy*. New York: Paragon House.
———. 1993. *The Less Noble Sex: Scientific, Religious, and Philosophical Conceptions of Woman's Nature*. Bloomington/Indianapolis: Indiana University Press.
Varden, Helga. 2015. Kant and Women. *Pacific Philosophical Quarterly*, early view.
Wilson, Holly. 1998. Kant's Evolutionary Theory of Marriage. In *Autonomy and Community: Readings in Contemporary Kantian Social Philosophy*, ed. Jane Kneller and Sidney Axinn, 283–307. Albany: State University of New York Press.
Wood, Allen W. 2008. *Kantian Ethics*. Cambridge: Cambridge University Press.
Zack, Naomi. 2011. *The Ethics and Mores of Race: Equality After the History of Philosophy*. Lanham: Rowman & Littlefield.

Chapter 6
Love & Respect Redux: Kant on Sex, Marriage, and Friendship

Abstract In light of contemporary understandings of marriage, Kant's definitions of marriage and the marriage right strike some as grossly mistaken. I think, however, that a closer inspection of what Kant has to say about marriage and the limited way in which he intends it to solve the problem of sexual objectification shows that his position is not as nonsensical as some critics make it out to be. This is not to say that Kant's account of marriage is without problems; I argue that Kant's account of marriage only deals with half of the problem of sexual objectification as he presents it. But I also argue that Kant's account of marriage points to the way in which a complete solution to the problem of sexual objectification is possible, the resources for which can be found in Kant's ethics, namely, in his account of moral friendship. I proceed as follows. First, I present Kant's view of the legal institution of marriage. I then explain how legal marriage and the special right that grounds it are supposed to solve the legal problem of sexual objectification as he presents it in his practical sexual ethics. Next, drawing on Kant's distinction between right and virtue, I argue that legal marriage cannot solve the moral problem of sexual objectification. I then consider Kant's account of moral friendship, and argue that friendship provides the kind of context in which two people can engage in morally permissible sexual activity.

Much like his practical sexual ethics, Kant's account of marriage, which is his solution to the moral problem we face in light of his understanding of sexual appetite, has for the most part been sharply criticized by contemporary philosophers. For example, Susan Mendus (1987, 30–31) says that Kant's treatment of marriage "is notorious, an embarrassment to moral philosophers and philosophers of law alike." Hannelore Schröder (1997, 287) claims that Kant's marriage solution is "completely illogical and contradictory." And Reinhold Aris (1965, 102) dismisses Kant's view as "shallow and repulsive."[1] A quick glance at Kant's definition of marriage helps to explain these harsh criticisms of his view. Kant defines marriage as "the union of two persons of different sexes for lifelong possession of each other's sexual attributes" (MM 6:277), and he identifies the marriage right as a special kind of right, one he calls "a right to a person akin to a right to a thing" (MM 6:276). So, it would

---
[1] This quotation of Aris is cited in Mendus (1987, 31).

seem that Kant reduces marriage to a contractual relationship whereby each spouse comes to own the genitals of the other for the purpose of their respective enjoyment, and the right that grounds this contract is one that conceives of the spouses as akin to things. It is hard to believe that this is the same person who enjoins us to respect human dignity as invaluable and who confesses "ever new and increasing admiration and reverence" (CPrR 5:161) for the moral law that requires us to pay such respect.

In light of contemporary understandings of marriage as a joining of two people who are in love, it is understandable that Kant's definitions of marriage and the marriage right would strike some people today as grossly mistaken. I think, however, that a closer inspection of what Kant has to say about marriage and the limited way in which he intends it to solve the problem of sexual objectification shows that his position is not as nonsensical as someone such as Schröder makes it out to be. This is not to say that Kant's account of marriage is without problems. I am going to distinguish between the legal problem of sexual objectification and the moral problem of sexual objectification. I contend that although Kant's account of marriage only deals with the legal problem of sexual objectification as he presents it, his account of marriage points to the way in which a complete solution to the problem of sexual objectification is possible, the resources for which can be found in Kant's ethics, namely, in his account of moral friendship.

Because the problem of sexual objectification is one that needs to be addressed before any other conclusions may be drawn about Kant's practical sexual ethics, and because Kant understands potentially good sexual relations and, so, marriage, as only possible between a woman and a man, my discussion in this chapter focuses exclusively on the problem of sexual objectification with respect to different-sex couples. As I hope will become clear, if the solutions found in Kant's ethics work, then they can in principle apply to same-sex couples, which I will argue in the next Chapter when I turn directly to evaluate Kant's position on same-sex sexual relations and the possibility of same-sex marriage within the context of his ethical theory. I proceed as follows. First, I briefly review Kant's understanding of the problem of the way sexual desire objectifies people, distinguishing between the legal problem of sexual objectification and the moral problem of sexual objectification. I then present Kant's view of the legal institution of marriage, focusing on Kant's account of the way in which "the right to a person akin to a right to a thing" grounds his legal conception of marriage. I then explain how legal marriage and the special right that grounds it are supposed to solve the legal problem of sexual objectification as he presents it in his practical sexual ethics. Next, drawing on Kant's distinction between right and virtue, I argue that marriage cannot solve the moral problem of sexual objectification. I then consider Kant's account of moral friendship, which he takes to be an intimate union of equals that combines respect and love. I conclude by arguing that moral friendship provides the kind of context in which two people who are equals can engage in sexual activity without thereby morally objectifying each other.

6.1 Kant on Marriage

I want to start my treatment of Kant's view of marriage by reviewing what he sees as the problem with sexual appetite, namely the way in which it inclines us to objectify our sexual partners, to view them as mere instruments for our gratification. According to Kant, when we consider the sexual impulse in and by itself, "there lies in this inclination a degradation of man; for as soon as anyone becomes an object of another's appetite, all motives of moral relationship fall away; as object of the other's appetite, that person is in fact a thing, whereby the other's appetite is sated, and can be misused as such a thing by anybody" (CL 27:384–385). Kant goes on to say that sexual appetite is a sensible desire that is *sui generis*, since "there is no other case where a human being would already be determined by nature to be the object of another's enjoyment" (CL 27:385).

There are a few things to note about the quotations in the preceding paragraph. First of all, Kant here is talking about sexual appetite as "nature implanted it" in us. In other words, within the context of this discussion, he intentionally brackets or sets aside all the ways in which our sexual desire can be shaped by our socialization (either for good or for bad); he merely considers the sexual appetite in its simplest and most basic form. Second, although Kant acknowledges that some of our inclinations and passions are the result of socialization (A 7:267–275; Cf. Wood 1999, 259–265), and some of these (e.g., the passion for dominance) take humans as objects, he believes that sexual appetite is the only *natural* inclination that objectifies other people in this way. Third—and this, I think, is missed by critics such as Schröder—Kant's understanding of the way in which we objectify our sexual partners underscores the way in which he espouses a holistic (rather than, e.g., dualistic) conception of human beings. The problem with our natural sexual impulse, as he sees it, is that it is "a *principium* of the debasement of humanity, a source for the preference of one sex over the other, and the dishonouring of that sex by satisfying the inclination." He continues,

> The consequence is, that any man or woman will endeavor to lend attraction, not to their humanity, but to their sex, and to direct all actions and desires entirely towards it. If this is the case, humanity will be sacrificed to sex. So if a man wishes to satisfy his inclination, and a woman hers, they each attract the other's inclination to themselves, and both urges impinge on one another, and are directed, not to humanity at all, but to sex, and each partner dishonours the humanity in the other. (CL 27:385)

Sexual appetite is a problem, according to Kant, precisely because human beings are whole organisms, not souls or minds "inside" of bodies. Because we are whole organisms, when we sexually desire another person and aim to use the person's sexual organs (and, one might say, sexuality) to satisfy our inclination, we treat this other person as a mere thing *precisely insofar as it is impossible to abstract or separate the person from her body.*[2]

---

[2] I think Allegra de Laurentiis (2000, 298) fails to appreciate this aspect of Kant's thinking, but this is because she heavily emphasizes the way in which she reads Kant's metaphysical distinction between phenomena and noumena as informing his understanding of persons.

It is, according to Kant, because our personhood includes our being embodied, rational animals, that mere sexual appetite objectifies: it treats the person as though she were in fact not a person but a mere assemblage of bodily parts there to be enjoyed. And, as the preceding block quotation indicates, it is not merely that my natural sexual desire objectifies my sexual partner. It also motivates me to objectify myself. More specifically, according to Kant, in an effort to attract my sexual partner, I tend to encourage my sexual partner to focus on my sexual attributes and my sexual attributes alone in order to get her or him to want me. But I do this, thinks Kant, to the detriment of my humanity, that is, I do this in a way that encourages my sexual partner to see me merely as sexual object and not as a person, not as a being possessing humanity.[3] Significantly, that both my sexual partner and I willingly do this to each other does not in any way mitigate the way in which we are each objectified and engage in objectifying the other (Denis 2002; Cf. Hay 2013, 9). As Kant puts it, "man cannot dispose over himself, because he is not a thing....He is, however, a person, who is not property, so he cannot be a thing such as he might own" (CL 27:386).

On the other side of this dilemma is Kant's conviction that the sexual drive is in some sense good. For one, he thinks it is the means by which nature propagates the species, which makes it desirable for that reason. Moreover, insofar as our sexual appetite is rooted in our sensible natures, Kant is committed to thinking it is part of the good of that nature, at least in principle. He even goes so far to say that a person who lacked sexual desire would be defective, "an imperfect individual" (CL 27:385). So, he needs to reconcile the goodness of our sexual drive with the propensity we have when acting on that drive to objectify our sexual partners.

One further point needs to be made before moving on to Kant's account of marriage, and it is a point that some commentators on Kant's view of marriage have not adequately emphasized, namely the way in which Kant's practical philosophy requires Kant to distinguish between the legal problem of sexual objectification and the moral problem of sexual objectification, each of which requires its own solution.[4] Recall that Kant distinguishes his practical philosophy into two parts. The first part he calls "juridical" and deals with what is permissible in a legal way, that is, it concerns positive law and the ways in which it constrains human action ("The Doctrine of Right"). The second part he calls "ethical" and deals not merely with

---

[3] Cf. Martha C. Nussbaum (2007, 50): "Sexual objectification is a complex notion. To objectify a woman is to treat as an object a being who is really a human being. That treatment, however, has many different dimensions that are complexly related. It includes the denial of autonomy (this being is not self-determining), the denial of subjectivity (this being does not have thoughts and feelings that need to be taken into account), the idea of property (this being can be owned, bought, and sold), the idea of violability (one of these things being like the other), and the idea of instrumentality (this object is nothing more than a tool)." Although Nussbaum in this context focuses on the sexual objectification of women, and although her analysis is more complex than Kant's, I think at bottom her view and Kant's are compatible, particularly since she sees instrumentality as what is "most centrally" wrong about sexual objectification (50).

[4] I speak more directly to this below (Sect. 6.1.3).

6.1 Kant on Marriage

human action but also human intention or motive, that is, it concerns virtue and the ways in which practical reasoning should inform our actions and our motives ("The Doctrine of Virtue"). This distinction in Kant's practical philosophy has important implications for his practical sexual ethics. Kant thinks that a solution to the problem of sexual objectification is one that "restricts our freedom in regard to the use of our inclination, so that it conforms to morality" (CL 27:386). But with the distinction between juridical law and ethical law in mind, Kant needs to develop a twofold solution to the problem, since the problem itself is twofold. On the one hand, there is the problem of establishing a legal context in which the rights of sexual partners are not violated. On the other, there is the problem of establishing a context in which the dignity of sexual partners is recognized and respected. As I will argue, Kant's account of marriage aims at solving only one half of this problem, though the resources for addressing the other half are in his account of moral friendship as the context in which two people can morally enjoy each other's humanity.

6.1.1 Marriage and the Marriage Right

Kant engages in two lengthy discussions of the marriage right, in "The Doctrine of Right" and in the Collins Lecture Notes. Kant begins his discussion in "The Doctrine of Right" by providing his definition of sexual union, which he takes to be "the reciprocal use that one human being makes of the sexual organs and capacities of another (*usus membrorum et facultatum sexualium alterius*)" (MM 6:277). He then gives a brief taxonomy of species of sexual acts. Sexual union "is either a natural use (by which procreation of a being of the same kind is possible) or an *unnatural* use, and unnatural use takes place either with a person of the same sex or with an animal of a nonhuman species" (MM 6:277). As I have already explained (Chap. 5, Sects. 5.3.1 and 5.3.2), because he believes that the unnatural use of our sexual capacities always constitutes a violation of the humanity in our own person, Kant thinks that "there are no limitations or exceptions whatsoever that can save them from being repudiated completely" (MM 6:277). With respect to natural sexual unions, Kant further distinguishes between those that take place "in accordance with mere animal nature" and those that take place "in accordance with law" (MM 6:277). Sexual union in accordance with law is natural sexual union within marriage. All other natural sexual unions are merely in accordance with animal nature.

Kant defines marriage as "the union of two persons of different sexes for lifelong possession of each other's sexual attributes" (MM 6:277). Kant explicitly denies that marriage essentially concerns procreation, though he acknowledges that procreation is "nature's end" in implanting sexual impulse in human beings. He denies that marriage is essentially about procreation because, if it were, Kant argues, marriages would be dissolved when spouses could no longer procreate (e.g., when they reach old age).[5] Actually, in Herder's Lecture Notes on Kant's ethics, Kant goes even further in denying that procreation is the purpose of sex within marriage:

---

[5] Cf. VL 27:639: were procreation the only morally justified reason for engaging in sex (and, therefore, for being married), "it would follow from this that persons who by reason of age or infirmity

> Those who hold God's end to be always the principal one should consider here, whether the natural man has the providential intention to sustain the human race, or merely an inclination to immediate pleasure. The former is indeed the main end, but not the only one, and the remainder must certainly not conflict with it, but they can nevertheless be non-injurious to it; and it is thus altogether too scrupulous to forbid married couples those intimacies which are not immediately connected with propagation. (HL 27:48)

Here Kant explicitly warns against denying married couples the permissibility of engaging in sexual activity merely for pleasure. Sex for pleasure, according to Kant, is permissible so long as, and only if, it occurs between two spouses. This underscores the fact that the point of marriage is not the making and rearing of children but the establishment of a context in which two people may legally engage in permissible sexual activity. As he puts it, the marriage contract is "necessary by the law of humanity, that is, if a man and a woman want to enjoy each other's sexual attributes they *must* necessarily marry, and this is necessary in accordance with pure reason's laws of right" (MM 6:277–278).

The law of right to which Kant refers concerns a special kind of right, namely, the right a person has to another person akin to their rights to things (MM 6:276). In order to understand how this right is special (perhaps even peculiar), I want briefly to explain, on the one hand, Kant's understanding of property rights (a right to a thing), and on the other, Kant's understanding of contract rights (a right against a person).[6]

Kant defines a right to a thing as "a right to the private use of a thing of which I am in (original or instituted) possession in common with all others" (6:261). Kant puts this right in terms of the common possession of a thing because he thinks that only in this way could I claim to be wronged by someone who takes my property. This is because Kant thinks that it is absurd to understand a right to a thing as consisting of an obligatory relationship between the possessor and the possessed, since this would involve asserting that a thing (i.e., an object) can have obligations to me, which is absurd. So, Kant thinks that we need to conceive of a right to a thing as a right I claim against others, which he construes as my right to the private use of a thing that we all own together as members of civil society.

When it comes to a right one may have against a person, Kant defines this as "my possession of another's choice, in the sense of my capacity to determine it by my own choice to a certain deed in accordance with laws of freedom (what is externally mine or yours with respect to the causality of another)" (MM 6:271). In other words, I have a right against a person if I am legally empowered to require another to perform certain actions, as, for example, happens when I contract someone to paint my house. Such a contract empowers me to force this person to paint my house or face legal sanctions for failing to do so.

---

did not possess this impulse, or could not fulfill it, would have to separate, or would not be able to conjoin."

[6] De Laurentiis (2000, 300–306), provides a good summary of the basics of Kant's theory of right as it appears in "The Doctrine of Virtue."

6.1 Kant on Marriage

These two rights relate to the marriage right because in a *certain* way the marriage right combines the right to a thing and a right against a person. Kant claims that the right to a person akin to the right to things is a right that governs a number of domestic relationships, since "what is mine or yours in terms of this right is what is mine or yours *domestically*," and since "the relation of persons in the domestic condition is that of a community of free beings who form a society of members of a whole called a *household*..." (MM 6:276). Accordingly, Kant claims that by this right "a *man* acquires a *wife*; a *couple* acquires *children*; and a *family* acquires *servants*" (MM 6:276).[7] To enjoy a right to a person akin to the rights of things is to enjoy "possession of an external object *as a thing* and use of it *as a person*" (MM 6:276). In the case of marriage, the right to a person akin to a thing involves the following: I have a right to the private use of my spouse's sex organs (analogous to a right to a thing), and I have a right against my spouse to engage in sexual intercourse with me for the purpose of exercising my right to the sex organs of my spouse (analogous to a right against a person); and this right entails exclusivity (i.e., that I only have sex with my spouse and my spouse only with me).

The way in which the marriage right seems to be a mere combination of the right to property and the right against a person motivates Schröder's (1997, 287) criticism of Kant's view: "It is not possible to be both a person and a thing under the law as the two are mutually exclusive in Kant's own definition of person (someone who isn't subjected to the arbitrary rule of others)."[8] Indeed, Kant is clear that one cannot "make himself the physical property of others, i.e., give up his freedom and personality so entirely that the other can treat him as a thing" (VL 27:602). I think one misreads Kant if one understands the marriage right as entailing the kind of blatant contradiction Schröder alleges. First of all, Kant insists that although the marriage right combines the two rights I discuss above, it nonetheless "is a right lying beyond any rights to things and any rights against persons" (MM 6:276). In other words, the marriage right cannot be reduced either to a property right or a right against a person—it is *sui generis*. Second, although in "The Doctrine of Right" Kant expresses the marriage right in terms of a man acquiring a wife (and so expresses the right as one-sided), in fact, the marriage right is one that each spouse enjoys, which is why, according to Kant, the marriage right guarantees their respective equality under the law, even when they engage in sexual activity. According to Kant, in marriage "while one person is acquired by the other *as if it were a thing*, the one who is acquired acquires the other in turn; for in this way each reclaims itself and restores its personality" (MM 6:278). But how, according to Kant, does marriage restore

---

[7] In making this threefold distinction, Kant underscores the fact that he conceives of the function of marriage to sanction morally permissible sexual relations, not procreation and the raising of children.

[8] Lina Papadaki (2010) makes the same mistake as Schröder, reading Kant's understanding of marriage in terms of a property right: "When it comes to marriage, Kant seems to ignore his previously expressed conviction that it is impossible for one to be both a proprietor and a property. The husband and the wife, he tells us, are each other's proprietors and properties at the same time. Kant's conception of marriage, then, becomes paradoxical" (281). Helga Varden (2006, 203) rightly points out that Kant's texts clearly rule out such an interpretation.

one's personality, and how does this restoration solve the legal problem of sexual objectification?

6.1.2 The Marriage Right, Reciprocity, and Legally Permissible Sex

Kant's reasoning about the way in which the marriage right guarantees reciprocity between spouses is notoriously difficult to follow. As Jane Kneller observes (2006, 462), although it is tempting to construe Kant's account of the marriage right merely in terms of contract law, "there is good reason to take Kant's own claims to be presenting a formal, legalistic, account of juridical right with a grain of salt, or several." We ought to be cautious about reading Kant reductively, according to Kneller, because Kant views marriage "less like a contract and more like a gift exchange: The marriage pact involves two people 'giving' themselves to each other for life and love" (466). Kneller's point here is well taken: whatever the virtues or vices of Kant's account of marriage, he develops it as a way of establishing genuine equality between spouses. In this respect, it is instructive to think of Kant's account of marriage as informed by the account of marriage St. Paul presents in 1 Corinthians 7:

> Because of cases of sexual immorality, each man should have his own wife and each woman her own husband. The husband should give to his wife her conjugal rights, and likewise the wife to her husband. For the wife does not have authority over her own body, but the husband does; likewise the husband does not have authority over his own body, but the wife does. Do not deprive one another except perhaps by agreement for a set time, to devote yourselves to prayer, and then come together again, so that Satan may not tempt you because of your lack of self-control. (1.2–5, NRSV)

Paul, like Kant, is trying to establish the equality of different-sex spouses in a society where women occupy an inferior position to men. In the passage I just quoted, Paul addresses a particular problem among some members of the church, namely, the conviction of some people that it is best to avoid sexual intercourse while married. As Craig S. Keener (2011, 53) notes, "Paul insists that husbands and wives are obligated to grant each other intercourse." Although this response may seem cold and legalistic, Gareth Moore (1992, 146) notes that Paul's command here actually insists on spousal equality, insofar as the obligation is mutual.[9] Similarly, Kant's understanding of the marriage right as each spouse's right to the reciprocal use of the other is an attempt to establish equality between women and men within the context of marriage. Remember, according to Kant, in the state of nature, women are naturally (physically) inferior to men and, so, end up being treated by men as though they were mere "domestic animals" (A 7:304). This means that within the context of a sexual relationship in the state of nature, according to Kant, women cannot be the equal of men, and, so, in the state of nature all sexual relations involve

---

[9] For a detailed reading of 1 Corinthians 7 that traces the Cynic and Stoic influences on Paul's thinking, see Will Deming (1995, 110–130).

6.1 Kant on Marriage

objectification. And, because women are essentially financial dependents in the society to which Kant belonged, they cannot be citizens, which means that even in civil society they are inferior to men, except that now their being physically weaker is complicated by their inferior social status (MM 6:314–315). So, even within civil society, given the inferior social status of women, outside of marriage women and men cannot be sexual equals, since men are at a social, political, and financial advantage to women. The marriage right, as Kant construes, it is supposed to remedy this inequality.

According to Kant, when one possesses a right to a person akin to a thing, what is one's own is not "one's own in the sense of property in the person of another (for a human being cannot have property in himself, much less in another person), but means what is one's own in the sense of usufruct (*ius utendi fruendi*), to make direct use of a person *as of* a thing, as a means to my end but still without infringing upon his personality" (MM 6:359). Within marriage, my spouse acquires a right to use my sexual organs for her or his pleasure, which involves me surrendering my personhood, insofar as allowing my spouse to enjoy me sexually can only take place if I allow myself to be treated as a mere thing. But, I, too, have a right to use my spouse's sexual organs for my pleasure, which involves her surrendering her personhood, insofar as allowing me to enjoy my spouse sexually can only happen if she allows me to treat her as a mere object. If this mutual sexual use occurs outside of marriage, Kant maintains that it is "*cannibalistic* in principle (even if not always in its effect)" since "in this sort of use by each of the sexual organs of the other, each is actually a *consumable* thing with respect to the other" (MM 6:359–360). Marriage, as the "reciprocal giving of one's very person into the possession of the other" (MM 6:359) rules out such "cannibalism."

It is telling that Kant contends that marriage involves the giving of "one's very person" and not merely the giving of "one's genitals." We have to remember that Kant believes that "a person is an absolute unity" (MM 6:278). This means that marriage, according to Kant (and contrary to first appearances), "signifies a contract between two persons, in which they mutually accord equal rights to one another, and submit to the condition that each *transfers his whole person entirely to the other*, so that each has a complete right to the other's whole person" (CL 27:388, emphasis added). So, when sexual intercourse occurs within marriage, there occurs a kind of substitution of the personhood of one spouse for the other such that in surrendering their respective personhood, each spouse simultaneously has her and his personhood restored by the other. Here is how Kant explains the marriage right in the Collins Lectures:

> If only one partner yields to the other his person, his good or ill fortune, and all his circumstances, to have right over them, and does not receive in turn a corresponding identical right over the person of the other, then there is an inequality here. But if I hand over my whole person to the other, and thereby obtain the person of the other in place of it, I get myself back again, and have thereby regained possession of myself; for I have given myself to be the other's property, but am in turn taking the other as my property, and thereby regain myself, for I gain the person to whom I gave myself as property. The two persons thus constitute a unity of will. Neither will be subject to happiness or misfortune, joy or displea-

sure, without the other taking a share in it. So, the sexual impulse creates a union among persons, and only within this union is the use of it possible. (CL 27:388).[10]

Barbara Herman (2002, 66) makes sense of Kant's argument in the preceding passage by way of an analogy. "Suppose," she suggests, "I give you every pencil I own or will come to own knowing that (or on condition that) you will give me every pencil that you own or come to own. One could say that we thereby create a community of pencil ownership—a unity of will about pencils." This argument, according to Herman, works within the context of Kant's "Doctrine of Right" because "within the State (or civil society) it is possible to reestablish and secure the equal autonomy of the partners in a sexual relationship by defining them (and so setting the conditions of their sexual relationship) under the law as equal legal persons, giving them new public natures, as it were, conveniently called 'husband' and 'wife'" (66). In other words, the State mediates the relationship between wife and husband, thereby guaranteeing their equality and throughout all aspects of their relationship, including their sexual encounters.

> Now, in this [marriage], that they both fully acquire each other, and one becomes the other's property, there is constituted the *union* of the two conjoined sexes, in respect of all their relationships. Yet each, for all that, is self-possessing, although given over to the other as a thing, since each retains freedom to dispose over the other's property as *their own*. (VL 27:639)

In coming legally to possess the person of my spouse, according to Kant, I come to be responsible for her or his happiness, for her or his well-being. Marriage is a genuine union of persons insofar as "the relation of the partners in a marriage is a relation of *equality* of possession, equality both in their possession of each other as persons…and also equality in their possession of material goods" (MM 6:278). I am bound by the law to attend to the happiness of my spouse, just as she or he is bound by the law to attend to my happiness. Should either of us fail in this responsibility, we can be punished by law, which is the way in which Kant envisions the marriage right creating a context for permissible sex: under threat of punishment by law I am required to make the happiness of my spouse my end, which, on Kant's view, just is one way that we acknowledge the personhood of another.

---

[10] Cf. VL 27:638: "So if the sexual inclination is to be recognized on the side permitted by morality, it must be able to co-exist with the freedom sanctified by humanity. Now since one party is conceding possession of their substance to the other, each of them can only remain free if, in the bond of common sexual possession one of another and in precisely the degree to which each possesses the other, the one who allows the other to have *dominium* over them at the same time subjects that other to their own possession, so that they each recoup themselves. The two of them mutually acquire each other; each becomes *dominus* of the other and in that case remains also self-possessing, and is free. This is the institution of *matrimonium*, and consists, therefore, in a *jus mutuum perpetuum ad commercium sexuale* [an enduring mutual right to sexual intercourse]…."

6.1.3 Kant's Incomplete Solution: The Legal Problem & the Moral Problem of Sexual Objectification

At the end of Sect. 6.1.1, I argued against the reading of Kant's conception of marriage that accuses him of construing marriage in terms of a property right. Not only is such a reading inconsistent with Kant's texts, it also entails Kant blatantly contradicting himself, which, although possible, seems in this case to be an uncharitable reading of him. I want to make a similar case with respect to evaluating Kant's account of the marriage right as a solution to the problem of sexual objectification. Some scholars mistakenly believe that Kant's account of marriage is supposed to solve both the legal *and* the moral problems of sexual objectification. Barbara Herman (2002),[11] Thomas Mertens (2014),[12] Mari Mikkola (2011),[13] Lina Papadaki (2010),[14] and Brook J. Sadler (2013)[15] each read Kant's account of marriage in this way. If they are right, then Kant's account of marriage fails in a serious way. Elizabeth Brake (2012, 70) expresses the problem with this reading of Kant's account of marriage:

> Objectification is a psychological state, and hence not directly remediable through external structures of formal legal rights. Legal marriage does not create the psychological state constitutive of respect....Legal marriage is an institution of justice: It creates legal rights enforceable by the state. Virtue concerns psychological states internal to the agent, which cannot be brought about by external legislation—including marriage.

I can underscore Brake's point with an analogy. Think, for example, of the teacher-student relationship. One might think that mutual respect between teacher and student is something that is required if genuine learning is to occur. And one might also think that, all things being equal, teachers possess a superior status to their students, at least insofar as teachers tend to be empowered with institutional authority and also tend to have better command of the content of their courses than their students do. So, with respect to their relationship to their students, we can think of teachers occupying a position analogous to the ones husbands occupy with respect to their

---

[11] "The idea seems to be that through mediation by law, the natural tendencies to objectification, and so to dominance and exploitation, in sexual relations are blocked. The institution of marriage in this way resolves the moral difficulty arising from sexual activity" (67). Cf. De Laurentiis (2000, 298, and 299 note 7), who criticizes Herman for this.

[12] "These moral difficulties and dubious legal consequences result from Kant's difficulty to combine his understanding of sexual desire with the attempt to regulate its satisfaction by considerations of consent and nature....he holds that this desire can only be satisfied in a moral way on the basis of a lifelong mutual consent in marriage" (341).

[13] "Entering such a [marriage] contract constitutes 'the sole condition' under which humanity is safeguarded and the context of monogamous, non-adulterous marriage is the only one in which sexual impulses can safely be acted on morally speaking" (106–107).

[14] "Marriage, then, if we disentangle it from Kant's outdated views on men and women, can be a morally sound relationship, and we can understand Kant's reasons for believing that sex within this morally safe context is permissible" (288).

[15] "Why is marriage a morally necessary contract? The answer is that on Kant's view, the marriage contract is necessary in order to make sex morally permissible" (219).

wives, at least as far as Kant understands the husband-wife relationship. If our concern is to establish a respectful relationship between the teacher and her students, we could do so *via* contractual obligations prohibiting some behaviors while enjoining others. For example, where I teach professors are prohibited from using physical force to discipline a student. Professors are also required to hold office hours in order to be available to students to help them with course material. These requirements, which are contractual, go some way to establishing a respectful relationship between teachers and students—but they only go some way. Respecting another person involves more than merely how you treat them, that is, it involves more than merely performing certain actions that in general we identify as expressing respect. Respecting another person also entails taking a certain attitude toward her, believing that she is worthy of respect. These other features of respect (what Brake calls "psychological states) cannot be legislated. Insofar as they cannot be legislated, so the criticism goes, Kant's marital solution to the problem of sexual objectification fails.[16]

The preceding criticism of Kant's account of marriage assumes that Kant intended the legal institution of marriage to solve both the legal and the moral problem of sexual objectification. I think, however, that this criticism of Kant's account of marriage is misguided. In order to defend my case, I want to draw on the work of Allan Beever (2016), who most clearly and charitably makes the case that Kant's account of marriage is meant only to address the legal problem of sexual objectification. Part of the difficulty in distinguishing the two problems of sexual objectification is that Kant's account of marriage in "The Doctrine of Right" deals with a different issue than his account of marriage in his lecture notes (Beever 2016, 348). In the lecture notes, Kant does not clearly distinguish between the legal and moral problems of sexual objectification, but he does so distinguish in the "Doctrine of Right." In light of this distinction, Kant avoids the kind of mistake of which some commentators accuse him.

Before I briefly present Beever's account of the legal problem of sex and the way marriage purportedly solves that problem, I want to remind you of the basic distinction motivating Kant's dividing his *Metaphysics of Morals* into two parts (Chap. 2, Sect. 2.2.2). Kant stipulates that there are two elements to any lawgiving. First of all, there is the law, "which represents an action that is to be done as *objectively* necessary," and, second, there is the incentive, "which connects a ground for determining choice to this action *subjectively* with the representation of the law" (MM 6:218). In other words, when it comes to legislating laws, we can distinguish between the law itself, which prescribes or prohibits certain actions, and the intention with which one performs the action, which concerns one's motivation for doing what one does. Accordingly, Kant argues, we can distinguish between two kinds of lawgiving. The kind of lawgiving that "does not include the incentive of duty in the law and so admits an incentive other than the idea of duty itself is *juridical*"; the

---

[16] To be clear, Brake (2005, 2012) recognizes that Kant's conception of marriage is meant to address the legal problem of sexual objectification, not the moral problem. Cf. Martha Nussbaum (1995, 268–269), and Allegra De Laurentiis (2000, 298).

6.1 Kant on Marriage

kind of lawgiving that "makes an action a duty and also makes this duty the incentive is *ethical*" (MM 6:219). So, insofar as Kant's account of marriage appears in the "Doctrine of Right," Kant must intend marriage to be a juridical solution to a juridical problem. Were his account of marriage intended to be an ethical solution to an ethical problem, it would have appeared in "The Doctrine of Virtue."

What, then, is the juridical or legal problem of sexual objectification to which marriage is the solution? Here is Beever's (2016, 351) formulation:

> Though *A* can consent to sex with *B*, that consent cannot carry any moral weight. The consent can be morally operative only if *A* is a moral person, but that is inconsistent with the sex act in which *A* becomes a thing. Accordingly, on its face, all acts of sexual intercourse are violations of the partners' innate rights, whether consented to or not.

The legal problem turns on Kant's understanding of an innate right. In the "Doctrine of Right" he identifies only one such right: "*Freedom* (independence from being constrained by another's choice), insofar as it can coexist with the freedom of every other in accordance with a universal law, is the only original right belonging to every man by virtue of his humanity" (MM 6:237). This innate right, the right of humanity, in this legal context does not have to do with our dignity (though our possessing dignity is the ground of this right). Rather, the innate right precludes being constrained by another's choice; it concerns what is always legally impermissible for me to do to you, namely to constrain your choice.

Herein lies the key to the legal problem of sexual objectification, since Kant's account of sex depicts sex as treating one's sexual partner as a mere thing. As Beever (2016, 348) points out, the legal problem of sexual objectification arises because "the relevant kind of consent is impossible. This is because consent to engage in sex cannot be understood as *morally genuine consent* given the innate right and the nature of sex according to Kant's description." To engage in sex, according to Kant, is to allow another to use you as a mere thing. The solution to this problem might seem to be rather simple, namely the mutual consent of the sexual partners (Schaff 2001, 452). Kant, however, explicitly rules this out:

> If, instead of this [i.e., marriage], the conjunction were to be founded on a voluntary concession of the one party's sexual member to the other, that one would be in the position of letting himself or herself be treated by the other as *objectum reale* [a physical object], without taking account of their personhood; this would be a beast-like condition, a conjunction aimed merely at a satisfying of the natural impulse. (VL 27:639)

Mere consent does not do the trick because merely consenting to sex just is merely to consent to be treated as a thing, but to be treated as thing is to give up your personhood and, thereby, your innate right not to be constrained by the will of another. Hence, given the way (according to Kant) sex objectifies, genuine consent is impossible, because we cannot consent to be treated as a mere thing and retain our innate right as a person not to be constrained by another. Hence, the legal problem of sex.

Kant's account of legal marriage as the "reciprocal giving of one's very person into the possession of the other" (MM 6:359) solves this legal problem because marriage provides each spouse with a substitute personhood, as it were. Within the context of marriage, I hand over my personhood to my spouse by consenting to sex, but my spouse does exactly the same, which, according to Kant, means that I regain what I just lost—that is, I do not really lose it at all. As Beever (2016, 352) expresses Kant's point, "In these circumstances, it is impossible to pick out an object that is possessing *A*, because the only possible object is *B* and *B* is being possessed by *A*, and it is impossible to be possessed by something you are possessing." So, on Kant's account, each spouse retains her or his personhood through the reciprocity legal marriage entails, and this secures each's innate right not to be constrained by the will of another, thus making marriage, according to Kant, the only context in which a woman and a man can engage in sexual intercourse without violating their innate right.

Marriage, on Kant's view, solves the legal problem of sexual objectification because marriage creates a (legal) context in which the act of sexual intercourse is transformed from an act where each person violates the innate right of freedom of her or his partner to an act whereby this right is protected through the mutual and complete giving of each other's personhood, which is backed by the power of the state. This solution, however, as Elizabeth Brake points out (2005, 77), leaves untouched the moral problem of sexual objectification. The moral problem, you will recall, involves violating the dignity of your sexual partner by treating her or him as a mere thing, an instrument for your own sexual gratification. Kant must think there is a solution to this problem, since, as I have already pointed out, he never condemns sex as *in principle* immoral. Perhaps, as some scholars maintain, Kant intends his account of marriage to work double-duty. Perhaps, that is, Kant intends marriage to deal with both the legal and the moral problem of sexual objectification. This seems to be the thinking of Matthew Altman (2010, 318–319):

> By taking on her happiness as one of his ends, then, the husband recognizes his wife as someone to whom he has a moral responsibility. Although he uses her for his own sexual gratification, she is not *merely* a thing to be used. By agreeing to be legally bound to treat her as a person, he respects her dignity in furthering the ends she sets for herself....The threat of punishment discourages people from violating the freedom of others—in this case, by requiring someone to take responsibility for his or her spouse's well-being and forbidding any attempt to treat the person merely as a means.

Altman's reading of Kant on marriage (like the ones I mention above) seems to draw on Kant's account of the second duty of virtue, namely the duty we each have to promote the happiness of others. According to Kant,

> The *respect* that I have for others or that another can require from me (*observantia aliis praestanda*) is therefore recognition of a *dignity* (*dignitas*) in other human beings, that is, of a worth that has no price, no equivalent for which the object evaluated (*aestimii*) could be exchanged....But just as he cannot give himself away for any price (this would conflict with his duty of self-esteem), so neither can he act contrary to the equally necessary self-esteem of others, as human beings, that is, he is under obligation to acknowledge in a practical way, the dignity of humanity in every other human being. (MM 6:462)

This passage captures the notion of respect that underlies Kant's insistence that we each have a duty to promote the happiness of others. By adopting the happiness of others as my own end, by promoting their natural well-being as well as I can, I thereby make it my maxim to respect others as beings possessing dignity. Perhaps,

6.1 Kant on Marriage

then, as Altman suggests, by entering the marriage contract and thereby promising to make my spouse's happiness my end I thereby come to respect her or him in the way Kant describes above, which would mitigate the objectifying nature of mere sexual desire and solve the problem sex poses for Kant.

Unfortunately, however, the preceding explanation of Kant's marriage solution to the moral problem of sexual objectification does not work, for two important reasons. First of all, there is Brake's criticism, which is that the moral problem concerns more than the way in which we act towards our sexual partners. It also concerns our psychological states with respect to them: our attitudes towards them, and our feelings and beliefs about them. To use Kant's terms of art, a juridical solution cannot solve an ethical problem. Second, and just as importantly, the moral problem with sexual objectification concerns the way in which sexual partners treat each other and view each other *within the context of their sexual activity*. Sex can be morally objectifying because in the act of sexual intercourse I can and often do (according to Kant) treat my sexual partner as a mere thing, thereby failing to respect her. *Pace* Altman, being legally obliged to have a genuine concern with the natural welfare of my sexual partner does nothing to mitigate how I might treat this person as a mere object while we are having sex. So, the mechanism by which marriage works to solve the legal problem of sexual objectification cannot work to solve the moral problem.

In light of the incompleteness of Kant's solution to the dual problem of sexual objectification, what should we say about his practical sexual ethics? One option would be to conclude that Kant believed there can be no solution to the moral problem of sexual objectification. This, however, does not square with the fact that Kant never condemns sex as immoral in principle and also admits that it can be good. Another option would be to conclude that he was convinced that there had to be a solution to the moral problem, but he could not quite figure out what it is. This is a more charitable conclusion to draw, but it is no more satisfying, since it does not quite sit with the seriousness with which Kant describes the moral problem of sexual objectification—surely someone who finds sexual objectification so morally repulsive and who also does not condemn sexual intercourse as immoral in principle would bother explaining how sex can be morally good. Jane Kneller (2006, 465) summarizes why it is important for Kant to have a credible solution to the moral problem of sexual objectification:

> Sexual relations pose a huge metaphysical problem for Kant because he has staked his philosophy on a distinction between our selves as we are in the world of nature and our selves as agents capable of improvement. Natural inclinations are not themselves evil or wrong, but human beings can and should control them. Kant's moral theory depends on the assumption that persons can be responsible because they can control their own behavior. Sex is a glaring instance of this tension, as Flikschuh puts it, "between the claims of freedom and the constraints of nature."

I think that Kant offers us a hint as to his thinking on the solution to the moral problem of sexual objectification in one lone remark in "The Doctrine of Virtue," at the very end of his discussion of the casuistical questions concerning lust. In the final paragraph of that section, Kant states that "sexual inclination is also called "*love*" (in the narrowest sense of the word) and is, in fact, the strongest possible sensible pleasure in an object" (MM 6:426). He goes on to say that sexual desire cannot be equated with the love of delight or the love of benevolence. "It is," according to Kant, "a unique kind of pleasure, and this ardor has nothing in common with moral love properly speaking, though it can enter into close union with it under the limiting conditions of practical reason" (MM 6:426). So, when sexual desire is conjoined with moral love—that is, *Menschenliebe* (Chap. 4, Sect. 4.4.3)—and is pursued under the limiting conditions of practical reason, it can be good. But "the limiting conditions of practical reason" is just another way to describe Kant's notion of autocracy. This means that Kant's ethical theory allows that sexual desire can be acted on in a way that does not morally objectify one's sexual partner. In light of the conclusions I draw in Part I, we should not be surprised to discover that the condition for morally permissible sex involves the virtuous cultivation of sexual desire, which (according to the passage at the end of Kant's treatment of lust) involves the joining of sexual desire and moral love. Kant actually identifies a kind of relationship that exemplifies moral love and respect and, it would seem, that therefore can be the kind of relationship in which two people can engage in morally permissible sex. This relationship is friendship.

6.2 Kant on Friendship

As is the case with Kant's practical sexual ethic and his account of marriage, Kant's account of friendship and the role he sees friendship playing in our moral lives has not received much attention (Wike 2014, 140). This is unfortunate because Kant's account of friendship makes it an important aspect of the life of a virtuous human being, and it is what he calls "moral friendship" that can function as the solution to the moral problem of sexual objectification. Kant opens his discussion of friendship, which takes place in the conclusion to "The Elements of Ethics" in "The Doctrine of Virtue," with the following definition:

> Friendship (considered in its perfection) is the union of two persons through equal mutual love and respect. – It is easy to see that this is an ideal of each participating and sharing sympathetically in the other's well-being through the morally good will that unites them, and even though it does not produce the complete happiness of life, the adoption of this ideal in their disposition toward each other makes them deserving of happiness. (MM 6:469)

Kant defines friendship in such a way that sets this kind of relationship up as the ideal relationship between two people, and insofar as he defines the relationship in terms of equal mutual love and respect, it is clear that he has in mind the duty of virtue to promote the happiness of others. In other words, the ideal of friendship is the ideal through which individuals can most fully pursue the second end of virtue and do so in a way that is expressive of virtue, which is why Kant says that friendship unites people through morally good will and makes them deserving of happiness.

6.2 Kant on Friendship

In addition to saying that friendship is an ideal, Kant also claims that "friendship is only an idea (though a practically necessary one) and unattainable in practice, although striving for friendship (as a maximum of good disposition toward each other) is a duty set by reason, and no ordinary duty but an honorable one" (MM 6:269). Although he does not explain the difference between an ideal and an idea within the context of his discussion of friendship in the *Metaphysics of Morals*, he presents us with the following explanation of the difference between the two in the Collins Lecture Notes: "their measure is always the maximum; so far as this maximum is a measure in regard to other lesser qualities, such a measure is an Idea; but so far as it is a pattern for them, it is an Ideal" (CL 27: 423). When Kant says that friendship is an Idea, he means that "it is not drawn from experience, but has its seat in the understanding" (CL 27:423). According to Victoria Wike (2014, 144), "In the arena of practical reason, ideas are indispensable and necessary because they serve as archetypes, as the rule against which all practical objects and actions are judged."[17] In other words, we do not draw our concept of friendship as an Idea from experience; rather, it is only a conception we have as a result of maximizing the notion of a relationship that is perfectly good and founded on equal respect and love; hence, Kant's categorization of this Idea as "friendship considered in its perfection." Insofar as friendship is an Ideal, our Idea of friendship in its perfection sets before us a pattern for behavior that we can use as we strive to become better friends (Cf. Rorty 2011, 42–45). Patricia C. Flynn (2007, 423) argues that Kant's understanding of friendship as an Ideal cannot be reconciled with his account of real friendships, but this criticism has less to do with Kant's account of friendship and more to do with the way in which practical ideas function in Kant's ethics (Wike 2014, 143). Indeed, Kant's notion of friendship as an ideal is similar to his notion of virtue as something toward which we always strive, as well as his claim that the idea of a holy will is something that can serve as an ideal for us, despite it being impossible for us to be holy (ML 29:604).

Kant maintains that friendship "is the most intimate union of love and respect" (MM 6:469). Friendship, though, strives for an equal yet delicate balance between love and respect, which concerns the highest form of our relations with other. Recall that love and respect are the two emotions that motivate Kant's duty of virtue to others, namely, to promote their own happiness as if it were your own (Chap. 4, Sect. 4.4.4). According to Kant, love and respect work to balance each other and, so, balance the unsocial sociability of human nature. "For love can be regarded as attraction and respect repulsion, and if the principle of love bids friends to draw closer, the principle of respect requires them to stay at a proper distance" (MM 6:470). Our love for others, as it tends towards unsociability, can devolve into a desire to control or dominate them, to make them into what we want, into our own image of what they should be. But respect pulls us back, since our respect for our

---

[17] Cf. CPR A328/B385: "[an idea of practical reason] is the indispensable condition of every practical use of reason…Accordingly, the practical idea is always fruitful in the highest degree and unavoidably necessary in respect of actual actions. In it practical reason even has the causality actually to bring forth what its concept contains." Cf. CPrR 5:127.

friends *qua* rational being with dignity requires us to acknowledge their independence and autonomy. And *vice versa*.

So much for the way in which friendship entails the most intimate and equal union of love and respect. But I also claimed that this union is delicate, by which I mean it is difficult to establish and even more difficult to maintain. Once again, this difficulty has to do with the unsocial sociability of human beings and the way in which we are inclined to grant priority to our respective sensible feelings and desires over and against the results of our practical reasoning. Here is how Kant expresses this delicate balance:

> Although it is sweet to feel in possession of each other that approaches fusion into one person, friendship is something so delicate (*teneritas amicitiae*) that it is never for a moment safe from interruptions if it is allowed to rest on feelings, and if this mutual sympathy and self-surrender are not subjected to principles or rules preventing excessive familiarity and limiting mutual love by requirements of respect. (MM 6:471)

When Kant says that friendship should not be allowed to rest on feelings, he is not saying that friendships should be purged of emotions. Rather, he is talking about the basis of friendship. And here he is repeating a line of thinking that permeates his writings on ethics, a line of thinking that I have emphasized throughout this book. It is the line of thinking that maintains that the rational part of ourselves is superior to the sensible part of ourselves, and, so, our rational part, as the seat of our dignity, should be the guiding motivation in our practical dealings, including our dealings with others. This does not rule out feelings such as sympathy, but Kant's criticism of sympathy in the preceding passage is of the same mind as his criticism of the sympathetic benefactor in the *Groundwork* (G 4:398); "sympathy" here means the natural, uncultivated feeling of sympathy we may have for others, which (for reasons I discuss in Chap. 3, Sect. 3.2.2) is an unreliable ground for morally good choices and relations. This is why Kant says that these feelings must be subjected to principles. He is talking about the way in which our sensible nature (i.e., our sensible desires and emotions) should be cultivated in light of the autocracy of practical reason if our sensible nature is to be virtuous. It is in this light that we should understand his statement a few lines later, "But in any case the love in friendship cannot be an affect; for emotion is blind in its choice, and after a while it goes up in smoke" (MM 6:471). The love Kant means here is the love of delight, which is a love he understands as an uncultivated pleasure one takes in the perfections of another (Chap. 4, Sect. 4.4.3).[18] That he means this kind of love—and not the (moral) love of human beings—is clear from the passage that immediately precedes this line, where Kant criticizes those "friends" whose relationship involves a great deal of fawning over each other and, as a result (he thinks) involves a fair amount of fighting and making up.

---

[18] Kant gives a slightly different account in the Vigilantius Lecture Notes. There, he distinguishes five components of friendship, the last of which is "The love for mutual well-liking" (VL 27:680), which is the love of delight. He goes on to define friendship as "a complete love of well-wishing and also of well-liking among equals, in regard to their moral dispositions and inclinations" (VL 27:680).

6.2 Kant on Friendship

This account in "The Doctrine of Virtue" is similar to the one he gives in the Vigilantius Lecture Notes, where he defines genuine friendship as "a complete love of well-wishing and also of well-liking among equals, in regard to their moral dispositions and inclinations" (VL 27:680). Kant identifies five components of genuine friendship. First, there is the "well-wishing love to others" (VL 27:675), which, as I have argued (Chap. 4, Sect. 4.4.3), just is what Kant in other texts calls the "love of benevolence." Second, genuine friendship occurs between those who are equal (VL 27:676). Third, genuine friendship involves "the communal possession of one person by the other, or reciprocal possession, i.e., union of their person as to moral disposition" (VL 27:677). Fourth, genuine friendship involves "the reciprocal enjoyment of their humanity" (VL 27:677). And, finally, genuine friendship involves "the love for mutual well-liking" (VL 27:680).[19]

I am going to have occasion to comment on some of these components of genuine friendship when I turn to discuss the implications of Kant's account of friendship for his practical sexual ethics. At this point, I want to draw attention to a shift in my terminology in order to explain a distinction in Kant. In the preceding paragraph, I discussed the five components of "genuine" friendship. This is because Kant distinguishes between three[20] different kinds of friendship, only one of which is genuine (Cf. Moran 2012, 178–186). The first kind of "friendship" is friendship of need, which Kant claims "is that whereby the participants may entrust each other with a reciprocal concern in regard to their needs in life. This was the first beginning of friendship among men, but occurs, for the most part, only under the most primitive conditions" (CL 27:424–425). Kant claims that this kind of friendship, which concerns only each person using the other (though not as a mere means) to meet her or his own needs, does not really occur in society. It is not that friends don't benefit each other in society. Rather, first of all, in society friendship concerns much more than merely meeting each other's needs, whether it be aesthetic friendship or friendship of disposition.[21] Second, "he is a true friend, of whom I know and can presume, that he will really help me in need; but because I am also a true friend of his, I must not appear to him in that light, or impose such a dilemma on him" (CL 27: 425). In other words, genuine friends do not burden each other with favors, otherwise the relationship becomes unequal (MM 6:470). So, friendship of need is not genuine friendship.

---

[19] I do not think that this text contradicts the text of "The Doctrine of Virtue," where Kant claims that the love of friendship is not an affect, because in the Vigilantius Lecture Notes Kant operates with a very peculiar notion of the love of well-liking (i.e., the love of delight), which he says "lies solely in the intellectual disposition of the friends" and is "engendered from the material of reciprocal esteem" (VL 27:680). So, the love of well-liking at work in this definition of friendship is actually a species of intellectual pleasure (MM 6:213).

[20] Lara Denis (2001, 3), H.J. Paton (1993, 142), and Victoria Wike (2014, 143) each claim that Kant has four conceptions of friendship because they each count perfect friendship as a distinct type. I disagree, since perfect friendship is just genuine friendship considered as an Ideal.

[21] As Kate Moran (2012, 179) points out, Kant thinks that this type of friendship [friendship of need] becomes less and less likely as human needs develop from basic needs into 'luxuries.'"

The second type of "friendship" is what Kant calls a "friendship of taste" (Collins Lecture Notes) or an "aesthetic friendship" (Vigilantius Lecture Notes) or "friendship based on feeling" ("Doctrine of Virtue"). A friendship of taste, according to Kant, "is an analogue of friendship and consists in taking pleasure in the company of mutual association of the two parties, rather than their happiness. Between persons of similar station or calling a friendship of taste is not so common as it is between those of differing occupations" (CL 27:426). A friendship of taste is closest to what we might in English call an "acquaintance." This kind of relationship is not for the genuine and mutual concern of each friend for the other but rather is based merely on the enjoyment each friend experiences in the company of the other. This is why Kant says that these kinds of friendship tend to occur between people of different occupations or different social stations. These friendships are really about mutual amusement rather than the trust, confidence, and intimacy of a genuine friendship.

The third kind of friendship is genuine friendship, according to Kant, which he also calls "moral friendship," or, alternatively "friendship of disposition and sentiment," which involves "dispositions of feeling, and not those of actual service" (CL 27: 426–427). This kind of friendship centers around "the complete confidence of two persons in revealing their secret judgments and feelings to each other, as far as such disclosures are consistent with mutual respect" (MM 6:471). Kant says that when we can share our feelings with our friend in such a way that the usual worries about betrayal and mistrust are not an issue, "then we are fully in communion with him" (CL 27:427). According to Kant, in order to avoid the worries about betrayal and mistrust that can characterize our relations with others, "we therefore have need of a friend in whom we can confide, and to whom we may pour out all of our views and opinions; from whom we cannot and need not hide anything and with whom we are fully able to communicate. On this, therefore, rests the friendship of disposition and fellowship" (CL 27: 427).

As I intimated above, the need for friendship stems from our nature as unsocially sociable beings, which, in this context, gets expressed, on the one hand, as the need to confide our most secret thoughts, our deepest desires, and our most vulnerable emotions to another person (sociability) along with the worry that revealing ourselves in this way will result in betrayal and mockery on the part of those who learn our secrets (unsociability). As Allen Wood (2008, 234) explains, "these two contrasting features of human sociability lead, in Kant's view, to a profound need to find another person to whom we can reveal ourselves on conditions of mutual trust." Friendship, according to Kant, fulfills a significant need of humans, and, in a certain respect, it functions to neutralize the unsocial aspects of our nature.[22] Here is Kant's description from "The Doctrine of Virtue" of the way friendship fills this need:

---

[22] Cf. CL 27:428: "But that which diminishes the generality of good-will, and closes the heart towards others, impairs the soul's true goodness, which aspires to universal benevolence. Friendship is thus an aid in overcoming the constraint we harbour, from mistrust, towards those we associate with, and in opening up to them without reserve." Cf. CL 27:422.

> The human being is a being meant for society (though he is also an unsociable one), and in cultivating the social state he feels strongly the need to *reveal* himself to others (even with no ulterior purpose). But on the other hand, hemmed in and cautioned by fear of the misuse others may make of his disclosing thoughts, he finds himself constrained *to lock up* in himself a good part of his judgments (especially those about other people)... If he finds someone intelligent—someone who, moreover, shares his general outlook on things—with whom he need not be anxious about this danger but can reveal himself with complete confidence, he can then air his views. He is not completely alone with his thoughts, as in a prison, but enjoys a freedom he cannot have with the masses... (MM 6:471–472)

Our unsocial sociability makes us want—no, need—companionship while at the same time making us cautious (if not downright suspicious) of others in a way that closes off genuine companionship with most people. Moral friendship, however, is an ideal of the kind of companionship Kant here claims we long for, since moral friendship entails a relationship with a partner whom you think is smart, who shares your general worldview (including, importantly, your values[23]), and whom you can trust fully. In this context, you can make yourself most vulnerable without feeling or being vulnerable, because you share yourself with a genuine, moral friend.

Now we are in a position to see how Kant's account of moral friendship relates to the moral problem of sexual objectification. Recall that mere/natural sexual desire, according to Kant, is an expression of our unsociability, insofar as the tendency of this desire is to objectify our sexual partners as mere things. The moral problem of sexual objectification can only be solved if we can identify a context in which (1) sexual partners are genuine equals, and (2) sexual partners can engage in sexual activity while treating each other as ends, that is while they each respect the humanity of their respective partners and they each respect their own humanity. In light of Kant's understanding of genuine, moral friendship, particularly with respect to the way in which it reconciles our unsociable tendencies in our relations with others, I contend that moral friendship can be the context in which two people can engage in sexual relations without objectifying each other.

6.2.1 Sex, The Enjoyment of Humanity, and Moral Friendship

The feature of moral friendship that speaks most directly to the ability of friendship to serve as the context in which the moral problem of sexual objectification is neutralized is also the final end of friendship (Wood 1999, 280), namely, our ability to trust and be emotionally and cognitively intimate with our friend. This is the fourth feature of friendship, according to Kant, what he calls "the reciprocal enjoyment of the humanity" between friends. He explains this feature thusly: "in the mutual relation in regard to capacity, and the satisfaction of the power and need so typical of man, they [friends] stand together, to communicate not only their feelings and sensations to one another, but also their thoughts" (VL 27:677). Such communication

---

[23] I think, therefore, that Allen Wood (1999, 276–277) underemphasizes the way in which genuine friendship rests on friends being virtuous.

is possible, according to Kant, because of the trust and confidence that friends have in each other. And such trust and confidence is possible because moral friends are equals (CL 27:426). Accordingly, friendship "is a special bond between particular persons; in this world only, therefore, it is a recourse for opening up one's mind to the other and communing with him, in that here there is a lack of trust among men" (CL 27:428). In establishing this deep trust between each other, friends thereby effectively eliminate the "antagonism" that can be such a hindrance to social relations (VL 27:680; Cf. IUH 8:20–21).

How would this aspect of friendship make morally permissible sexual activity possible? According to Kant, sexual desire objectifies both our sexual partners and ourselves, since mere sexual appetite is the desire to use the sexual organs of another for my own gratification. Sexual desire, therefore, treats your sexual partner as a mere thing, insofar as you only want to use her or him for sexual satisfaction, but sexual desire also entails you treating yourself as a mere thing, insofar as you offer yourself up to your partner for her or his sexual enjoyment. In these ways, the humanity in both myself and my sexual partner is debased, since "a human being cannot be used merely as a means by any human being (either by others or even by himself) but must always be used at the same time as an end" (MM 6:462). The question, then, is, "What does treating someone as an end look like when it comes to sexual behavior?"

I think the enjoyment of humanity that constitutes moral friendship must form some part of what it means to treat another as an end. Or, more precisely, enjoyment of another's humanity is one instantiation of treating another as an end, and it is an instantiation that is particularly suited to dealing with the problem of sexual objectification. When friends enjoy each other's humanity, they thereby recognize each other as rational beings possessing dignity in at least two ways. First of all, insofar as I listen to and am open to my friend's most intimate and secret feelings, desires, and opinions, I cannot but recognize her as more than a mere object, as more than a thing or even a mere animal. Things and mere animals do not have intimate feelings, desires, and opinions. Second, my recognition of my friend's humanity—and, therefore, her dignity—is expressed in my ability to keep her confidence and not fall into the antagonism that is characteristic of human nature. My recognition of my friend's humanity and my genuinely having her trust mean that I recognize her as an end.[24]

Is this kind of recognition possible between two sexual partners? Indeed, is it possible between two sexual partners within the context of their sexual activity? You might think not because the ravenous way in which Kant describes mere sexual appetite would seem to imply that people caught up in sexual desire cannot but take advantage of their sexual partners, particularly since their sexual partners, within the context of sexual activity, tend to leave themselves vulnerable.

I think, however, that there are two responses to this objection. First, Kant is clear that moral friendship involves a significant degree of intellectual vulnerability and openness to another, insofar as I am sharing all of my secrets with my friend. I see

---

[24] Papadaki (2010, 288–292) develops a similar account of the way moral friendship can be a context for morally permissible sex.

no *prima facie* reason to think that the kind of intellectual or psychological vulnerability and reciprocal trust that Kant describes as characteristic of moral friendship cannot have an analogue within the context of a physical sexual relationship, where sexual partners are similarly vulnerable and need a similar kind of trust and confidence in each other (i.e., I do not think that sexual activity would violate Kant's prescription that friends should not be too intimate [Cf. Denis 201, 21]). Since Kant thinks that the kind of trust and confidence characteristic of moral friendship helps prevent friends from exploiting each other's intellectual and psychological vulnerability, why cannot the same level of trust and confidence serve to prevent such friends from exploiting each other's sexual vulnerability?

Second, remember that Kant admits that sexual appetite can be connected with moral love "and enter into close union with it under the limiting conditions of practical reason" (MM 6:426). So, in other words, Kant thinks it is possible for us to exercise the autocracy of practical reason over our sexual desire, thereby making sexual desire receptive to being joined with moral love of another person. And, as I have already argued, moral love (i.e., love of human beings) is the sensible desire (accompanied by the requisite sensible feeling of love) that has been cultivated by practical reason and forms part of the union of love and respect Kant says is characteristic of friendship. Hence, friendship, insofar as genuine friends can and do enjoy each other's humanity, can place limiting conditions on sexual appetite and neutralize the tendency of this appetite to objectify our sexual partners.

6.2.2 Sex, Reciprocity, and Moral Friendship

If the argument of the preceding section regarding the enjoyment of humanity works, that only deals with half of the moral problem of sexual objectification, namely, the way in which I can objectify my sexual partner. It does not, however, deal with the other part of the problem, namely, how in offering myself up to my sexual partner for her or his gratification, I thereby demean myself and violate my own dignity. I think Kant's account of moral friendship can deal with this half of the problem, too, though by drawing on a different feature of moral friendship, namely "the communal possession of one person by the other, or reciprocal possession, i.e., union of their person as to moral disposition" (VL 27:677).[25]

When Kant proposes marriage as the solution to the legal problem of sexual objectification, it is marital reciprocity that allows him to claim that marriage precludes each partner's submission to sexual objectification. This is because, according to Kant, spouses who agree to engage in sexual intercourse with each other surrender their personality equally so that each spouse in losing her or his personhood thereby regains it back in the form of the personhood of the other, and in this

---

[25] Both Gary Banham (2012, 173) and Lina Papadaki (2010, 288–289) identify this feature of friendship as similar to marital reciprocity.

way, thinks Kant, husbands and wives form a unity. According to Kant, there is an analog of such reciprocity with moral friendship. As he describes it,

> The maximum of mutual love is friendship, and this is an Idea, since it serves as a measure by which to determine reciprocal love. The greatest love I can have for another is to love him as myself, for I cannot love anybody more than that; but if I would love him as myself, I can do it no otherwise than by being assured that he will love me as much as himself; in that case I am requited for what I part with, and thereby regain occupancy of myself. (CL 27:423–424)

Kant even goes so far as to say that the reciprocity characteristic of moral friendship "is somewhat the same as in marriage" (VL 27:677). The difference between marriage and moral friendship, he claims, is that the reciprocity characteristic of friendship is founded "on moral principles and mutual love derived from that, and is thus an intellectual or moral possession" (VL 27:677). In other words, whereas the reciprocity of marriage entails the spouses' *physical* possession of each other, friendship entails the *intellectual* possession of each other.

This distinction between the physical reciprocity of marriage and the intellectual reciprocity of friendship invites the question, "Why cannot both coexist in a single relationship?" If they can, then such a relationship would be one in which the people involved could engage in sexual activity that is morally permissible. Given Kant's understanding of the differences between women and men, the answer, on Kant's account of things, is obvious: men and women are not equals and, so, there can be neither intellectual reciprocity nor genuine friendship between men and women. Here the relevant kind of inequality is social inequality, since the inability of women to own property and, thereby, be active citizens means, for Kant, that any relationship they have with men is one of dependence, which rules out equality. Moreover, according to Kant, in genuine friendship reciprocal possession rests "on moral principles," and genuine friends "need to have the same principles of understanding and morality, and then they can fully understand each other" (CL 27:429). On his view of things, however, women are incapable of principles (OBS 2:232).[26]

There is good reason, though, to question the cogency of these aspects of Kant's practical ethics. First of all, as I indicated in the previous Chapter, there is every reason to critique Kant's account of women as unequal, both physically and socially, to men. And this means that Kant's reasons for thinking that women cannot be citizens are bad reasons, since they no longer hold (Denis 2001, 19–20). Indeed, despite the persistence of misogyny and social inequality between women and men (e.g., with respect to equal pay), women can and do enjoy the kind of independence Kant believed was essential to active citizenship. Second, there are no *prima facie* reasons to think that women are incapable of the kind of reciprocal intellectual possession that Kant describes as part of friendship. Actually, according to Kant "the basis for that compatibility and bond of friendship" is "difference…which establishes friendship, for in that case the one supplies what the other lacks" (CL 27:429). So,

---

[26] Cf. (Papadaki 2010, 289–290), who points out that, according to Kant, a married different-sex couple cannot achieve moral friendship because such friendship requires a sharing of intellectual and moral principles, of which women are incapable.

according to Kant's reasoning and conception of gender differences, women and men ought to be especially suitable for friendship, since he believes that they complement each other in ways that accentuate the kind of difference Kant thinks serves as the basis for friendship. Third, if we keep in mind the description of the kind of enjoyment of humanity that I argued is possible between men and women who are sexual partners, and if such enjoyment were joined with the reciprocity constitutive of moral friendship, then different-sex sexual partners would each gain their personalities back within the context of sexual activity within their relationship, thereby solving the second half of the moral problem of sexual objectification.

6.3 Looking Ahead

In this chapter I presented Kant's proposed solution to the legal problem posed by his account of sexual desire, namely that sexual desire objectifies its object in a way that violates the innate right of humanity in a person (i.e., the right not to be constrained by the will of another). In arguing that Kant intends his account of marriage to be the legal solution to the legal problem of sexual objectification, I have tried to demonstrate that his account of marriage is more cogent than it might first appear, so long as one correctly understands its limited scope. I then raised the moral problem of sexual objectification and suggested that the tools to develop an adequate solution to this aspect of the problem of sexual objectification can be found in Kant's account of friendship. I argued that friendship, understood as the perfect union of love and respect wherein two people confide in each other and share in each other's well-being, provides a context that mitigates the tendency of mere sexual desire to objectify its object. More specifically, I suggested that two aspects of genuine friendship in particular—friends' reciprocal possession of each other and their enjoyment of each other's respective humanity—create the conditions under which a man and a woman can engage in sexual activity that is morally permissible, since under these conditions, sexually intimate men and women can treat each other as ends in themselves and thereby respect each other's dignity and their own.

Accordingly, I hope that the argument of this chapter has gone some way to demonstrating that Kant's practical sexual ethic and his account of the legal institution of marriage each have significant merits that should make us pause before instinctually and unreflectively rejecting them as offensive or as relics of some thankfully lost culture. I have not yet applied the fruits of this discussion to the issue of same-sex sexual relations, nor have I considered the implications of the foregoing arguments for whether my interpretation of Kant's ethics can allow for same-sex marriage. This, then, shall be the focus of the next and final chapter, which will aim to bring the fruits of my investigation to bear on the same-sex marriage debate.

References

Altman, Matthew C. 2010. Kant on Sex and Marriage: The Implications for the Same-Sex Marriage Debate. *Kant-Studien* 101.3: 309–330.
Aris, Rheinhold. 1965. *History of Political Thought in Germany, 1789–1815*. Oxfordhsire: Frank Cass & Co., Ltd..
Banham, Gary. 2012. Kantian Friendship. In *Critical Communities and Aesthetic Practices: Dialogues with Tony O'Connor on Society, Art, and Friendship*, ed. Francis Halsall, Julia Jansen, and Sinéad Murphy, 171–180. Dordrecht: Springer.
Beever, Allan. 2016. Kant on the Law of Marriage. *Kantian Review* 18 (3): 339–362.
Brake, Elizabeth. 2005. Justice and Virtue in Kant's Account of Marriage. *Kantian Review* 9 (1): 58–94.
———. 2012. *Minimizing Marriage: Marriage, Morality, and the Law*. Oxford/New York: Oxford University Press.
De Laurentiis, Allegra. 2000. Kant's Shameful Proposition: A Hegel-Inspired Criticism of Kant's Theory of Domestic Right. *International Philosophical Quarterly* 40 (3): 297–312.
Deming, Will. 1995. *Paul on marriage and celibacy: The Hellenistic background of 1 Corinthians 7*. Cambridge/New York: Cambridge University Press.
Denis, Lara. 2001. From Friendship to Marriage: Revising Kant. *Philosophy and Phenomenological Research* 63 (1): 1–28.
———. 2002. Kant's Ethical Duties and Their Feminist Implications. *Canadian Journal of Philosophy, Supplementary Volume* 28: 157–187.
Flynn, Patricia C. 2007. Honesty and Intimacy in Kant's Duty of Friendship. *International Philosophical Quarterly* 47 (4): 417–424.
Hay, Carol. 2013. *Kantianism, Liberalism, and Feminism: Resisting Oppression*. New York: Palgrave MacMillan.
Herman, Barbara. 2002. Could It Be Worth Thinking About Kant on Sex and Marriage? In *A Mind of One's Own: Feminist Essays on Reason and Objectivity*, ed. Louise M. Antony and Charlotte E. Witt, 53–72. Boulder: Westview Press.
Keener, Craig S. 2011. Paul and the Corinthian Believers. In *The Blackwell Companion to Paul*, ed. Stephen Westerholm, 46–62. Malden/Oxford: Blackwell Publishing.
Kneller, Jane. 2006. Kant on sex and marriage right. In *The Cambridge Companion to Kant and Modern Philosophy*, ed. Paul Guyer, 447–476. Cambridge: Cambridge University Press.
Mendus, Susan. 1987. Kant: An Honest but Narrow-Minded Bourgeois? In *Women in Western Political Philosophy: Kant to Nietzsche*, 21–43. New York: St. Martin's Press.
Mertens, Thomas. 2014. Sexual Desire and the Importance of Marriage in Kant's Philosophy of Law. *Ratio Juris* 27 (3): 330–343.
Mikkola, Mari. 2011. Kant on Moral Agency and Women's Nature. *Kantian Review* 16 (1): 89–111.
Moore, Gareth. 1992. *The Body in Context: Sex and Catholicism*. London/New York: Continuum.
Moran, Kate A. 2012. *Community and progress in Kant's moral philosophy*. Washington, DC.: Catholic University of America Press.
Nussbaum, Martha C. 1995. Objectification. *Philosophy and Public Affairs* 24 (4): 249–291.
———. 2007. Feminism, Virtue, and Objectification. In *Essays on Sexuality, Virtue, and the Good Life*, ed. Raja Halwani, 49–62. New York: Palgrave MacMillan.
Paton, H.J. 1993. Kant on Friendship. In *Friendship: A Philosophical Reader*, ed. Neera Kapur Badhwar, 133–154. Ithaca: Cornell University Press.
Papadaki, Lina. 2010. Kantian Marriage and Beyond: Why It is Worth Thinking about Kant on Marriage. *Hypatia* 25 (2): 276–294.
Rorty, Amelie. 2011. Kant on two modalities of friendship. In *Rethinking Kant: Volume 3*, ed. Oliver Thorndike, 33–51. Newcastle upon Tyne: Cambridge Scholars Publishing.
Sadler, Brook J. 2013. Marriage: A Matter of Right or of Virtue? Kant and the Contemporary Debate. *Journal of Social Philosophy* 44 (3): 213–232.

Schaff, Kory. 2001. Kant, Political Liberalism, and the Ethics of Same-Sex Relations. *Journal of Social Philosophy* 32 (3): 446–462.

Schröder, Hannelore. 1997. Kant's Patriarchal Order, trans. Rita Gircour. In *Feminist Interpretations of Immanuel Kant*, ed. Robin May Schott, 275–296. University Park: The Pennsylvania State University Press.

Varden, Helga. 2006. A Kantian Conception of Rightful Sexual Relations: Sex, (Gay) Marriage, and Prostitution. *Social Philosophy Today* 22: 199–218.

Wike, Victoria S. 2014. Kantian Friendship: Duty and Idea. *Diametros* 39: 140–153.

Wood, Allen W. 1999. *Kant's Ethical Thought*. Cambridge: Cambridge University Press.

———. 2008. *Kantian Ethics*. Cambridge: Cambridge University Press.

Chapter 7
Conclusion: Kant's Ethics & the Same-Sex Marriage Debate

Abstract My aim in writing this book was to make the case for Kant's ethics containing resources that speak to the issues pertaining to the contemporary debate over same-sex marriage. In order to make my argument, I needed first to address what I called "the Anscombian reading of Kant's ethics," which is a reading of Kant that mischaracterizes his ethical theory as a deontological theory that is morally rigoristic, formalistic, and closed off to empirical features of human beings and our lives. Hence, I devoted Part I of this book to debunking the caricature of Kant's ethics that the Anscombian reading puts forth. Only then could I specifically address Kant's practical sexual ethics and account of marriage, which has been the focus of Part II. I have argued that Kant's sexual ethics (including his account of gender differences between women and men) and his account of the legal institution of marriage are not as flawed as some commentators have made them out to be and, in fact, contain some valuable insights. In this final chapter I apply those insights to the contemporary debate over same-sex marriage by revisiting the arguments for and against same-sex marriage that I presented in Chap. 1 and by commenting on the ways in which I think Kant's moral philosophy can help us to evaluate those arguments.

My aim in writing this book was to make the case for Kant's ethics containing resources that speak to the issues pertaining to the contemporary debate over same-sex marriage. In order to make my argument, I needed first to address what I called "the Anscombian reading of Kant's ethics," which is a reading of Kant that mischaracterizes his ethical theory as a deontological theory that is morally rigoristic, formalistic, and closed off to empirical features of human beings and our lives. Hence, I devoted Part I of this book to debunking the caricature of Kant's ethics that the Anscombian reading puts forth. Only then could I specifically address Kant's practical sexual ethics and account of marriage, which has been the focus of Part II. I have argued that Kant's sexual ethics (including his account of gender differences between women and men) and his account of the legal institution of marriage are not as flawed as some commentators have made them out to be and, in fact, contain some valuable insights. Notably, though, I have not yet applied those insights to the contemporary debate over same-sex marriage. That is my task in this concluding chapter. I am going to return to the arguments against and for same-sex marriage that I presented in Chap. 1, and drawing on the account of Kant's ethics I have presented, I will comment on the ways in which I think that features of Kant's moral philosophy speak to those arguments. Before I do that, though, I want to address the elephant in the room, namely, Kant's moral condemnation of homosexuality.

7.1 Kant's Evaluation of Same-Sex Sexual Relations

As I explained in Chap. 5, Kant unqualifiedly condemns same-sex sexual activity, whether it occurs between two women or two men. To review, he claims that same-sex sexual activity is a species of *crimina carnis contra naturam,* that is, of sexual crimes against nature. He condemns sexual activity between two women or between two men because such activity "runs counter to the ends of humanity, for the end of humanity in regard to this impulse is to preserve the species without forfeiture of the person" (CL 27:391). Additionally, Kant claims that same-sex sexual activity is immoral in a further sense because of the way in which those who engage in it "forfeit their person," which, he claims degrades such people "below the beasts" (CL 27:391). So, it seems that Kant provides three distinct but related reasons for thinking that same-sex sexual activity is immoral: it is not procreative; in not being procreative it entails forfeiture of the persons involved; and the nature of such forfeiture degrades those who engage in it as though they were "less than" non-human animals. I want to examine each of these reasons in light of Kant's own moral theory.

7.1.1 Sexual Activity and Procreation

First of all, regarding the preservation of the species, Kant also claims that this is *nature's* end for us: "Just as love of life is destined by nature to preserve the person, so sexual love is destined by it to preserve the species" (MM 6:424). Here I take him to mean that if we were to personify nature and speak of nature having purposes, the natural purpose of sexual intercourse between women and men would be to procreate, since by this means and this means alone can we propagate the human species. But if the preservation of the species through procreative sex is nature's purpose, Kant seems to be saying that this natural purposes places moral constraints on the way in which we should behave. He seems to think that nature's purpose for sex implies that this purpose is, or should be, *our* purpose in having sex, so that to have sex that is inherently incapable of procreation is to act contrary to nature's purpose and, therefore, to what should be our purpose in having sex, which is immoral.[1] So,

---

[1] Since my focus here is on same-sex sexual activity, I leave to one side questions about what Kant's view entails when it comes to men and women engaging in coitus for purposes other than procreation. Though, it is worth reminding readers that Kant allows that such sexual activity is not immoral, insofar as he thinks that sterile married couples may engage in coitus.

according to this way of elaborating Kant's view, same-sex sexual activity, which cannot be procreative, is immoral.

I think, however, that Kant's normative ethical theory gives us good reason to pause before reaching this conclusion regarding the connection between what nature's alleged purpose may be and the kinds of purposes we are morally obligated to adopt. Throughout this book I have stressed that central to Kant's normative ethical theory is the claim that human beings are finite, dependent, morally imperfect beings (see especially Chap. 2, Sects. 2.2.1 and 2.2.2). He explains this imperfection in terms of human beings having two natures, a sensible one and a rational one. In virtue of our sensible natures, Kant argues that each of us has an interest in our respective conception of happiness, which is one of our goods as finite rational beings. But it is not our only good, thinks Kant. Our rational nature, as the ground of our powers to deliberate about what we should do and to act on the basis of such deliberation, makes us more than mere animals concerned with happiness (Cf. G 4:395–396). It makes us beings who, according to Kant, possess dignity and who, in virtue of this dignity, have a second good we should pursue, namely the cultivation of our capacity to choose on the basis of reasons. On Kant's understanding of human beings, we act well when we act autonomously, and we act autonomously when we correctly reason about what we should do and then act in light of this deliberation, rather than merely acting unreflectively on our sensible inclinations. So, we act well when we do not merely accept what is naturally desirable but instead submit the claims of sensible nature to rational scrutiny. Here then is one reason for someone persuaded by Kant's ethics to reject the claim that because procreation is allegedly a natural end of sex, we are thereby morally prohibited from engaging in sex that is not procreative. On Kant's own moral theory, we should not merely accept an end of nature as morally obligatory; rather, if we are to act autonomously we need to reason about whether this end is in any way morally obligatory.

Perhaps, therefore, when Kant claims that same-sex activity "runs counter to the ends of humanity, for the end of humanity in regard to this impulse is to preserve the species without forfeiture of the person" (CL 27:391), what he means is that we have a moral obligation to engage only in procreative sex, an obligation that thereby precludes any sex that is not procreative (such as same-sex sexual activity). So, I want now to consider what such an argument would look like. Does Kant's normative ethical theory warrant concluding that human beings have a moral obligation only to engage in sexual acts that are procreative?

Recall (Chap. 4, Sect. 4.4) that Kant distinguishes between perfect duties and imperfect duties. Perfect duties are those duties that "admit of no exception in favor of inclination" (G 4:422) so that we act immorally if we fail to fulfill them. On Kant's view, perfect duties are all ones that prohibit or forbid certain acts; they do not prescribe the pursuit of certain ends. So, it would not make sense for there to be a perfect duty to engage in procreative sex, since a perfect duty to engage in procreative sex would entail that any act that does *not* involve procreative sex is immoral.

Accordingly, a moral obligation to engage only in procreative sex would have to be what Kant calls an imperfect duty. When it comes to imperfect duties, "the law cannot specify precisely in what way one is to act and how much one is to do by the action for an end that is also a duty" (MM 6:390). Kant identifies two basic imperfect duties that we are obligated to pursue: the promotion of the happiness of others and our own self-perfection. Is there an imperfect moral obligation to engage only in procreative sex in order to promote the happiness of others? According to Kant, when it comes to promoting the happiness of others,

> It is for them to decide what they count as belonging to their happiness; but it is open to me to refuse them many things that *they* think will make them happy but that I do not, as long as they have no right to demand them from me as what is theirs. (MM 6:388)

Perhaps others might claim that their happiness consists in me only engaging in procreative sex acts, but such people do not have a right to *demand* this of me.[2] Nor do others have a right to demand of me that I refrain from same-sex sexual activity as a matter of promoting their happiness. So, I cannot be said, on Kant's terms, to have an imperfect duty to engage only in procreative sex as a matter of promoting the happiness of others.

What about an imperfect duty to engage only in procreative sex as a matter of my duty to perfect myself. Here again it is worth remembering how Kant elucidates the imperfect duty to perfect oneself. He claims that this duty

> consists only in *cultivating* one's *faculties* (or natural predispositions), the highest of which is *understanding*, the faculty of concepts and so too of those concepts that have to do with duty. At the same time this duty includes the cultivation of one's *will* (moral cast of mind), so as to satisfy all the requirements of duty. (MM 6:387)

Here again it seems that there cannot be an imperfect moral obligation to engage only in procreative sex. Our ability to procreate is not a faculty we have—it is not a capacity we possess that needs to be developed. The power to procreate is a function of our biology, and either we are capable of engaging in procreative sex or we are not; this is not something we can develop. Moreover, engaging exclusively in procreative sex has no connection to cultivating our wills so that we act autonomously. In order to claim that engaging only in procreative sex entails the cultivation of our wills to "satisfy all the requirements of duty," we would have to assume that engaging only in procreative sex is what it means to act autonomously when it comes to our sexual activity, but to assume that would be to beg the question. So, according to Kant's normative ethical theory, it seems that we cannot establish that there is a moral obligation to engage only in procreative sex.[3]

---

[2] Even if the person who demands this of me is my spouse, on Kant's account of marriage, my spouse has a right to sex, not a right to procreative sex.

[3] Nothing I have argued regarding a failure to establish a moral obligation only to engage in procreative sex entails that engaging in procreative sex is morally forbidden. As Kant claims, "that action is *permitted* (*licitum*) which is not contrary to obligation" (MM 6:222).

7.1.2 Same-Sex Sexual Activity and the Forfeiture of One's Person

It is unsurprising that Kant's ethical theory cannot justify judging same-sex sexual activity to be immoral on account of it not being procreative. In his discussion of lust in the "Doctrine of Virtue," Kant admits that "it is not so easy to produce a rational proof that unnatural, and even merely unpurposive, use of one's sexual attribute is inadmissible as being a violation of duty to oneself" (MM 6:425). This, I take it, is why Kant does not attempt to make such an argument in this work but instead argues that a so-called unnatural sex act, such as masturbation, is immoral because "by it the human being surrenders his personality (throwing it away)" (MM 6:425). This brings me to Kant's second reason for claiming that same-sex sexual activity is morally prohibited, namely that engaging in same-sex sexual activity involves "forfeit of their person." Since same-sex sexual activity and masturbation are both, according to Kant, *crimina carnis contra naturam,* we can safely conclude that the forfeiture of one's person with respect to same-sex sexual activity is the same thing as the throwing away of one's personality with respect to masturbation. Regarding the latter, Kant claims that one's personality is thrown away because engaging in such a crime against nature, one "uses himself as a means to satisfy an animal impulse" (MM 6:425). So, *crimina carnis contra naturam* are immoral because they violate one's own dignity.

It is telling, however, that Kant thinks that it is not enough merely to say that such sexual acts involve treating oneself merely as a means, since this way of expressing the wrong does not capture "the high degree of violation of the humanity in one's own person by such a vice in its unnaturalness" (MM 6:425). Such unnatural sex acts, according to Kant, involve the "complete abandonment of oneself to animal inclination, which makes the human being not only an object of enjoyment but, still further, a thing that is contrary to nature, that is, a *loathsome object,* and so deprives him of all respect for himself" (MM 6:425).

One might well wonder, though, whether same-sex sex acts entail such abandonment to animal inclination. Kant's thinking seems to be that when one engages in *crimina carnis contra naturam,* such as same-sex sex acts, one does so *only* in order to satisfy one's animal craving for sexual pleasure. When one engages in same-sex sex acts, according to this way of thinking, one simply gives in to one's animal desire for sexual pleasure (presumably in the form of an orgasm) so that one behaves as a mere animal and, so, acts in a way that precludes self-respect. But why should one accept this as an accurate description of some, never mind all, same-sex sexual activity? Of course, two women who engage in sexual activity or two men who engage in sexual activity may sometimes do so passionately and may even be said at times to have sex with a kind of reckless abandon. This does not mean that they are surrendering themselves to animal passion in the way in which Kant's argument supposes. More importantly, Kant offers no reason for thinking that sexual acts between two women or between two men—whatever those acts may be—by their very nature are acts that reduce the participants to mere animals, to savages of some sort. And I cannot think of any reason in support of his characterization. Finally, even if one grants for the sake of argument that some same-sex couples sometimes engage in passionate sex that threatens their self-respect, there are no good reasons for thinking that such sex threatens self-respect insofar as it occurs between two women or between two men (Cf. Brake 2005, 66–69).

7.1.3 Same-Sex Sex Acts and the Behavior of Non-human Animals

This brings me to Kant's third reason for rejecting same-sex sexual activity as immoral, the reason that makes sexual activity between two women or between two men a crime against nature, according to Kant, namely, that this kind of sexual activity degrades the people who engage in it below non-human animals. As I explained in Chap. 5, Kant thinks that *crimina carnis contra naturam* debase our humanity below the beasts because these types of sexual activity are types of activity in which non-human animals do not engage. I think this is the weakest of Kant's reasons for condemning same-sex sexual activity. First of all, as I noted in Chap. 5, Kant is wrong to think that non-human animals do not engage in same-sex sexual activity. Not only do many species of non-human animals engage in same-sex sexual activity, most of the evidence indicates that this activity is good for the animals in question (i.e., it plays a positive evolutionary role for members of their respective species). Second, and more importantly, what should it matter whether non-human animals engage in some activity? There are plenty of activities in which non-human animals do not engage, but this does not mean that these activities are thereby immoral. My cat cannot (and, so, does not) read *Invisible Man*, and my chicken cannot (and, so, does not) cook a mushroom pizza. But this does not mean that reading *Invisible Man* and making a mushroom pizza are both immoral. On Kant's normative ethical theory, what makes an action moral has to do in part with whether it aims at an end that practical reason correctly determines to be genuinely good, and there is nothing in Kant's ethical theory, and there is nothing about same-sex sexual activity, to indicate that all same-sex sexual activity by its nature cannot fit this bill.

In light of the foregoing considerations, I think Kant's ethical theory does not support Kant's conclusion that same-sex sexual activity is in principle immoral. Accordingly, I think it is possible, at least in principle, for someone working within the framework of Kant's ethics to argue that same-sex marriage is something that should be made legal. Actually, in light of what I have argued thus far in this book, I think one can draw on Kant's normative ethical theory and his practical sexual ethics in evaluating the arguments against and for same-sex marriage that I presented in Chap. 1. In this way, one can draw on resources in Kant to develop a position regarding same-sex marriage. In order to make good on this claim, I now want to return to the arguments I examined in Chap. 1 to see what, if anything, Kant's ethical theory has to offer with respect to engaging those arguments.

7.2 The Arguments Against Same-Sex Marriage

Given Kant's own views regarding human sexual desire and his personal rejection of same-sex sexual activity as immoral, one might think that Kant's ethical theory would look favorably on those arguments against same-sex marriage. But I have not been concerned to defend what *Kant's* view would be regarding same-sex marriage. The main thesis of this book is that there are resources in Kant's ethics that can be of value to those of us engaged in the debate over same-sex marriage. When one draws on those resources as I have presented them in this book, I think there is good reason to think that the arguments against same-sex marriage are not good arguments.

7.2.1 The Definitional Objection and Kant's Conception of Marriage

The definitional objection to same-sex marriage contends that same-sex couples *cannot* marry because marriage is not the kind of thing of which same-sex couples are capable. Defenders of the definitional objection claim that marriage is a basic good with an "objective core" that is determined by our nature as embodied, sexually reproductive beings. Marriage, according to this position, entails both a union of the wills of the spouses (in the form of their consent to marry) and a union of the bodies of the spouses (in the form of their sexual union in the act of coitus). In light of this characterization, defenders of the definitional objection insist that marriage is inherently ordered to procreation and family life. Since same-sex couples cannot achieve the bodily union characteristic of marriage, so this argument goes, same sex couples cannot marry.

Kant's account of marriage gives us several reasons to be critical of the definitional objection. First of all, defenders of the definitional objection seem to think of marriage as a kind of natural institution, one whose existence is not reducible to the state's conception of it or to changing societal standards with respect to it. Marriage, according to Kant's ethics, is a legal institution, and, as such, only exists within the context of civil society. So, the claim that marriage has a fixed objective core does not make much sense. With Kant's ethics in mind, one might argue that marriage is an institution that the state creates in order guarantee the rights of spouses.

Second, although Kant defines marriage as the union of two persons, he does not do so on the grounds that defenders of the definitional objection do. Defenders of the definitional objection, for example, conceive of the bodily union allegedly achieved in marriage as a genuinely biological union, on par with the kind of bodily union that exists with respect to a individual human being's organs. But this does not make sense. Not only is it impossible for two human beings to become one human being (which is what the analogy with bodily organs entails); it is also the case that, according to Kant's account, marriage protects the rights of spouses because it establishes reciprocity between them, and there can be no reciprocity where there are not two people.[4]

Closely related to this second point is a third: the function of marriage, as Kant's ethics presents it, has nothing to do with procreation. Marriage is the legal institution that can guarantee the legal rights of sexually active spouses. Having children, or being able to have children, is not a necessary condition for being married on Kant's account. So, accordingly, the idea that marriage is inherently ordered to procreation and the raising of the family does not make sense as an account of the legal institution of marriage.

7.2.2 Marital Norms and the Alleged Harms of Same-Sex Marriage

An argument closely related to the definitional objection is the one that claims that same-sex marriage harms marital norms. The harm here is not material harm but instead is allegedly the harm done when a false good is presented as a true one. More specifically, the argument claims that legalizing same-sex marriage makes it more difficult for women to be good wives and men to be good husbands, insofar as same-sex marriage runs counter to the conception of marriage at work in the definitional objection. So, the argument goes, same-sex marriage is a mere counterfeit version of marriage.

I think in principle someone committed to Kant's ethics can have some sympathy with the general claim that counterfeit goods can have a deleterious effect on the moral character of people. After all, Kant's ethics, as I have presented it, is a kind of virtue ethics, one that is concerned with the development of certain character traits. So, someone drawing on the basic tenets of Kant's ethics can appreciate the way in which certain practices or institutions can harm our capacity to develop virtuous characters. The problem with the argument concerning harms done to marital norms is that it presupposes the conception of marriage operative in the definitional objection, namely the so-called "conjugal view" of marriage. So, the argument only works if one accepts that conception of marriage, and I have argued that Kant's conception of marriage gives us reasons for rejecting the definitional objection's conception of marriage.

Insofar as the other harms alleged of same-sex marriage also depend on one holding the conjugal view of marriage, the same criticism can be made of them. Take, for example, the claim that legalizing same-sex marriage would undermine genuine friendships, insofar as acknowledging same-sex unions as genuine marriages rules out any clear way of distinguishing romantic, sexual relationships from

---

[4] Although this point does not bear on the issue of same-sex marriage, it is worth noting that Kant's account of marriage does not entail that marriage is a permanent union of spouses, insofar as "permanent" here means that spouses may not divorce. Kant explicitly allows for justified divorce in cases of adultery and in cases where one or both spouses prove incapable of sexual intercourse (VL 27:640).

genuine, non-sexual friendships. This concern arises because of a conception of marriage that sees it as distinguished from non-sexual friendships by the way spouses allegedly can and do achieve "genuinely bodily union." But if one denies the possibility of such a union, this disappears. Indeed, there are any number of ways in which a marriage might be distinguished between non-marital friendships, the most obvious and important one being that marriages are sexual relationships that are exclusive.

7.2.3 Same-Sex Marriage and the Alleged Harm Done to Children

This objection to same-sex marriage once again turns on a certain conception of marriage, namely one that takes marriage to be essentially about the making and raising of children. According to this argument, children do best when raised by their biological mothers and fathers, and one of the main points of marriage is (or should be) to guarantee that children are raised in this way. Insofar as legalizing same-sex marriage would make marriage no longer primarily about making and raising children (since same-sex couples cannot procreate), children will fare worse in our society.

Once again, this objection to same-sex marriage turns on a certain conception of marriage, one that takes an essential function of marriage to be the fostering of procreation and the raising of families. Kant's account of marriage, however, gives us reasons to be critical of such an understanding of marriage. The harm that most concerns Kant is the harm that can come to sexual partners (especially women in relation to men) when their legal rights are not protected. This is why Kant conceives of marriage as a legal institution whose purpose is to provide a context in which spouses can engage in sex without violating the legal rights of each other. Whatever the case may be with respect to the evidence concerning the conditions under which children thrive most (and it is not clear to me that the evidence speaks definitively in favor of the view that children do best when raised by their biological parents), this issue is not pertinent to the legal institution of marriage, at least as it is conceived on Kant's account. So, drawing on Kant's thinking, one can conclude that the issue of how best to raise children does not speak against same-sex marriage.

7.2.4 The Liberal Case Against Marriage

This objection to legalizing same-sex marriage may be the one that raises the most interesting issues in light of the account of marriage we find in Kant's ethical writings. The argument here is that marriage has been and continues to be an institution that has systematically oppressed women. Insofar as this is the case, lesbians (and presumably gay men) should not put their activist energy into achieving the right to marry. This objection to same-sex marriage stands out against the previous objections I've considered in this chapter because the cogency of this objection does not depend on one subscribing to the conjugal view of marriage. Actually, this argument, as Claudia Card (1996) develops it, has very much to do with the way in which the institution of marriage allows for—if not outright encourages—the unjust treatment of wives. In this way, the liberal case against same-sex marriage cuts right to the heart of the issue, according to the account of marriage one finds in Kant, namely protecting the legal rights of married people.

I argued that we should charitably read Kant's concern regarding the problems of sexual objectification and his proposed solution in the form of legal marriage as an attempt on Kant's part to acknowledge and address the way in which women in society tend to occupy a precarious position, one where they are at the mercy of men: physically, financially, politically. Even if it is true that women in general (at least in most Western nations) occupy a better position than they did in Kant's day, Card's argument raises legitimate and serious concerns about the continued systemic oppression of women. And it should not go unremarked that the very institution Kant cited as a way of addressing the unjust treatment of women may well be, on Card's argument, a cause of the very injustices he tried to alleviate.

I think, however, that one can appreciate and agree with Card's assessment of the ways in which marriage has contributed to the systematic oppression of women while not drawing her conclusion concerning whether lesbians and gays should pursue the right to marry. Card's criticisms of the institution of marriage can be seen as an invitation to think about the ways in which the institution is but a historical necessity to deal with our unsociability given our development as a species but that, with time, marriage as we have it in the contemporary West may not be necessary or even desirable. This is the kind of view that someone such as Holly Wilson defends (1998). Perhaps Wilson is right. Perhaps there will come a time when sexual relations between humans will evolve to the point where the legal protections of marriage are no longer necessary. Kant's view of human beings and his understanding of human development certainly do not seem to me to be open to this possibility. But even if we assume that Wilson is correct, in the meantime, it seems to me that one would be justified in concluding that we keep marriage—for both different-sex and same-sex couples—legal.

7.3 The Case in Defense of Same-Sex Marriage

Given the way in which the previous section suggests ways in which one can draw on Kant's ethics in order critically to evaluate the case against same-sex marriage, you might expect there to be simple agreement with arguments in defense of same-sex marriage. While some of the arguments are consistent with some features of Kant's ethics, I think that it is not merely a matter of each of the arguments being in some way in agreement with views one finds in a charitable reading of Kant's writings.

7.3.1 The Equal Treatment Argument

I identified three different versions of the equal treatment argument, maintaining that each of them shared one basic feature: they each contend that there are no morally relevant differences between same-sex couples and different-sex couples with respect to the issue of whether people should be allowed to marry. So, each of the equal treatment arguments concludes that if the state allows different-sex couples to marry, it should, on pain of inconsistency, allow same-sex couples to marry. This is the force, for example, of the argument that argues from the analogy with antimiscegenation laws. Insofar as the view of marriage we find in Kant's writings is one whose function is to secure the legal rights—and equal treatment—of couples in sexual relationships, I think the reasoning of equal treatment arguments is consistent with the kind of reasoning about marriage that we find in Kant's writings. Of course, such reasoning only works to justify same-sex marriage if it is also the case that we have good reasons for thinking that same-sex sexual relationships are not immoral. Hence, my extended discussion of that concern in Sect. 7.1 above.

Interestingly, although Kant does not make an argument similar to the sterility objection in an attempt to justify same-sex marriage, he does make an argument that resembles it in order to establish that the function of marriage as a legal institution is not tied to procreation. His point is that if it were, we would not allow elderly couples who are no longer capable of procreating to remain married. Insofar as this argument of Kant works with respect to elderly sterile different-sex couples and marriage, I see no reason to think it cannot work equally well when adjusted to the case of same-sex couples, who cannot procreate.

The final version of the equal treatment argument is the one that connects most with the kind of thinking we find in Kant's writings on sex and marriage. Cheshire Calhoun argues that barring same-sex couples from marrying implies a kind of sexual orientation caste system, insofar as such a bar entails that the relationships of different-sex couples have a unique, superior status with respect to the kinds of sexual relationships we should acknowledge, promote, and defend in civil society. If only different-sex couples are allowed to marry, then this implies that only such couples "are naturally fit to participate in the one institution that all societies, liberal or otherwise, must presuppose" (Calhoun 2000, 127).

As I have presented him, Kant certainly thinks that marriage is the one institution that all societies must presuppose, insofar as marriage is the one institution, on his account, whose function is to protect the legal rights of sexual partners. If the primary function of marriage is to secure these legal rights (and, so, is not tied to procreation), and if it is also the case that same-sex couples are no different from different-sex couples in any morally relevant respect when it comes to evaluating these relationships as sexual relationships, then it seems that someone informed by Kant's thinking on these matters would agree with Calhoun's assessment of the situation. What's more, insofar as I am right to claim that moral friendship, as Kant understands it, provides a context in which the moral problem of sexual objectification can be addressed, there seems to be nothing that should lead us to think that same-sex couples are any less capable than different-sex couples of establishing that kind of relationship. And if I am right to draw that conclusion, then it follows that there are no good reasons to think that different-sex sexual relationships are in principle any better than same-sex sexual relationships *qua* sexual relationships, which means that any protections afforded different-sex couples ought to be extended to same-sex couples.

7.3.2 The Benefits of Same-Sex Marriage and the Conservative Case

Some of the arguments that try to establish the benefits of same-sex marriage are made largely in response to the claims that same-sex marriage would cause a number of social harms. For example, William Eskridge and Darren Spedale (2006) argue that legalizing same-sex marriage would have positive effects on the friends, families, and even fellow citizens of same-sex couples. Even if this is true, someone drawing on Kant's argument in defense of legal marriage would find these considerations in some sense superfluous. Kant's case for marriage concerns the protection of the rights of the married couple. If the institution has additional concomitant benefits, that may well please us, but on this line of reasoning that is not relevant to the justification of the institution of marriage. The same is true of any alleged benefit that legalizing same-sex marriage has to the well-being of the children of same-sex couples.

The case is slightly different when it comes to the kind of benefit argument that Jonathan Rauch defends (2004). Rauch claims that the benefits of same-sex marriage go beyond the kind of legal privileges that such couples enjoy in some countries. According to Rauch, insofar as marriage—monogamous marriage—is closed off to same-sex couples, same-sex couples are denied the kind of stability and support that legal marriage affords. More specifically, same-sex couples are effectively discouraged from thinking of sex as something that is fuller and more meaningful when it takes place within a loving relationship. Legalizing same-sex marriage, thinks Rauch, would change that. It would encourage same-sex couples to embrace some of the norms of different-sex couples, including (though not only) norms concerning monogamy. In this respect, Rauch's case for the benefits of same-sex marriage are very similar to the so-called "conservative" case made for same-sex marriage by people such as Andrew Sullivan.

I claimed that arguments such as Rauch's are a bit different from the ones made by Eskridge and Spedale, at least as far as Kant is concerned, because the benefits to which Rauch (and also Sullivan) point are ones that concern the sexual behavior of same-sex couples and the norms governing their relationships. According to Kant's sexual ethics, the central moral concern with respect to sex is the dual problem of sexual objectification (i.e., the legal problem and the moral problem). Insofar as Rauch and Sullivan argue that marriage can be a context in which spouses can treat each other in ways that are consistent with and expressive of love and respect,

7.3 The Case in Defense of Same-Sex Marriage

they defend a view that is consistent with the claim that marriage can be a context in which spouses can establish a moral friendship and, so, establish a relationship in which the moral problem of sexual objectification can be addressed. Strictly-speaking, Kant's account of marriage is merely legal and so does not guarantee that marriages are also moral friendships. But it seems to me that the ideal marriage, at least according to the reasoning we find in Kant's ethics, would be one where the spouses are in a moral friendship.

This brings me to a point that I only very briefly touched upon in Chap. 6 in my discussion of moral friendship as a possible solution to the moral problem of sexual objectification. If my argument works, then two people who are in a moral friendship can engage in morally permissible sex, at least insofar as their sexual encounters are ones that are expressive of the kind of respect and love characteristic of a moral friendship. But this raises the question: if two people (either same-sex or different-sex) can establish a sexual relationship that is also a moral friendship, and if such a relationship is a context in which the problem of moral objectification is neutralized, then isn't the legal institution of marriage superfluous? Remember that the legal problem of sexual objectification arises because of the way in which Kant understands sexual appetite. According to his view, to engage in sex with someone is to allow that person to indulge her or his sexual appetite and, thereby, treat you as a mere thing, a mere object for their enjoyment. And, on Kant's view, consenting to sex doesn't alleviate this worry about objectification because the only thing that such consent entails is you agreeing to be treated like a mere thing, which, of course, does not solve the legal problem of sexual objectification. According to Kant, marriage addresses the legal problem because marriage, he thinks, establishes legal reciprocity in such a way so as to guarantee the personhood of each spouse (Chap. 6, Sect. 6.1.3).

Kant seems to think that only within a marriage can this problem be adequately addressed because he seems to think (at least in some of his discussions of sex) that sexual appetite by definition objectifies and results in one allowing oneself to be objectified. I have argued, however, that he cannot be right about this, and I have done so on grounds found within Kant's writings: for example, Kant himself admits that it is possible for sexual appetite to be conjoined with moral love "under the limiting conditions of practical reason" (MM 6:426). If moral friendship is a context in which a combination of moral love and sexual appetite can take place, it seems that moral friendship is a context in which sexual appetite is transformed into a morally permissible desire, which would seem to make marriage moot.

On this account, it is possible for two people to avoid sexual objectification within the context of moral friendship. I think, however, that two considerations drawn from Kant's ethics speak against concluding that marriage, as Kant understands it, is not a necessary legal institution. The first consideration is that moral friendship is, according to Kant the perfect union of love and respect. It is the kind of relationship that two virtuous people can achieve and work at maintaining, but the emphasis here should be on "work." I say this because we should not forget Kant's emphasis on our unsocial sociability and the way in which we are incapable of achieving holiness. So, any moral friendship is going to be imperfect, and at any point in time one or both friends may fail to act in ways expressive of the love and respect characteristic of a moral friendship. If such a friendship is also a sexual relationship, then the danger of occasional failures in love and respect seem to me to be more pronounced, at least insofar as Kant's concerns about sexual objectification and the power of sexual appetite are correct. Given these considerations, legal marriage provides a kind of insurance, as it were, since it provides the opportunity for same-sex and different-sex couples to enter into a legal contract that at least protects them from the legal problem of sexual objectification, if not the moral one.

The second consideration that should keep us from concluding that legal marriage is an unnecessary institution is closely related to the first. In light of Kant's philosophical anthropology, it is fair to say that virtuous character is difficult to achieve and probably quite rare (Cf. G 4:406–407). It is also true that sexual appetite, on Kant's view, is part of our animal natures and a source of great pleasure for us. It stands to reason that, in light of the power of sexual desire (as Kant conceives it), a number of humans will want to satisfy their sexual desire, regardless of whether they have cultivated virtuous character. Insofar as that is the case, and especially insofar as this puts certain members of civil society (e.g., women) at a disadvantage, I think that one can argue that the state has a responsibility to provide for the legal protections of marriage in order to provide its citizens with a context in which they can engage in rightful sexual relations (i.e., sexual relations in which one's legal rights are protected).

7.3.3 Marriage the Changing Institution

These last two considerations about the need for marriage as a legal institution brings me to the final arguments for same-sex marriage that I want to evaluate in light of Kant's ethics. One family of arguments maintains that there is no such thing as "traditional marriage," where "traditional marriage" means some fairly stable and relatively unchanging conception of marriage across historical periods and cultures in which marriage was understood to be a monogamous sexual union between a man and a woman for the purpose of procreating and raising a family. Such a conception of marriage is but one version of the institution among many, with various conceptions of marriage appearing at various times and in various societies, and with each variation on marriage reflecting the particular cultural and political interests of the society whose conception it was. The point of these arguments is to demonstrate that marriage has always been an evolving institution and that opening legal marriage to same-sex couples is but one more shift in this evolution.

I think that someone informed by Kant's thinking can happily acknowledge that marriage is a changing institution, so long as the emphasis remains on marriage as affording legal protections for spouses with respect to the problem of sexual objectification. There is, however, one version of a change to marriage that I considered in Chap. 1 that I want to revisit as I conclude this section, namely, Elizabeth Brake's suggestion that liberal democracies should open the institution of marriage up so that amorous love relationships are not the only kind of care relationships that the state affords legal protections. Brake argues instead for what she calls "minimal marriage," which would accommodate what we think of as different-sex and same-sex marriage, but it would also include all sorts of other kinds of care relationships, both sexual and non-sexual. Minimal marriage, as Brake conceives it, would allow an individual "to exchange all her marital rights reciprocally with one other person or distribute them through her adult care network" (2012, 161).

What sense can we make of Brake's suggestion in light of Kant's ethics? On the one hand, Brake's account of minimal marriage is designed to address the needs of people in a variety of care relationships, some of which Kant was not thinking of when he developed his view of legal marriage. But insofar as he emphasizes our moral imperfection and propensity to evil, Kant's ethical theory is at least receptive to the idea that the state might have an interest in providing some legal protections and privileges to people who are caretakers, though this may require some creative developments of Kant's theory. On the other hand, insofar as Brake's proposal transforms marriage into a legal institution that is not primarily or exclusively concerned with protecting the legal rights of sexual partners, Kant's account of marriage gives one reason to be critical of Brake's proposal. For Kant, marriage, as I have repeatedly emphasized, is a legal institution whose sole purpose is to provide a context in which rightful sexual relations can occur. Brake's proposal underplays that function of marriage, which should give pause if one finds Kant's concern analysis of sexual objectification compelling.

7.4 Conclusion

To a certain extent, Brake (2005, 68–69) does not find Kant's account of the problem of sexual objectification persuasive. According to her,

> Kant does not provide a convincing argument that being seen as a sexual object diminishes one's freedom. The features of sexual desire do not make it impossible for an autonomous agent to consent to sex. Such consent does not dispose of one's humanity (as suicide does) or alienate one's freedom (as slavery does)."

According to someone such as Brake, Kant's way of understanding sexual desire and the alleged dangers that it poses to the moral status of humans is simply mistaken. So, the solutions Kant proposes are unnecessary. According to this line of thinking, we do not need legal institutions or special relationships to transform sex into an activity that is morally permissible. All we need, if we are autonomous adults, is to engage in consensual sex. Consent, as it were, does the trick.

In defending this way of thinking about morally permissible sex, Brake gives voice to a very common liberal intuition about sex. Indeed, many of the thinkers who defend same-sex marriage and whose work I considered in Chap. 1 and in this Chapter share this view of consensual sex with Brake. On this issue, as I have already suggested in Chap. 6, I think Kant's sexual ethics begs to differ, and if I have accurately and cogently represented Kant's views, then his moral theory gives us good reason to be suspicious of the view that consent alone can make sexual activity morally permissible. The central claim of this book has been that Kant's ethics—both his normative ethics and his practical ethics of sex and marriage—are viable ethical theories and, to this extent, can serve as valuable resources to those of us engaged in the same-sex marriage debate. If I have succeeded in establishing this claim, then I have done so because of the way in which my reading of Kant's ethics takes his philosophical anthropology as central to a charitable reading of his moral theory. At the heart of his anthropology is the claim that while we have a predisposition to good, we also are morally imperfect beings with a propensity to evil, and nowhere does this propensity pose more of a danger than in our sexual lives.

Perhaps Kant's more conservative sexual ethic represents an unpopular position among defenders of same-sex marriage. To my mind, though, this forms part of the appeal of Kant's ethics as a resource for people engaged in the contemporary debate over same-sex marriage because it means that Kant's ethical theory can provide us with reasons to challenge aspects of both sides of this debate. Perhaps, then, his ethics can push those of us engaged in the debate to re-examine and improve the arguments we make in defense of our respective positions and help us come to a better understanding of the positions of our interlocutors.

References

Brake, Elizabeth. 2005. Justice and Virtue in Kant's Account of Marriage. *Kantian Review* 9 (1): 58–94.
———. 2012. *Minimizing Marriage: Marriage, Morality, and the Law*. Oxford/New York: Oxford University Press.
Calhoun, Cheshire. 2000. *Feminism, the Family, and the Politics of the Closet: Lesbian and Gay Displacement*. Oxford/New York: Oxford University Press.
Card, Claudia. 1996. Against Marriage and Motherhood. *Hypatia* 11 (3): 1–23.
Eskridge, William N. Jr., and Darren R. Spedale. 2006. *Gay Marriage: For Better or for Worse? What We've Learned from the Evidence*. Oxford/New York: Oxford University Press.
Wilson, Holly L. 1998. Kant's Evolutionary Theory of Marriage. In *Autonomy and Community: Readings in Contemporary Social Philosophy*, ed. Jane Kneller and Sidney Axinn, 283–306. Albany: State University of New York Press.

Index

A
Adultery, 129, 172
Affects, 48, 65–68, 78, 85, 90, 92, 99, 116, 154
Altman, M., 150, 151
Animality, 54, 56, 69, 122–124, 126–128
Anscombe, E., 20, 24–30, 36–37, 39, 42, 44, 47, 48
Anscombian reading, 19, 24, 29, 37, 59, 60, 71, 72, 75–78, 80–83, 89, 105, 165
Antagonism, 50, 51, 53, 158
Anthropology, 19, 30, 33, 44, 48, 49, 53, 59, 65, 68, 71, 75–77, 81, 82, 87, 89, 92, 98, 99, 106, 107, 109, 112, 113, 119, 133, 134, 178, 180
Aquinas, T., 5, 8, 10
Aristotle, 4, 28, 29, 35, 81, 82, 108, 110
Autocracy, 76–99, 112, 120–122, 125, 152, 154, 159
Autonomy
  and self-legislation, 26, 37, 39, 42–43

B
Baxley, A.M., 35, 63, 76, 82, 83
Beever, A., 148–150
Bestiality, 132
Bodily discipline, 119–124
Bodily union, 5, 13, 171, 173
Brake, E., 18, 19, 147, 148, 150, 151, 178, 179

C
Calhoun, C., 13, 14, 175
Card, C., 11, 13, 174
Categorical imperative, 23, 40

Character of the sexes. *See also* Gender
  and domestic relations, 110, 115–118, 133, 143
  and oppression of women, 11, 174
Children, 6–8, 15, 17, 19, 33, 99, 105, 110, 114, 117, 129, 142, 143, 172, 173, 176
Choice, power of, 56, 58, 80, 93
Concubinage, 129, 130
Constraint
  external, 34
  self-constraint, 157
Constructivism, 41
Coontz, S., 17
Corvino, J., 15
Couples
  different-sex, 3, 5, 6, 12–19, 138, 144, 161, 174–179
  same-sex, 3–5, 11–15, 17–19, 131, 138, 170, 171, 173–176, 178
Crimina carnis
  contra naturam, 127, 128, 130–132, 166, 169, 170
  secundum naturam, 127–130

D
de Beauvoir, S., 111
Definitional objection, 4–5, 7, 9, 11, 13, 171–172
Denis, L., 77, 126–128, 134, 140, 159, 160
Deontology, 29, 75, 165
Dependence, 30, 31, 33, 35, 43, 48, 51–53, 59, 61, 71, 72, 75, 78, 87, 99, 105–135, 145, 160, 167
Depravity, 58, 59, 80, 92
Desires, 8, 31, 77, 106, 138, 169

D

Dignity, 41, 43, 44, 47, 53, 55, 61, 67, 71, 77, 81, 87, 88, 90, 91, 93, 94, 99, 113, 119, 120, 125, 127–129, 131, 132, 134, 138, 141, 149, 150, 154, 158, 159, 161, 167, 169
Displeasure, 60, 61, 63–65, 86, 145–146
Divine command ethics, 24
Doctrine of right, 34, 79, 140, 141, 143, 146, 148, 149
Doctrine of virtue, 34, 76–83, 86–99, 120, 124, 126–128, 131, 141, 149, 151, 152, 155, 156, 169
Duty
  imperfect, 89, 120, 167, 168
  perfect, 89, 120, 124, 127, 167

E

Emotions, 6, 8, 15, 17, 31, 36, 43, 47, 48, 53, 56, 60–68, 72, 78, 84–86, 90, 92–98, 113, 134, 153, 154, 156
Equal treatment argument, 12–14, 175–176
Eskridge, W., 12, 14, 18, 176

F

Feelings
  pathological, 62–66, 86, 95
  practical, 86
Finnis, J., 6, 8, 9
Frailty, 57
Freedom
  inner, 43, 79
  outer, 79
Friendship
  moral, 138, 141, 157–160, 177
  of need, 155
  of taste, 156

G

Gallagher, M., 7, 8, 15
Garve, C., 70
Gays, 3, 11–17, 173, 174
Gender. *See also* Character of the sexes
  and sex, 48, 53, 67, 105–128, 132–135
George, R.P., 5–9, 131
Girgis, S., 3–8
God, 28, 30, 31, 36, 37, 78, 84, 142
Gregor, M.J., 79, 97, 131

H

Happiness, 16, 31–33, 35, 36, 40, 43, 44, 47–49, 51–55, 58–60, 68–72, 76, 77, 80, 82–84, 87–100, 120, 121, 123, 133, 145, 146, 150–153, 156, 167, 168
Harm argument, 6
Herman, B., 29, 83, 105, 106, 113, 133, 146, 147
Heteronomy, 38–39
Highest good, 69, 70
Hill, A., 41
Hill, T., 85, 88
Homosexuality, 8–11, 13, 15–17, 131, 166
Human nature, 5, 32, 44, 47–59, 72, 82, 84, 87, 90, 99, 153, 158
Humanity, 43, 48, 55, 69, 77, 88, 89, 119, 120, 123–127, 130, 131, 134, 135, 139–142, 149, 150, 155, 157–159, 161, 166, 167, 169, 170, 179

I

Impurity, 57, 58
Incentive, 31, 56–58, 71, 79, 90, 93, 112, 115, 148
Incest, 128, 129
Inclinations, 32–35, 38–40, 48, 51, 55–59, 61, 63–65, 67–70, 77, 78, 80–87, 89, 90, 92–97, 99, 100, 110, 112, 115–124, 126, 129, 131, 134, 139, 141, 142, 151, 155, 167, 169
Interests, 13, 31, 35, 38, 57, 59, 61, 67, 70, 89, 95, 96, 111, 114, 118, 167, 178, 179

K

Kain, P., 40
Kantian paradox, 26, 37, 39, 42, 44
King, L., 49
Korsgaard, C.M., 27, 29, 41

L

Lesbians, 3, 11–17, 173, 174
Louden, R.B., 113
Love
  that delights, 94–96
  of human beings (*Menschenliebe*), 86, 95–98, 154, 159
  pathological, 94–96

Index

practical, 94
that wishes well, 95, 96
Lust, 54, 55, 89, 120, 124–132, 151, 152, 169

M

Marital norms, 6–7, 172–173
Marriage
    contract, 115, 142
    right, 14, 137, 141–147
    and problem of sexual objectification, 34, 48, 53, 54, 138, 141, 147–151, 157, 158, 161, 177, 179
    and reciprocity, 144–146, 150, 159–161
Masturbation, 9, 125, 126, 131, 132, 169
Maxims, 26, 38, 53, 57, 58, 67, 70, 80, 82, 87, 88, 91, 93, 94, 97, 120, 127, 150
Mikkola, M., 108, 113, 147
Minimal marriage, 18, 19, 179
Moral character, 47, 53, 63, 88, 172
Moral law, 23, 29, 30, 33–35, 37–41, 56–58, 62, 64, 65, 70, 77, 87, 91–94, 125, 127, 138
Moral obligation
    and Anscombian reading, 19, 24, 29, 37, 59, 60, 71, 75–78, 80, 81, 83, 89, 105, 165
    and formalism, 20
    and rigorism, 20, 89
Moral realism, 36, 39–42
Moral worth, 48, 59, 61–65
Morrison, I., 61

N

Natural dialectic, 32, 39, 42–43, 47, 53
Natural law
    classical, 5, 8, 10
    new natural law, 4, 5, 7–9, 13, 131
Nature
    rational, 41, 84, 127
    sensible, 35, 39, 42, 47, 56, 59–68, 72, 77, 80, 82–87, 97–99, 112, 140, 154, 167
Necessitation, 30, 33–36, 77
Needs, 4, 8, 17, 20, 24, 28, 33–36, 38, 43, 48, 51–53, 59, 61, 65, 66, 69–72, 75–100, 110, 114, 115, 117, 118, 121, 122, 126, 132, 138, 141, 142, 155–157, 159, 160, 167, 168, 178, 179
Noumenal realm, 43
Nussbaum, M., 81–83

O

Obligation
    narrow, 89
    wide, 89, 91

P

Papadaki, L., 147
Passions, 15, 48, 65–68, 78, 85, 86, 90, 99, 117, 133, 139, 169
Personality, 43, 55, 69, 86, 120, 125, 127, 143, 145, 159, 169
Phenomenal realm, 43
Philosophical anthropology, 19, 30, 33, 44, 47–72, 75–77, 81, 82, 87, 89, 92, 98, 99, 106, 119, 133, 178, 180, (*see also* Human nature)
Pleasure, 9, 13, 54, 56, 60, 61, 63–65, 67–69, 77, 83, 86, 87, 93, 95, 96, 100, 121, 122, 125, 131, 142, 145, 152, 154, 156, 169, 178
Practical reason, 9, 30, 32, 35, 36, 38, 41, 42, 55, 56, 59, 61, 65, 67, 71, 76, 78–81, 83, 84, 86, 88, 90, 92, 93, 99, 112, 113, 121, 123, 134, 141, 152–154, 159, 170, 177
Predisposition to good, 54–56, 59, 77, 127, 180
Procreation
    and purpose, 5, 6, 13, 16, 17, 19, 109, 125, 126, 128, 141, 166–168, 171–173, 175
Propensity to evil, 56–59, 77, 87, 179, 180
Prostitution, 128–130

R

Rational beings, 23, 30, 31, 33, 35, 40, 41, 44, 53, 55, 69–71, 77, 78, 80, 83, 87, 88, 98, 99, 109, 112, 120, 127, 128, 132, 154, 158, 167
Respect, 13, 30, 55, 108, 138, 169
Right, 3, 28, 79, 110, 137, 168
Right to a person akin to a right to a thing, 137, 138 (*see also Marriage right*)

S

Saint Paul, 144
Same-sex sexual activity, 3, 8, 10, 15, 119, 131, 132, 166–171
Self-conceit, 92, 93

Self-love, 54, 55, 64, 91, 92, 96, 115
Sex, 3, 23, 51, 75, 105, 137, 165
Sexual appetite, 68, 106, 115, 119, 122–125, 131, 133, 137, 139, 140, 158, 159, 177, 178
Sexual objectification
   legal problem, 138, 140, 144, 147–152, 159, 161, 176–178
   moral problem, 91, 138, 140, 147–152, 157, 159, 161, 175–177
Sexual pleasure, 67, 125, 131, 169
Stone, A., 107, 111
Sullivan, A., 16, 176

T
Teleology, 110, 131

U
Unsocial sociability, 44, 48–60, 68, 98, 114, 116, 119, 132, 153, 154, 157, 177

V
Varden, H., 113, 116
Vices, 54, 55, 80, 87, 97, 106, 118, 124, 125, 127, 134, 144, 169
Virtue
   and apathy, 85, 97–98
   and fortitude, 78, 80, 81, 88
   and habit, 81–83, 87
   and morally obligatory ends, 76–83, 87–89
   and self-mastery, 83–86, 90, 99, 122

W
Wike, V., 152, 153
Will
   finite, 30–33, 43, 47, 69, 78, 81, 82, 84, 87, 89, 127
   holy, 30–33, 35, 78, 84, 153
Williams, B., 24, 93
Wood, A., 39, 41, 49, 50, 53, 57, 60, 62, 63, 68, 77, 80, 110, 119, 139, 156, 157